Global
Electioneering

CRITICAL MEDIA STUDIES
INSTITUTIONS, POLITICS, AND CULTURE

Series Editor
Andrew Calabrese, University of Colorado

Advisory Board

Recent Titles in the Series

Forthcoming in the Series

Global Electioneering

Campaign Consulting, Communications, and Corporate Financing

Gerald Sussman

ROWMAN & LITTLEFIELD PUBLISHERS, INC.
Lanham • Boulder • New York • Toronto • Oxford

ROWMAN & LITTLEFIELD PUBLISHERS, INC.

Published in the United States of America
by Rowman & Littlefield Publishers, Inc.
A wholly owned subsidiary of The Rowman & Littlefield Publishing Group, Inc.
4501 Forbes Boulevard, Suite 200, Lanham, MD 20706
www.rowmanlittlefield.com

PO Box 317, Oxford OX2 9RU, UK

British Library Cataloguing in Publication Information Available

Library of Congress Cataloging-in-Publication Data

Sussman, Gerald.
    Globalizing politics : campaign consulting, communications, and corporate financing /
Gerald Sussman.
        p.   cm.—(Critical media studies)
Includes bibliographical references and index.
    ISBN 0-7425-2691-7 (cloth: alk. paper)—ISBN 0-7425-2692-5 (pbk.: alk. paper)
    1. Political campaigns—United States. 2. Political consultants—United States. 3.
Advertising, Political—United States. 4. Business and politics—United States. 5.
Corporations—United States—Political activity. 6. United States—Foreign economic
relations. I. Title. II. Series.
    JK2281.S87 2005
    324.7'0973—dc22

                                                                    2004026495

Printed in the United States of America

⊗™ The paper used in this publication meets the minimum requirements of American
National Standard for Information Sciences—Permanence of Paper for Printed Library
Materials, ANSI/NISO Z39.48-1992.

Contents

List of Tables

Preface

In the 1950s, a middle-aged local political party organizer rounded up several very young boys in my neighborhood, myself included, to go house to house ringing doorbells and handing out flyers for a U.S. presidential candidate. As a son of grateful immigrants who fled a repressive southeast European state, I did it readily and with my father's approval. I had only vaguely received knowledge that the candidate had been a war leader, and that I was an operative involved in a great political event—the election of Dwight D. Eisenhower. I've never been a Republican, but I have no regrets about my childhood political participation on Ike's behalf, because the experience helped fix in my consciousness how politics was conducted before its industrialization, professionalization, and transnationalization.

Pippa Norris, writing mainly about the British experience of electioneering, captured much of what it once was like in the United States as well:

> The party base was a loose organizational network of volunteers dispersed in local areas. The party organization was predominantly constituency-oriented, involving politicians, party workers, and citizens in direct face-to-face contact through activities like town-hall hustings, canvassing, and branch-party meetings. In national-party/branch party organizations (or "mass-branch" parties) the grassroots membership provided the unpaid labour, helping the local candidate, advised by an agent from the national party. (Norris 2000, 141)

My intention in this study is to convey what transnational capitalism and hyperindustrialism (the extension of industrial principles and processes into spaces of life not previously incorporated or socially accepted) has done to American elections and how, given the expansive character of the U.S.

ix

industrial system, its political agenda is impacting other countries. The immediate focus is on the work of the professional political consultants who serve
as the stewards of the electoral process—though not its actual managers.
Stewards ultimately act on behalf of larger power and ideological interests. I
see the political consultants only as midlevel functionaries, because the main
force driving politics in the United States is the transnational corporate sector,
their political action committees, lobbyists, and various allies in political life,
and very wealthy individuals, who materially and politically have the most to
gain and to lose from electoral outcomes.

The focus on political consultants provides a perspective on how the
United States conducts its internal and external political affairs and how
this is mediated by their uses of information and communication technologies. But even this limited focus is complicated and diffuse. To make sense
of what political consultants do in U.S. and foreign elections, I contextual-
ize their roles in a broader analysis of the political forces operating domestically and internationally, with an emphasis on the changes in the world political economy that are functionally and ideologically driven by the core
principles of neoliberalism. For a number of political scientists, the central
explanation of change in electoral systems is the expansion of professionalization of the campaign process. According to the professionalization thesis, the political system is the logical result of technological change, a complex social stratification, and professional specialization. I argue that such
an approach, while informative in certain respects, largely ignores the financial, industrial, and social historical aspects of political change—the
embedded *politics* of politics—and is therefore misleading.

There is no central cast of players and no cabal that runs U.S. and other
countries' electoral processes, but there are enduring interests that last well
beyond the individuals who occupy elite power positions. Contemporary elite
interests bring about their policy and administrative preferences most effectively through coordination, such as in industry groups, trade associations,
political action committees, and other high-powered councils that circulate
comfortably within the inner circles of political and business administration.
Organized interests may not be as organized as some would imagine and not
as random in their influence as others may think, but they can and do act with
considerable synchronicity when big common stakes are on the table (such as
the American Medical Association and the insurance and pharmaceutical industries' response to proposed national health care legislation). Nothing could
be a bigger stake than the capture of political office. Without it, the legal, economic, and ideological preconditions for elite control would be undermined,
and their continued authoritative position in society would be jeopardized.
Dean Acheson, who was the leading architect of U.S. foreign policy in the

1940s and early 1950s, stated the elite position on politics quite explicitly: "If you truly had a democracy and did what the people wanted, you'd go wrong every time" (cited in Ferguson 1995, 377).

Business elites tend to define democratic societies as ones that confer market opportunities with minimal government interference, not as governments that maximize citizen participation and public policy debate. Elections are seen as moments to engineer public consent to rule by the few. Those running for office who challenge this formulation are quickly marginalized by business elites and discredited in the corporate mass media. Neoliberal capitalism rationalizes resource uses in ways that deepen polarities of opportunity and reward and assault the earthly environment. This has induced many people who previously shunned radical structural analysis to take seriously the growing and conspicuous social class divisions that play out in neoliberal political prescriptions and polemics (tax policy and wealth redistribution, relaxation of environmental protection standards, the rising costs of and access to higher education and health care, the decline in real wages, the export of manufacturing and high-tech jobs, military recruitment and casualties, and other issues of public concern).

People differ on how they view economic rights, but recent, and not well-publicized, polls have shown that most Americans see private corporations as having far too much power and representing a threat to democracy and "the American way of life." The United States now has the widest income gaps among the leading industrialized countries and in its own history. Is periodic voting a sufficient exercise to protect democracy? Do citizens apply "rational choice" when they vote or choose not to vote? Political parties, which once played a central role in mobilizing people to attend political rallies, selecting leaders, and distributing patronage, have been largely replaced by private sector professionals and institutions that organize election tasks.

This study critically looks at the professionalization of elections from historical and political economic perspectives. It treats as controversial the notion that the way elections are conducted these days is a normal and natural outgrowth of modernization, technological development, and management efficiency and that they serve the interests of a democratic republic. It provides an analysis of organized wealth and control of resources as an alternative way of describing the driving forces behind electoral changes, arguing along the lines of what Tom Ferguson (1995) calls an "investment theory" of politics. The objective is to critically discuss a complex subject and make it understandable and accessible to readers without a political science degree. A critical understanding of the transformation of politics and the political economy in which it is lodged is extremely important for people to grasp, and for this reason, I try to avoid the jargon that is typical of many political science texts, though some of it is unavoidable.

Chapters 1 and 2 provide an overview of the book and the issues in modern-day electioneering in the United States and in other countries. In chapter 3, I discuss some of the leading professional political consultants in recent years and the arsenal of information and communication tools they bring to their business. Chapter 4 describes as a backdrop the postwar actions taken by the United States to influence elections in states regarded as vulnerable to socialist, communist, or radical nationalist rule. Chapter 5 focuses on the globalization of electioneering and the methods used in overseas consulting, with extended attention to the case of Britain. In Chapter 6, I look at the financial and funding aspects of U.S. elections and give particular consideration to the role of transnational corporations and trade associations in the electoral process. Chapter 7 offers a summary of the main findings and arguments and alternatives to the present rules and methods by which elections are conducted in the United States.

It is traditional to cite individuals who have contributed to one's research. This is intended not merely for courtesy's sake but also because the expression of appreciation represents a conception of how knowledge and interpretation are formed in the body of one's understanding and work. Analysis and interpretation are social constructions, not personal "inventions," though I take responsibility for matters of error and misinterpretation that others, including those below, may find in this manuscript. One cannot even begin to recognize let alone list all the people who have contributed to one's formulations, such as my mentors along the educational trajectory (you know who you are). But there are a few people in recent years, at least in my immediate recollection, who have been especially important to this project—with deep apologies to those I've overlooked.

Larry Galizio was an able graduate research assistant who shared a deep interest in political consulting and collaborated in an early spin-off of the book's research. During the course of this writing, Larry took politics into his own hands and decided to seek political office himself, something most of us should do at some point in our lifetime. Tanya March, another graduate research assistant, tracked down many important items and read and commented on drafts of the manuscript. Dan Schiller and Vinny Mosco, two great colleagues and friends, encouraged me to build on an early conference presentation on the globalization of politics and develop it into a book manuscript. Frank Webster was a wonderfully supportive host during my research visit at the University of Birmingham (U.K.). Joel Myron, whose passions dedicated to the struggles of working people and others living at the margins, helped inspire values of social justice and political inclusiveness that I hope are evident in this study.

My communication and urban studies students, especially those in Political Communication and Information Cities, were unflinching in asking good questions about the relevance of politics to media and communications and to everyday life. Colleagues at Portland State, especially Sy Adler, Charles Heying, and Regina Lawrence, made themselves available for many fruitful conversations about American politics. I thank Portland State University, which provided two separate faculty enhancement grants to help me pursue face-to-face conversations with political specialists in the United States, England, and Scotland.

On the home front, Connie Ozawa engaged and constructively challenged a number of ideas I have had about the American polity. Daniel Sussman, with whom I shared many long walks, discussed and debated big political ideas and philosophy along the way. Jacqueline Sussman was one of my most reliable informants about core values in youth culture and encouraged me with her own social awakening to write for people of her coming-of-political-age generation. Sid Sussman, with considerable talent for political wit, helped me over the years see some of the absurd and banal aspects of politics and appreciate the importance of political humor as a form of personal and popular resistance. To all of the above with much affection.

1

Political Communication in the Neoliberal Era

PUBLIC AND PARTY ENGAGEMENT IN POLITICAL CAMPAIGNS

Rapid global transformations over the past quarter century have included important changes in the political and electoral practices in the United States and many other countries. With a deregulated, privatized, neoliberal economic regime in place on a world scale and the demise of the Soviet Union and its Eastern bloc allies, the mobility of a now more globalized capital has proceeded apace. This mobility comes as the result of both the collapse of the leading socialist alternative and the advent of and new faith in advanced technologies and the "magic of the market." Within this dominant market-oriented paradigm, it is assumed that economic restructuring and new technologies are linked as the driving forces of history. In the United States, it is a faith shared by most Democrats and Republicans and an ideological cornerstone of America's "New Democrats" and, across the "lake," Britain's "New Labour" Party. With its core attachment to the business elites as the social forces of change, neoliberalism is being adopted as the weltanschauung not only in the West but in countries previously guided by the ideals of communism, socialism, and social democracy, especially by among those "globalizing politicians" who share the view of capitalism as a permanently expanding system (Sklair 2001, 137).

The apolitical rhetoric of this faith attributes a "revolutionary" character to digital electronics, genetic engineering, and telecommunications that washes away conflict theories about society—most baldly expressed in the work of Francis Fukuyama—and replaces them with the inevitable, progressive, and entertaining images of the "virtual" world. Neoliberalism also extends to political "markets," where campaign professionals and corporate management have

1

taken greater control of the electoral process. Borrowing from the practices of product sales, political consultants engage in customized mass marketing of election candidates. And with flexible adaptations of campaign messages to suit the medium of transmission and targeted demographics, professional election specialists market specific appeals to likely voters sorted through data collection and identity profiling.

One observer finds that "political currents generally flow in tandem with the spread of American business and popular culture" (Harwood 1999, A18), of which elections are prime activities. With diminishing ideological differences to separate the two dominant parties, campaign managers prefer to emphasize candidates' character qualities over parties and issue identifiers. Indeed, capital interests within the world market system tend to prefer a weakened state structure, at least to the extent that this enables them to operate in a less regulated environment. Organizing elections becomes a means of consolidating interest group power in the policy arena as well as managing the symbolic utilities and legitimating functions of voting. In the absence of a strong welfare state, elections provide a mechanism for seemingly registering public opinion, the vox populi—thereby legitimating actions taken by the ruling party leadership. As the political scientist Murray Edelman critically observes, the "symbolic reassurance" that elections provide the public helps to "quiet resentments and doubts about particular political acts, reaffirm belief in the fundamental rationality and democratic character of the system, and thus fix conforming habits of future behavior" (cited in Dye and Ziegler 1993, 206).

Politicians in many countries, including the United States, employ specialists in public relations and advertising, whose charge is to package and sell them like soft drinks. Even in some critical assessments of the influences of American-style elections in other countries, the source is often seen to be the mixture of communication technologies and information management that consultants bring to the campaign, rather than the extension of neoliberal values into political spaces.[1] In the United States in particular, media and communication technologies are central in the articulation of political conflict and resolution. But for the most part, especially at the national level, politics is treated in the mass media as playful contests of personality and style and examinations of personal "values" rather than struggles between dominant and competing interests in society and socioeconomic classes.

The use and control of the legitimating power of elections in the modern state system has always accompanied the exercise of power. In fact, ruling elites, going back to ancient Rome and China or even earlier, have long understood that the successful deployment of power requires not only material security but also a degree of political legitimacy sufficient for regime maintenance. No incumbent interest can ignore the question of legitimacy, and no other practice more than elections confers upon a ruling elite the mantle of public endorsement and mandate. In what we call democratic societies, the election is the most important symbolic event in establishing the basis of legitimacy. With more and more power concentrated in the largest corporate entities in the United States and other Western states (including Japan), elites understand that the financing of favorable electoral outcomes is a required business expense. Financial underwriting of U.S. elections gives top corporate management access to policymakers, a powerful voice in tax policy and deregulation, insider status in the awarding of contracts and subsidies, and other means of influencing legislation. The campaign funding mechanism (within a winner-take-all voting system) helps ensure that quid pro quo (Bates et al. 2001, 48). It also excludes many potential candidates, including minority, populist, or grassroots-oriented politicians, third party formations, or others with strong commitments to serious or radical reform but who lack the means or willingness to play by standard political practices.

Political demographics and attitudes in the United States have changed in the postwar era. Central to this change is the overwhelming U.S. domination of world markets through the 1960s that created a high level of domestic elite confidence. To a great extent, organized labor shared the arrogance of being a world power and assumed that U.S. export trade would continue to redound to the benefit of workers and increase their share of the pie. Driven by the decline of urban life and their racial fears and facilitated by the automobile and bank credit (or GI loans), millions of white working-class families fled to newly opened suburban residential spaces and beyond. The interstate highway building program begun in the Eisenhower administration encouraged a level of physical mobility that weakened the spatial hold of neighborhoods and communities, and the white migration was underwritten by federal subsidies in support of suburbanization (e.g., Title 1 and Title 2 grants). This coincided with Robert Moses's ongoing massive road, bridge, and public housing building projects that effectively destroyed much of the existing fabric of New York's urban life.

Relocations broke up traditional urban voting blocs and weakened the political party as an institution of patronage for its urban constituencies. In recent decades, parties have focused more attention on middle-class suburban voters. At the same time, expanded commercial television has altered the spatial barriers between candidates and constituents and changed the information-collecting habits of Americans through their reliance on the tube for news and media constructions of significant political issues and images. News media and professional communicators suggested the political ideas that largely replaced the ideological function of local party operatives. Television came to be widely recognized as the principal and most influential medium of news and political information, but once its informational monopoly was well established, the industry's sense of public service obligation radically declined. The same trend has been seen in Britain, though not in the same measure, and in just about every other leading industrial country. Television remains the most important medium for transmitting political messages and images, and in the conglomerate-controlled digital multimedia future, it is likely to have an even more pervasive and direct influence on how people receive political information and vote (or not vote).

Beyond the power of news reporting, the broadcasting industry has significantly influenced the process of choosing the nation's political representatives. In 1924, the Republican Party started up its own radio stations and spent $120,000 on broadcasting publicity for the presidential campaign. (The Democrats spent $40,000.) Four years later, the Democrats fully caught on and outspent the Republicans $650,000 to $435,000 on radio promotion. In 1936, radio's "Ford Sunday Evening Hour" ran ads that harshly attacked Franklin Roosevelt's plan to promote Social Security legislation (Diamond and Bates 1992, 36; West 2000, 152), its eponymous benefactor being a well-known enemy of the administration. As one political journalist commented on the advent of campaign broadcasting,

> No longer were party tradition and loyalty the dependable glues holding voters to predictable patterns of political behavior. No longer could party beneficence, in the form of jobs or various forms of welfare assistance, dependably deliver voters at the polls. Most important, no longer could cities, states, or even the nation be organized adequately by doing party politics at the local level, neighborhood by neighborhood, as in the past. With the rise of radio, television, and other means of assaulting the sensitivities and allegiances of millions of American voters, politics swiftly shifted from retail to wholesale. (Witcover 1999, 31)

Specializing in the art of television advertising and in the use of a range of other technologies and techniques in political campaigns became the work of a small class of professionals generally known as political consultants. In Britain, they are popularly referred to as spinmasters. An American political writer refers to them as "the mad scientists of Winner Take All campaigns" (Hill 2002, 146). In a research article based on extensive interviews with political professionals in several countries, one political scientist found that political consultants, especially in the United States, strongly believe they have transcended the role of the political party in the election process. The study also found a direct correlation between "the degree of campaign professionalization in a specific area and the diminishing relevance of a strong and effective party organization" (Plasser 2001, 46, 52). In a three-year study of political consultants, political scientist James Thurber found that "[s]trategy, message, GOTV [get out the vote] and especially media consulting have all been taken over by private firms" (cited in Leahy 2004).

Politics in America, following neoliberal logic, is now more privatized. To the extent that professionals make politicians feel beholden to what they have to offer, namely (re)election, the candidate cannot help but experience dependency on private consultants and less reliance on the party. The growing wedge between candidate and party opens the door wider to monied lobbyists and special interests that can pay much of the costs of campaigning and parlay their financial support for favorable policy outcomes. It is clear that political parties are less central in American politics compared to the past, and much of the business of conducting elections is now contracted to private professionals, the business community, and organized interests. Candidates for the House or Senate will hire five to ten firms to organize the various components of a typical campaign, including specialists in polling, opposition research, direct mail, telemarketing, media purchasing, advertising, voter profiling, fund-raising, and general consulting (M. Green 2002b, 117).

Professionally and technologically mediated elections also alter the relationship of the voter to the party and political candidate. Elections and politics in general have become to a far greater extent than before exercises in communication and public relations ("language that works"), and professionalization has reduced the importance of representative leadership for both party and politician. In recent years, politicians usually have attempted to cast themselves as brokers for "public opinion" rather than stand out as opinion leaders (Chambat 2000, 267). This outlook represents a triumph of market ideology in that politicians regard themselves less as representatives of the people in a public sphere sense (that is, dense networks of citizen interaction and discourse on social and public policy) or legislators for social welfare in the New Deal tradition, which faded after the Lyndon Johnson administration. Most politicians, regardless of party, are more apt to think of the social contract as providing the public with limited and the most basic services while defending the interests of their best-paying patrons.

With the growing influence of market interests and the less socially activist role of government, parties and politicians have been very reticent of late to be identified with explicit political values and a coherent program of public policy. One European observer finds that "As election campaigns lose political content, political parties are withering and the impact of marketing is increasing. These developments are linked to the ideology of the 'middle way,' which unites 'modern' politicians of left and right in unquestioning acceptance of the rules of the global market economy" (Halimi 1999). An indication of the decline of the party and voter is the fact that in the 2000 U.S. election, only eight cents on the dollar of unregulated "soft money" contributions to the two major U.S. parties went to either party-building efforts, get-out-the-vote efforts, or voter education; the largest part of these funds went to candidate-centered so-called issue ads and only 8 percent of these ads even mentioned the sponsoring party (Brennan Center 2002b, 1).

Robert Reich, labor secretary under Clinton, suggests that the Democratic Party "doesn't exist as a 'party,'" though the Republican Party, he contends, is a more "disciplined organization" (*Newsweek* 2004, 4). The decline of political parties in the United States and other countries has opened the electoral fray to celebrities, especially those who already have mastered the use of media and can rely on name recognition. Among them are millionaires, race car drivers, athletes, beauty queens, movie stars, TV actors, talk show personalities, professional singers, and comedians. Minnesota, a state not known for frivolous pursuits, registered its rejection of politicians-as-usual by electing a professional TV wrestler for its governor. California, in a bizarre recall situation, put a celebrated bodybuilder and Hollywood action hero in the governor's seat. In the past quarter century, the country as a whole has elected a number of media and sports celebrities to high office—from mayors to the president. In Japan, the election of a heavily marketed prime minister, Junichiro Koizumi of the Liberal Democratic Party, with much media fanfare given to his looks and charm, was a significant departure from that country's more traditional preference for rather somber business-oriented leaders (Plasser and Plasser 2002, 345).

Other explanations for the transformation of politics in the United States support a structural interpretation. According to one critical analysis, the decline of political parties in U.S. national elections had occurred for three essential reasons. The direct primary system enables candidates to bypass in many ways local political party machines or the national party's determination of who should be on the ticket. Second, federal financing means that candidates are far less dependent on party funding sources. And third, access to the voting public via mass media, especially television, reduces the need for mobilization of voters by local party organizations (Parenti 1995, 180–81), and the media on their own prefer to focus more on candidates than parties (Wattenberg 1994, chapter 6). With a virtually unknown political organization, "United We Stand" (one could hardly call it a party as much as an ad hoc personality-based enterprise), Ross Perot garnered almost 20 percent of the presidential vote in 1992 by communicating to the public almost exclusively via television.

As a result, the party plays less of a mediating role and serves largely to connect candidates to consultants and big checkbooks. This suggests that citizen and nonprofit organizations cannot rely on the party machinery to gain access to the political process to the extent that they have in the past. The growing dealignment of voters (loss of identification or affiliation over time with one political party) should not be unexpected, therefore, given that parties themselves have jettisoned much of their democratic vocabulary and symbols, even the use of the word *democracy* itself. With both major parties' increasing dependence on corporate campaign contributions, it also is not surprising that candidates would studiously avoid using terms like *democracy* that could be construed as antibusiness.

The adoption of the primary system in the 1970s was widely heralded for transferring the power of nomination from the party elites to the people. It is doubtful whether that perception is accurate. To begin with, only about one-fifth of eligible voters even participate in primaries. What was clear was that the change forced candidates "to organize and operate their own campaigns," which meant that "campaigns became personalized and candidates became 'freebooting political privateers.'" Political parties were turned into "service centers to facilitate the efforts of individual candidates, offering public opinion polling, media advisors, direct mail specialists, and other professional assistance" (Jacobs and Shapiro 2000, 34). In fact, many if not all of the parties' previous campaign functions have been contracted out to private groups and individuals. In Europe, elections are not only organized by professionals but by foreign professionals (Bowler and Farrell 2000, 155–56).[2]

Do voters see themselves in control? According to a Harvard University study in 2000, what the public actually and overwhelmingly believes is that the electoral system is controlled not by the voters but (72 percent to 15 percent) by big money and top party officials (Joan Shorenstein Center 2000a). Even state and local ballot initiatives, which were supposed to insulate the democratic process from big power interests, ran up expenditures of $225 million during the 2000 election cycle (Nelson 2002, 26). Voters seem to be well aware of the private funding sources that back candidates and dominate political communication, but without eliminating the funding bias, there is little they can do about it. This finding is consistent with Thomas Ferguson's "investment theory" of politics (1995) in which he argues that because corporate and the highest income class's money drive the campaign process and dominate the information channels, no radical or grassroots oppositional choices can realistically be formulated and acted upon, which consistently defaults electoral processes, political rhetoric, and outcomes to elite power groups. The formal election system is captive of those individuals and interests able to negotiate their way within the larger political economy. As he sees it,

the fundamental market for political parties usually is not voters. . . . The real market for political parties is defined by major investors, who generally have

good and clear reasons for investing to control the state. . . . Blocs of major investors define the core of political parties and are responsible for most of the
signals the party sends to the electorate. . . . [T]here is nothing any group of voters can do to offset this collective investor dominance. (Ferguson 1995, 379)

Expensive media outlets are the channels of choice by which wealthy investors retain their monopoly on political discourse. The growing concentration of (multi)media firms, from some fifty in the early 1980s to just six by the
year 2000, made matters worse by allowing broadcasters to charge monopoly
rates for airing political advertisements. Adjusted for inflation, political campaigns in 2000 spent five times more on broadcast advertising than they did in
the 1980 electoral contests (Alliance for Better Campaigns 2001). In the 1996
campaign, Clinton and Dole spent 63 percent and 61 percent of their respective campaign expenses on political advertising (Corrado 2002, 90).

Michael Parenti comments that "Besides making things vastly more costly,
this transition to elections-by-television has done little to elevate the quality
of political discourse, emphasizing manipulation and giving little attention to
questions of economic and social justice" (Parenti 1995, 181). Voter detach-
ment or disdain over the present political system is evident in the growing
separation of voters from the political parties that used to be seen as their
source of patronage. Indeed, the same Harvard group found that more people,
disgusted by the undemocratic character of the present candidate-selection
system, favored an earlier one controlled by party bosses over the long,
drawn-out, money-driven primary system (Joan Shorenstein Center 2000b).
Leading Harvard political science faculty did not seem to draw lessons from
the study's findings about the impact of corporate financing on voters.[3]

With larger numbers of voters uncommitted to parties, the candidate is forced
to appeal to disparate interests. The political primary system polls the voters in
the fifty states during a highly compressed campaign, driving up costs and di-
luting the central message of candidate and party. Changes in the dates of a
number of state presidential primaries, including California (previously held in
June) and New York—the two biggest electoral vote payloads—to the first
Tuesday in March provided an enormous advantage to candidates with heavily
front-loaded financial war chests (such as Gore and Bush in the 2000 election)
and a great disadvantage to candidates trailing in campaign funding. The primary system and voter indifference add also to the cachet of the political consultants, on whom candidates heavily rely while making whirlwind political
tours of most if not all of the states.

Primaries feed professional consulting firms with millions of dollars, most
of which in the past came in the form of "soft money," given mainly to parties and issue advocacy ads but used less directly than the "hard money" that
goes directly to candidates and candidate-identified campaign issues. But in

reality the practical differences between the two are minimal, and parties have often laundered soft money into hard money when needed on behalf of Senate and House candidates. The proportion of political action committee (PAC) money in financing elections, particularly on the side of winners, has been growing. (See chapter 6.) By 1992, PACs already provided 42 percent of the successful candidates' campaign budgets, leading to an auctioning off of political interests (Bennett 1996, 137–38). PAC contributions in 2000 amounted to $260 million, 12 percent higher than the previous election cycle (Nelson 2002, 26).

Where does this leave citizens and citizen participation in the most important decisions affecting the political community? Dennis Johnson (2000) finds that major elections leave "no place for amateurs," which is to say, civic-minded citizens. Less than 5 percent of the electorate engages in any form of politics beyond voting. Gone are the days when "armies of volunteers, usually local party activists and the candidate's network of friends and family," were mobilized in "face-to-face canvassing and the distribution of printed [campaign] material (pamphlets, posters, and newspaper advertisements)" (Shea and Burton 2001, 3). Mark Petracca, a political scientist, found in his studies of politics that "the much exalted role of the amateur [citizen activist] is being replaced by the necessity of the political professional," diminishing citizens' involvement in and control of the political process (Petracca 1989, 12–13).

However, political parties were never bastions of grassroots democratic power. In 1957, Victor Perlo found that

> The men [*sic*] of great wealth have an iron grip on the political parties, and can usually determine the presidential nominees, or at least make certain that they will be individuals amenable to big business domination. This involves long-standing connections with the local political machines, control of publicity, media, and possession of the incomes needed to finance national campaigns. (cited in Prewitt and Stone 1973, 58)

Corporate domination, centralization, and professionalization of political space have eliminated almost all but limited symbolic participation of ordinary people, who once were involved in the door-to-door distribution of campaign literature, attended local political meetings and rallies, and felt a general sense of grassroots engagement and excitement with the entire process of electing officials and debating issues. Elections were events that filtered down from national party headquarters to each and every voting district. The change is particularly evident in the United States, with its mass marketing and media culture, its extensive integration of expensive information and communications technologies (ICT) into business and public affairs, and its glut of political contests. Expensive computer technology and software is employed in almost every aspect of campaigning: voter targeting and direct mail, polling, survey and opposition research, list development, fund-raising, telemarketing, websites, and other now standard electioneering techniques.

Candidates and national parties are less inclined to leave election outcomes, especially in important "swing" (relatively independent) districts, in the hands of local political party activists, preferring instead to pay professionals to develop a political strategy, monitor day-by-day voter attitudes, and manage every other aspect of the campaign. Even ballot initiative qualification is typically undertaken by professional organizations with a staff of paid signature gatherers. Political professionals are most often drawn to the election frenzy not by a deep interest in the party platform but by the vast amounts of money thrown into candidate selection and campaigning, now "marked by more frequent use of specialist consultants, public relations experts, and professional fund-raisers influencing decisions formerly made by candidates or party officials" (Norris 2000, 146). The central feature of professionalization is its emphasis on the command of all communicative aspects of the campaign—from polling to photo opportunities to spin-doctoring.

Image construction is territory where political consultants, advertising specialists, and pollsters can excel, using their talents to spin their candidates to victory. Such a method of creating political mandates, as Murray Edelman observes, is actually designed to *deny* power to citizens: "The intense publicity given to voting and elections is itself a potent signal of the essential powerlessness of political spectators because elections are implicitly a message about the *limits* of [citizen] power." And that is because the election spectacle and other "dramatic incidents involving individuals in the limelight displace attention from the larger configurations [of power] that explain the incidents and much else as well" (Edelman 1988, 97, 102; emphasis original). Elections of *individuals* (who are cast upon the voters as leaders) rather than *social agendas* construct an understanding of politics by marginalizing the meaning of citizenship to the act of voting. Symbolic leadership displaces the public as the source of political judgment and authority. The professionally managed and corporate-funded election as a form of legitimation is central to such an illusionary constitution of democratic governance.

NEOLIBERALISM AND POLITICS

It should come as no surprise that corporate elites and their political allies would seek to influence the political affairs of nations in which they have a significant economic stake. They would be seriously remiss in the protection of their own and their stockholders' interests if they did not. And politicians who are beholden to corporate benefactors or are themselves part of the corporate elite, as many are, share the goal of broadening opportunities for corporate commerce and investment. This "accumulation function" of the state has been a pillar of U.S. foreign policy throughout its history. The World Trade Organization's insistence on removing most remaining barriers to trade in goods and services can be seen as the institutional pacesetter in establishing the right of entry of foreign political consultants. Transnational corporations move information and money throughout the world in microseconds, often via third parties or countries, and the revenue source of these behemoths is often very obscure. Such uses of information technology make it difficult to trace election funding in the United States that comes from abroad or U.S. corporate money flowing to foreign campaigns.

Under U.S. law (since 1966), foreign corporations or individuals are banned from making political or election contributions, but this is often hard to enforce. The restriction does not extend to Americans working in overseas subsidiaries of U.S. corporations or American citizens and permanent residents in the United States contributing as subsidiary partners on behalf of foreign corporations. Local management of overseas American companies and foreign parents of American-managed companies, together with foreign governments in some cases, presumably have a shared and direct interest in the electoral outcomes in the United States and elsewhere where pertinent policy issues are on the political agenda. And it would be difficult to trace whether American management has illegally transferred politically targeted funds from foreign subsidiary or parent branches in many instances. In the 1990s, the Federal Election Commission (FEC) found illegal foreign payments of hundreds of thousands of dollars, an amount that actually could be considerably higher.

The United States has led the way in international deregulation, but other states, including those in the former Soviet bloc, have been enthusiastic followers of free-trade policies and what Bill Clinton called the "inexorable logic of globalization" (Harwood 1999, A1). Such logic explains, according to some, why the French electorate saw so little difference between the Conservatives and Social Democrats in the 2002 election that they voted in the extreme right, the National Front, as one of the two runoff parties. The intrinsic logic of globalization also requires that transnational corporations have a more direct hand in the election processes around the world so as to standardize the legal and policy codes by which they can seamlessly transfer investment, technology, operations, commodities, information, and profits on a global basis with the least amount of friction.

The country that has embraced neoliberal economics most enthusiastically outside the United States is Britain, and its principles have been coequally

assumed by Conservative and Labour governments. Perry Anderson observed in 1992 that the new program of Britain's Labour Party reflected the
impact of Thatcher's conservative changes in state policy starting in 1979,
and that Labour essentially had accepted

> the basic parameters of the Thatcher settlement. . . . [Labour] does not seek to
> extend the public sector or reverse privatisation to any significant degree. It
> does not propose to raise the overall level of taxation, but promises to adjust
> its incidence in a mildly more egalitarian direction. It does not substantially
> depart form the laws that now regulate industrial action, while rendering them
> a little more favourable to trade unions. It does not abandon the British nuclear
> deterrent. All these changes of the Thatcher years are uncontested. (Anderson
> 1992, 346)

The former welfare regimes, including those formerly with the Council for
Mutual Economic Assistance (the Soviet bloc countries) and the European
Economic Community, have been eliminating state supports to education,
health care, children's day care, job training, and other social support systems, at the same time that they have been loosening the barriers to foreign
investment and international trade. A corollary to this is the informal relaxation of restrictions on the entry of foreign political consultants. Whereas the
Central Intelligence Agency had to go undercover in engaging in electioneering activities during the Cold War era, American political consultants find
themselves *invited* into the most sensitive areas of state planning—the election of national leaders. It would have been inconceivable twenty-five years
ago, for example, that leaders in the Kremlin (and once ardent communists),
in what was regarded as the vanguard revolutionary state and the bulwark
against U.S. imperialism, would be dancing to the tune of conservative American political consultants brought in to help consolidate state power for a nas-
cent capitalist regime. But that, remarkably, is what transpired in the 1996
Russian election when Republican consultants from the United States went to
Moscow to manage Boris Yeltsin's presidential campaign. (See chapter 5.)

Neoliberal economics, with its emphasis on privatization, deregulation, and
liberalization (market-centeredness), has penetrated more deeply the political
sphere. The techniques of commercial advertising and public relations and the
use of private sector professionals, assisted by a loose regulatory structure, are
now central to the political process. Citizens are treated as political consumers
and candidates are marketed as products. One British business-oriented publication described this new era as one in which the

> tactics and tools of modern political warfare have an even longer political shelf
> life than general strategies. Every message is ruthlessly polled and tested in fo-

cus groups. Statistics experts in Washington, looking for hidden trends and messages, then analyze the results. Ads, speeches and messages are quickly reformulated and adapted. Similarly the recent bombardment, by some Irish candidates, of constituents with unsolicited pre-recorded phone messages is long-established practice in American elections. (*Business and Finance* 2002)

PROFESSIONALIZATION AND THE MARKETING OF POLITICS

Political marketing is the offspring of product marketing. Candidates (and voters) have become commodities in the production of the election spectacle. Candidates pitch, voters buy or ignore the pitch, and a program of (de)regulation, (un)enforcement, and (dis)investment is the end product. In a highly mediated and entertainment-oriented public culture, political marketers have to work assiduously to capture the attention of likely voters. In fact, the percentage of registered voters who actually vote in the United States is the lowest among the industrial countries, and although public interest groups point this out again and again, almost nothing is done to stimulate a sense of urgency about the election event. As one design for mobilizing and at the same time commodifying voters, the Bush presidential campaign in 2004 required that people wishing to attend his political rallies must be invited, and only those willing to canvass Republican homes, put up lawn signs, or participate in get-out-the-vote phone banks were assured of invitations (Halbfinger 2004, A1).

Political professionals often blame an "apathetic" public for this situation. Others find it a more compelling explanation to suggest that neither interest groups nor professional consultants have a reason to encourage a broad-based electorate to whom they would ultimately be held accountable. With low (but more predictable) turnouts, political elites can feel complacent in the assumption that the voters deserve the best elections that only money can buy. The "apathy" argument works as a useful rhetorical device for releasing them from responsibility for weak voter participation rates.

The political consulting specialists employ modern message management with the aid of phone banks, "people metering" devices, "perception analyzers," direct mail, telephone surveys, and a host of other techniques and electronic technologies. (See chapter 3.) They are also the "experts" in the production of "photo ops," images, and impressions and in the staging and marketing of personalities, slogans, and sound bites in print and broadcast media. Surveying of voters and political marketing of candidates has recently become pervasive in European elections, which historically have had tighter controls than the United States in privacy protection. In Italy, media mogul

Silvio Berlusconi created and marketed a new political party in 1993, Forza Italia, to carry out his 1994 election campaign for prime minister. For consultants, strategy takes precedence over substance and publicity rules over essence. A convergence of techniques drawn historically from propaganda, public relations, and advertising is used to deluge the public with a continuous repackaging and repetition of populist themes, which are insinuated as part of the candidate persona. Many of these techniques were developed during the fascist era in which leaders were enshrined with mystical powers and projected as embodiments of the national spirit. One of the principal lessons that political advisors today teach their candidate-clients is how to read the public pulse and "stay on message."

The use of election consultants is nothing new. Political advisors have been around since ancient times. Texts, from the Old Testament to the ignominious tales of the Russian monarchy, tell of the sometimes wise and sometimes imprudent counsel given to leaders. In the late nineteenth century, Republican William McKinley had the advisory services of Cleveland industrialist and millionaire Mark Hanna, who was with him during his years as a congressman, his electoral struggles in the Ohio gubernatorial campaign, through the 1896 presidential election and White House years. Hanna, who raised almost $7 million for McKinley's 1896 election campaign (compared to the $650,000 raised for the Democratic candidate, William Jennings Bryan) by levying assessments on Standard Oil, New York Life, and other major corporations, became a political boss in his own right. Aside from his corporate fund-raising efforts, Hanna issued regular press releases; trained stump speakers; staged some 300 "front porch" meetings between McKinley, the press, and the public; and created millions of posters, buttons, billboards, and campaign fliers (Center for Responsive Politics 2001; Hess 2000, 38; Shea and Burton 2001, 2). For his efforts, Hanna was made national party chairman and in 1897 was appointed as U.S. senator from Ohio on the occasion of the death of the incumbent.

Since the days of Hanna, election management has become a highly specialized profession, holding a prominent place in the drama of politics. In the Cold War era, the idea of propaganda or the "engineering of consent" suddenly became anathema and was usually reserved for describing Communist Party media and rhetoric. Following the collapse of the Soviet Union, however, political consulting enjoyed a burst of openness, legitimacy, and even appeal, in part because of the opening of many new political markets— including those of the former Soviet bloc countries. Although political consulting has a long history, the concept of professional election consultants as people unattached to party, cause, or candidate, and instead merely brought in as "hired guns," is relatively new (Witcover 1999, 74 *et passim*).

Currently, 79 percent of political consultants work for private corporations. One of them, Republican pollster Bill McInturff, takes in more than 50 percent of his revenues from corporate clients (Glasser 2000). Richard Pinsky, who managed Dole's 1996 presidential campaign in Florida, concurrently worked for D.C. public relations and lobbying firms on behalf of companies pursuing legislation in Congress (Mitchell 1998). There is a fundamental violation of the public interest, however, when without disclosure consultants wear one hat for corporate interests and don another as advisors for public officials—but that is happening more frequently. And as consultants find corporate work increasingly lucrative, they are less likely to attach themselves to a single political party or party issues. The trade journal *Campaigns & Elections*'s won-loss records of political consultants remind one of the statistics posted for major league baseball pitchers. According to Stephen Hess, senior fellow of government studies at the Brookings Institution, as American consultants "are unconnected to governance . . . [t]hey will do anything they think will work to get a candidate elected without connection to consequences" (cited in Prusher 1999, 1). There are big rewards for those who can parlay their political victories and ties to leading politicians with the corporate community. In a study by American University, 73 percent of consultants acknowledged that unethical practices are common in their industry, including the payment of kickbacks by businesses to the professionals for providing them campaign contracts (Glasser 2000).

In the 1990s, James Carville might have been the archetype winning-by-any-means strategist—or at least the most open about it. Before he announced his retirement from the campaign hustings and took his message to a national TV talk show, he was well known as the Democratic Party "pit bull." Undoubtedly unimpressed by the poorly run campaign of Michael Dukakis in 1988 and the influence of Harvard University people in that campaign, Carville has expressed no patience for reasoned argumentation in political campaigning or to appeals to the rational sensibilities of the voter. He once told an aspiring research director for a Senate campaign, who happened to be an academic, "To them [academics], everything is gray; I want black and white. I want to nail our opponent, I want to rip his head off. I want answers, and I want them now" (Johnson 2001, 61). In some ways, the Louisianan Carville sounds like a campaigner from an earlier generation, people who knew all the tricks of the trade, including how to dig up dirt on the opposition. Carville is in fact hostile to the importance given to the new wave of social science research weapons that are part of the contemporary electioneering armory.

One of Carville's Republican counterparts, Arthur Finkelstein, is perhaps even more of a take-no-prisoners campaign warrior and typically advises his clients to mock his opponents—sometimes adventuring into very sensitive areas. He devised a moniker against Democrat gubernatorial candidate Mario Cuomo as "too liberal for too long." On behalf of Bob Dole, Clinton was labeled the "tax and spend liberal." New York attorney general Robert Abrams, in a 1992 U.S. Senate race versus Alfonse D'Amato, was tagged "hopelessly liberal" and "a tax-hiking urban liberal." For the Israeli campaign of Benjamin Netanyahu, he ran television ads showing the then-prime minister Shimon Peres "walking with Palestinian leader Yassar Arafat. The logo: 'A dangerous combination for Israel'" (Schwartzman 1998, 15).

Revealing his moral ambiguity, Finkelstein, who is Jewish, ran a campaign at home for a candidate in 1978 who was widely regarded as anti-Semitic. He even constructed a "push poll" (a form of "polling" that leads the voter without identifying the pollster's political alignment) question for the candidate that asked voters if they would vote for a "foreign-born Jew" (his client's opponent). In 1990, he worked for Jesse Helms in an openly antigay campaign, even though Finkelstein himself is gay, and in another campaign wrote disparaging ads about Brooklyn, his birth town (Schwartzman 1998, 15). Is he a man of contradictions or simply a product of a political system that selects for and rewards ruthless opportunism?

But despite the occasional stories or exposés about celebrity consultants, political consulting is largely out of public view. From the perspective of power maintenance, there is good reason why that should be. The more the public is able to scrutinize the manner by which politics is actually conducted, the more the wizard behind the curtain is revealed. The product that consultants provide, on the other hand, is very much before the camera and the purview of voter spectators. Augmented by advanced technology and mass media, campaign management by political professionals is in fact a very expensive way of electing public officials. The cash nexus is precisely what makes elections the affair of the most well-to-do on all but the symbolic level. Candidates without professional campaign organizations are at a severe disadvantage to compete with those who have their services, which in the twenty-first century is almost unthinkable.

A highly visible campaign organization greatly improves the candidate's stature and, thereby, ability to attract wealthy backers and their money, which in turn strongly correlates with success at the polls (Herrnson 1992, 866–67). For the financial backers, their contribution buys access to legislators—especially politicians likely to deliver votes for their interests—and the policy and administrative process. It also buys advertising and, thereby, the ability to sway public perception and, in turn, capture the attention of lawmakers—while neutralizing enemies (Jacobs and Shapiro 2000, 40–41). For their part, candidates without early success at raising a war chest stand little chance of remaining viable, and they usually become the first campaign also-rans. Indeed, this has long been understood. It is not that money was not important in the electoral process in the past; it is that highly concentrated sources of money are driving the process today.

And despite all the tools and talents the professionals bring to politics, it is not the case in this author's view that they actually *run* election campaigns in any more than an administrative sense. It is even more exaggerated to suggest, as some claim, that they have taken over the political process. The term *professionalization*, used by many academic specialists on politics (Farrell 1998; Mancini and Swanson 1996; Scammell 1998), is an inadequate and inaccurate way to describe what has transpired in U.S. and other Western electoral systems. Such a term tends to make the transformation of elections seem natural, as part of the inevitable march of technological progress. A more convincing way of explaining the transformation of elections is related to the worldwide economic restructuring that is taking place, a process known both as neoliberalism and globalization, and the role that finance plays in these transnational transactions.

Political scientist James Thurber may need to reconsider his ordering of priorities in the political campaign. He argues that the most important resource in a campaign is the candidate, and the second is financial backing. But almost no one, at least in national elections, gets to wear the mantle of "candidate" until the powers-that-be have signaled that they are willing to back such a person, and even Thurber recognizes that presidential candidates need to attract money early and "from the right sources" (corporate backers) if they are going to be taken as serious players (Thurber 1995, 6). Big corporate funders (see chapter 6), including media conglomerates, ultimately dictate the "electable," and only when a politician has gotten that far can the candidate surround her/himself with an entourage of professional consultants. PACs channel their money toward candidates they deem likely to win, which in part is why they overwhelmingly support incumbents over challengers (Himes 1995, 65).

Although the U.S. president has considerably more power than the head of government in parliamentary systems (the prime minister), there is an exaggerated emphasis typically given by most political observers to the president as a decision maker. A system and stratum of preexisting political economic power, often referred to as *the state*, precedes and circumscribes any candidate's attempt to seek high office. The state (corporate, military, union, and other major organized political interests), comprising but also larger than the formal governing apparatus, represents the larger locus of power where most important policy decisions are made. And it is in policies, not the president per se, that corporations and other organized interests invest their financial resources. Elected presidents and other federal officeholders ultimately must respond to the voices of organized power. The range of presidential or congressional options in the American system is quite constrained for that reason, which gives politics a relatively stable and static character but makes the consultant a free agent in the pursuit of brokerage fees in any number of elections throughout the United States or abroad and equally at home with corporate patrons.

A British academic specialist in these matters contends that in the case of the United Kingdom, the technical expertise involved in electioneering is limited mainly to advertising companies and that political fixers are first and foremost party regulars, quite unlike independent external consultants (Harrop 2001). Harrop does not inquire, however, about the extent to which British politicians nonetheless have become voices for corporate interests and are often rewarded with gifts, albeit more at arm's length than their open-palmed American counterparts. But he does acknowledge that British elections have certainly changed since the 1945–1955 era, when there were "no private opinion polls, no campaign press advertising, no television, no daily press conferences, no instant rebuttal units, no websites." Nightly radio broadcasts by candidates during the campaign in that period reached an average of 45 percent of the population, "only exceeded by the most popular variety shows" (Harrop 2001, 56–57). Indeed, in the early 1980s, almost no countries permitted paid political advertising on television; today, outside of Western Europe, it is almost ubiquitous. Broadcast political advertising, as inadequate a genre as it is for informing the public about the political issues and process in the "information age," has since emerged as the world's most common form of campaign education.

POLITICAL CONSULTING AS A GROWTH INDUSTRY

The number of political consultants over the past twenty years has grown rapidly. Moreover, the profession has merged with other campaign specialists in areas such as advertising, direct mail, media, focus groups, and voter analysis. Candidates have become highly dependent on the professionals, which has greatly reduced the relative influence of longtime, close, personal supporters. Much of what consultants do, both for aspiring politicians and existing officeholders, is to orchestrate pseudoevents: leaking information and disinformation, floating trial balloons, arranging for important press interviews, spinning news stories, staging appearances, planting stories with favorite columnists, planning TV news coverage, coining slogans and sound bites, and the like.

As one study found, most major party House candidates spent 18 percent of their campaign budgets on their professional staffs, fund-raising, and additional administrative expenses, along with 18 percent on direct mail operations, 18 percent on television, and 11 percent on radio. Senate candidates spent 30 percent of their budgets on television (Paul Herrnson, cited in Corrado 2000a, 92). And in recent U.S. presidential campaigns, television and radio advertising accounted for 60 percent of all election expenditures, more than 90 percent of which goes to local stations (Morgan 2000; Norris 2000, 152). Even in the U.S. Spanish-speaking communities, consulting and political advertising is a growth industry, especially for the main Spanish language networks, Univision and Telemundo. In south and central Florida, Jeb Bush and the Republicans spent $1.3 million on Spanish-language ads up to late October in pursuit of his 2002 gubernatorial reelection (Alvarez 2002b, A20).

Another tactical feature of political advertising is that it's concentrated in large urban markets, especially in the "swing states" (those with large numbers of undecided voters). This means that large sections of the American people—especially in those places where voting patterns in the past ensure the success of one party and often in the districts where the constituent base is highly diffused—see little of the information or political ads that politicians are transmitting about their campaigns. By fall 1996, neither Clinton nor Dole had bothered to give a major stump speech or run a significant number of campaign ads in seventeen states (Witcover 1999, 218). Under the electoral college system, regardless of the popular vote, just eleven of the fifty states (plus the District of Columbia) have enough electoral votes (271) needed (270) to capture the presidential contest. Most small states merit little serious attention on the part of presidential candidates under these rules, except where the electoral vote (the allocation system of "electoral college" votes for each state and the national capital) is anticipated to be extremely close. Although he captured the election day turnout by a half-million votes, Al Gore won only twenty states plus Washington, D.C., in the 2000 presidential poll—and needed only one more to capture the winner-take-all electoral vote.

But even while political advertising is urban-focused, it pays little mind to the actual demographic composition of cities. Despite the fact that blacks vote overwhelmingly Democrat, only one of thirty-eight members of the Congressional Black Caucus was supported by party-sponsored issue advertising. None of the party funding went to its Hispanic members. The Senate in 2002 had no blacks or Latinos, which effectively excluded a quarter of the U.S. population from representation in that body.[4] Of all the political ads in 2000, only 8.4 percent of those of the Democrats were ethnically diverse, compared to 15.5 percent on the Republican side (which more actively courted blacks and Latinos), and none for the Reform Party or Libertarian Party. Only the

Green Party, with 92 percent diversity representation, seriously attempted to portray the United States according to its actual multiethnic composition (Brennan Center 2002a, 2; Holman and McLoughlin 2002, 36). The two dominant parties and their consultants are definitely green with respect to money. There is a symbiotic, mutually constituting and benefiting aspects of the money-driven election system, in which consultants work closely with broadcasters to drive up media spending as a major cost factor in elections. There's good reason for this. Each political ad placed usually brings media consultants a hefty 15 percent commission, although their actual earnings are a well-kept industry secret (Glasser 2000). There also are areas, such as direct mail, e-mail, telemarketing, and other candidate-to-voter targeted communication, where professional consultants serve as media producers themselves and can often bypass the mass media in getting the candidate's message out to the public, leaving mainstream media only the choice of whether or not to follow the consultants' lead.

The more that candidates bring professionals into politics and vice versa, the more expensive elections become. And the more expensive elections become, the greater the need for corporate patrons, including media outlets, who decisively exercise the power behind the throne. Consulting is a major business in itself, but it is also a subcontracted extension of corporate business investment in managing the political system. As a matter of self-perpetuation, corporate power has no choice but to control the political process, but in doing so, it is critical to the credibility of the democratic process that it not appear to be managed directly by or run on behalf of its biggest stakeholders. Hence the need for the professionals and "professionalization."[5]

The origins of professional political consulting in the United States go at least as far back as the 1930s. What has changed is the technostructure for information transfer (television, computers, satellites, etc.), which radically reduces the friction of space as an impediment to campaign management. The universalizing of telephone, television, fax, Internet, polling techniques, electronically generated mass mailing, and other electronic media has tended to mass-produce and standardize the electoral process, at the same time enabling a customizing of messages to suit the values, tastes, and lifestyles of "group demographics." It is the flexible system of modern-day politics—centralized control with decentralized operational organization and a capacity for small batch production of customized sound bites and issue packaging—that stylizes the candidate as someone for everyone.

The Dole campaign in 1996 e-mailed a newsletter that provided information about upcoming events to anyone who registered at their website (Connell 1997, 64). Other candidates have set up electronic bulletin boards, which, in addition to the "personal touch" of e-mail, can be used in polling, announcing candidate appearances, responding to potential voter questions, coordinating communication with both voters and staff members, and doing trial runs on issue approaches (Graff 1992, 24). One of Congress's leading PAC recipients, Dole had plenty of money to spend on electioneering, and even he had to admit that "When these political action committees give money, they expect something in return other than good government. It is making it difficult to legislate" (cited in Bennett 1996, 95).

The failed Ross Perot campaign in 1992 spent almost $60 million, 98 percent of it from the candidate's personal account, and relied heavily on the use of "800" numbers and a computer database of supporters. However, when Perot brought two veteran consultants into the campaign, Hamilton Jordon and Ed Rollins, there was a wave of protest among rank-and-file supporters, who complained about the professionalization of the United We Stand organization (Poor 1992, 1B). At the other end of the organizational spectrum, Bill Clinton's war room monitored newswires, talk radio, cable news, and satellite broadcasts from anywhere in the world on a twenty-four-hour basis, enabling the candidate to respond to every attack on his candidacy, so that "no charge went unnoticed; no charge went unanswered." The war room also used fax machines, modems, interactive satellites, and wireless phones to respond to issues and events at a moment's notice and in time for the nightly news— or to alert the media of Clinton's arrival in a city or town to ensure maximum coverage (Myers 1993, 181–82). The war-room tactics of Bush and Kerry in the 2004 election far surpassed those of Clinton's strategists.

Like the U.S. military, the country's corps of political consultants is the best equipped in the world. Their tools of trade, many taken directly from commercial advertising and PR, have become the standard in the control of informational and spin factors in American elections—and increasingly in other countries. Just as a host of information gathering and processing technologies—from checkout counter scanners to credit card readers to website cookies—gather data and create consumer profiles based on purchases, Internet usage, and personal demographics, information techniques, and technologies (polling, telemarketing, database management, etc.) are also put to use in collecting and sorting data on political preferences and voting behavior. Surveillance technologies, commercialism, and politics are in a process of rapid convergence. One monitoring technology used by political campaigns in oppositional research, Polaris, was developed from a system for nuclear submarine detection and warfare. (See chapter 3.) A former commentator from CBS News, Marvin Kalb, observed in the early 1990s that in the election environment, technology was being substituted for dialogue and predicted that "voters will become the targets, rather than the participants, in the process" (cited in Selnow 1994, 156). That moment has since arrived.

One company, Aristotle Industries in Washington, D.C., sells CD-ROM disks with a voter database of 138 million registered American voters, and campaign consultants can purchase information on any geographical region they wish. Aristotle also provides enhanced lists broken down by income, homeowner and renter status, family composition, voting history, and ethnicity. The data can be sorted for easy targeting and merged with other databases. This allows both consumer and political advertisers to target individuals with messages that are likely to resonate with their individual values, tastes, and lifestyles—breaking out citizens from their broader constituency identities. Another company, Fat Cats, lists all individual, PAC, and party contributors that gave more than $200 to federal candidates or political action committees (Johnson 2001, 153; Selnow 1994, 53).

Two Stanford University political scientists turned polling into an entrepreneurial niche by setting up a company that permanently surveys a cross-sectioned cluster of 100,000 people in order to register their preferences for "cars, clothing, computers, and candidates." Lured by prizes and other small perks, this control population was asked to provide feedback on subjects ranging from presidential debates to the last episode of *Survivor*. CBS used the academic entrepreneurs' "public pulse" techniques to instantly gauge how viewers of the debates were reacting to candidates' words and phrases (Hill 2002, 161). This is but one example of the seemingly endless range of possibilities on the horizon for political profiteering in the "new frontier" economy.

INTERNATIONAL CONSULTING

Encouraged by the business opportunities increasingly made available in the neoliberal world economic environment, American consultants have taken their show on the road. Political strategists from the United States have worked in the United Kingdom, Ireland, Germany, Austria, Canada, Israel, Russia, Mexico, Spain, Sweden, France, the Czech Republic, Venezuela, Argentina, Colombia, Malta, Honduras, El Salvador, the Philippines, Japan, Greece, Brazil, Ecuador, Dominican Republic, Panama, Nigeria, South Africa, and many other countries. One political strategist, Doug Schoen, who has worked in some two dozen countries, boasts that "There is not an election that's seriously contested around the world [where] Americans are not present as advisors on one side, or both" (Stevenson 2000b). This does not necessarily mean that other countries are adopting wholesale the American-style election system, but it does mean that the new form of electioneering—drawing heavily on public relations and advertising, technology, voter management, and private financial backers—is the standard against which any election tends to be measured.

One distinction that is made about elections (Plasser and Plasser 2002) is that between the "shopping model" and the "adoption model," which is the difference between selective and full-range reproduction of American electioneering techniques. Such typologies seem to miss a central point, however, which is that it is not its "American" elements that are at the crux of modern elections but rather its commercial, financial, and industrial aspects. When we see the adoption of laissez-faire trade and investment principles in Western Europe or China, which are pushed mainly by the United States, we do not say that those countries are Americanized, but rather that they are more integrated into the system of global capitalism. The fact that it is largely American specialists who bring "leading edge" techniques to modern electioneering, though not insignificant, is of less importance than the fact that electoral processes discourage public engagement and have become more open to the influence of industrial and wealthy interests, including those at the supranational level. It is this openness that facilitates transnationalization of the political sphere, which the United States is best positioned to exploit in the short term. (The forms of overt and covert U.S. political intervention in the Third World and former Eastern bloc countries are discussed at length in chapters 4 and 5.)

In the 1980s, the United States began to undertake election intervention on a more aboveground basis. Two observers have found that the outcome of this U.S. strategy (namely its Democracy Assistance Program) is to promote a political culture in the target countries featuring high campaign spending and top-down, donor-driven political organizations, which Third World countries do not need and can least afford (Ottaway and Chung 1999). Although election costs run the highest in the United States, the cost of campaigning almost everywhere is rising. One of the results is that when Russian and Brazilian elections become more expensive and make heavier use of media, communication technologies, and the specialists who know how to use them, the possibility of having truly local mass-based candidacies is diminished. Indeed, the United States has provided millions of dollars to influence the outcomes of elections, and, according to Cox News Service, certain private organizations "have used these federal funds to supply equipment, services, training and expert advice on strategy and polling to political parties and other private groups in more than 100 countries" (cited in Solomon 1999, 74).

Once campaigns hook into sound-bite journalism, it is not essentially the American influence that matters so much as their commercial, financial, and industrial characteristics. Politicians and parties in other countries may invite

American specialists to demonstrate the utilities of high-tech campaigns, but in the long run, once a country has sold off the political arena to wealthy interests, including corporate actors, the nationality of the money or the consultants matters less. In Third World countries, the long-term costs and consequences of high-tech, big-spending elections and the import of foreign consultants is likely to interfere with and slow down the pace of socially equitable development, interfere with publicly oriented planning, and discourage the creation of locally based civil society institutions and organizations (Ottaway and Chung 1999).

The emphasis on the "Americanization" of elections is somewhat of a diversion, a miscasting of the central issues. For one thing, many would challenge the idea of conflating professionalization with Americanness. Adoption of campaign styles and techniques is, of necessity, always going to be selective, always a matter of degree, and involving adaptation, but the real question is, who are the adopters? Are the adopters interested in bringing citizens more closely into the fold of the political process, that is, making the process more participatory, or are they wedded to a more privatized, elitist, and managerial model of politics? And, with the increased intervention of technology and expertise in the electoral process, whom do the successful elected representatives of such a process actually represent?

Plasser and Plasser (2002, 244) see three major changes in elections worldwide that derive from the contemporary neoliberal approach to electioneering. One is the increased use of mass media in political campaigns, a second is the increased reliance on professional campaign management, and a third is that the first two changes have brought about significantly greater costs in conducting electoral campaigns. To understand the implications of these changes, the central question again becomes, who and what interests are bringing about these changes? Part of the answer is found in another widely observed change in modern elections: political messages have become increasingly centrist in tone (that is, moving away from socialist or welfare values and closer to the validation of market forces or public-private partnerships). This suggests that a consensus exists among elite political organizations that enshrines the market system as the most dynamic force for wealth creation and protection of political liberties.

In the neoliberal vision, apart from policing, national security, building necessary infrastructure, and the passage and adjudication of certain laws, the role of the government should be minimal and promote a legal environment for market expansion while providing a safety net for the poorest citizens. There is no talk of class conflict but rather of harmony of multiclass interests. National interests are global interests and vice versa. Technical solutions and skills overcome political divisions.

Although it is not about Americanization per se, in a world governed by marketing, commercialization, and technology, the United States is clearly best positioned for global leadership and domination (as the British elites were when they first declared the supervening logic of international "free trade"). U.S. foreign policy rhetoric about its democracy-building interventions around the world reduces in practical terms to removing barriers to international trade and investment, while engaging in a certain level of procedural (electoral), though not necessarily very substantive, forms of democracy. Democracy building within the neoliberal framework ensures open markets and periodic elections, and election activity offers globetrotting work opportunities for American political consultants. Rick Ridder, former president of the International Association of Political Consultants, said in reference to the consulting gold rush in Mexico in preparation for the 2000 elections in that country, "If there's one thing Americans can teach Mexicans it is this: Democracy is a booming business" (quoted in Schrader 1999, A17). (Chapter 3 provides an extended treatment of some of the leading American political professionals who engage in both national and international electioneering.)

SHOW ME THE MONEY

There can be little doubt that money fuels what has been called the "permanent campaign" (the full-time occupation of candidates, politicians, and their staffs to solicit financing for election and reelection). Based on the ability-to-pay principle, U.S. elections are beholden to elite interests. And while there is a zero-sum outcome for the winners and losers in the campaigns, there are certain groups such as consultants and media outlets that always stand to benefit from money-driven elections. About 20 percent of a candidate's campaign goes to consulting fees, commissions, and expenses (Denton and Woodward 1990, 48). Campaign consultants themselves see campaign money as the single most important factor in the election outcome, although that perception differs between Democratic (83 percent) and Republican (65 percent) Party consultants (Pew Research Center 1998).

Anticipating the issue of corporate money–navigated elections, a 1950s-era political science text argued that in the "monopolistic competition" of elections, the politician "must first ask himself [*sic*] if he has the means to *sell* his point of view, for the problem, as the public relations man will not let us forget, is to be heard as well as to speak" (Kelley 1956, 229; emphasis in original). George W. Bush had such an advantage in campaign finances well before the 2000 presidential election that his Republican rivals had little chance of capturing the party primaries. And in the wake of the largest federal tax redistribution to the wealthiest Americans in 2003, Bush improved upon his fund-raising feat in the march toward the 2004 election. Money also dominates another theater of lawmaking: the ballot initiative, which draws in the talents of professional consultants and is fast becoming a back-door means of organized interests bypassing elected legislators.

Elections follow the logic of Parkinson's law: the more money that candidates raise, the more that elections cost; consultants with their armory of trendy, expensive campaign tools give candidates reason to believe that additional polling, telemarketing, or advertising time will mean the difference between winning and losing. Corporate executive officers (CEOs), seeing neither permanent friends nor permanent enemies but only permanent interests, seem all too happy to donate to both major political parties to promote their legislative or administrative agendas—and thereby corner the political markets for their own narrow class interests. In 1996, 235,000 individuals, less than one-thousandth of the U.S. population, each contributed $1,000 or more to federal election candidates. Since the mid-1990s, business PACs have been favoring Republicans over Democrats by a two-to-one margin and represent the main funding source of successful and incumbent politicians. The result is that the barriers to entry for would-be politicians are extremely high, effectively rendering the political system monopolistically off-limits to all but a well-financed minority.

Among the different types of political action committees, the so-called leadership PACs are designed to enable individual congressional representatives to dole out money to their favorite colleagues. These are major contributors to the two dominant parties. But even third parties would have little chance of competing without PAC support. In 1996, twelve Republican and two Democratic congressional members had party leadership PACs of more than $200,000. Rep. John Shadegg (AZ) led the Republicans with $4,575,019 in leadership (GOPAC) PAC support; and Rep. Richard Gephardt (MO) led the Democrats with $1,164,024 from the Effective Government Committee PAC. But while PACs by themselves may not be the center of political gravity in the United States (Schlesinger, ca. 1997), many observers argue that organized money contributions and the range of interests collectively represented by that money constitute the main situ of agenda setting in U.S. politics. William Greider refers to the American political system as a "mock democracy" that favors the narrow wealthy stratum, that has an "immediate financial stake in the political outcomes [and that] can afford to invest this kind of money in manipulating the governing decisions" (Greider 1992, 36–37).

Even major league baseball (MLB) has gotten into the act. In 2002, MLB pitched $108,000 toward sixty-five congressional candidates, plus another

$170,000 in soft money to the two major league parties. As the only sporting industry with a PAC, baseball's moguls became politically active when the House and Senate judiciary committees took up the question of the team owners' unique exemption from antitrust legislation. More than half the profits that the owners make, as well as other special operating privileges, including the right to move teams at will, is directly attributable to favorable federal legislation (*Associated Press* 2003).

The growing influence of corporate money in the political process has come at the expense of public sector interests and institutions, including political parties. PAC contributions, "the greatest lobbying tool ever invented," have greatly diminished the influence of parties, which provide a mere pittance of financial support to candidates compared to organized economic interests (Bennett 1996, 137, 151). The national parties in 1996, for example, served as "mere funnels through which soft money from major donors was passed on to state party organizations and special-interest groups to get around the federal limits on campaign funding" (Witcover 1999, 266). Election financing practices allow money to go directly to the candidates, rather than through the parties, and the parties have practically no voice in how the money is spent or who serves as the candidate's campaign consultants and spokespeople. As for how the public receives political information, the United States is one of the few Organisation for Economic Co-operation and Development (OECD) countries (the others being Switzerland and Austria) that provides no free airtime to political parties. Several countries provide free airtime and ban paid political advertising.[6]

For the 2000 presidential race, the Republicans organized a Team One Million, a thousand individuals each willing to contribute $1 million over a four-year election cycle (Johnson 2001, 178, 180, 183). (See chapter 6 for extended discussion of campaign contributions.) The Republican Party is said to have made 70 million telephone calls, sent 110 million letters, and mobilized 243,000 volunteers in the ten days prior to the day of voting (Plasser and Plasser 2002, 85). The Clinton-Gore Democrats, too, drawn by the money chase to adopt the neoliberal Democratic Leadership Council agenda, relied more than at any time in the past on the corporate dole. Altogether, some 4,500 PACs contributed about $250 million in the 2000 election (M. Green 2002b, 140).

Candidates with strong and articulate critiques of the corporate agenda, such as Ralph Nader, have virtually no chance of overcoming the big money that is spent to bring acceptable candidates to the ballot. The cost and diversions of campaigning and its funding mechanism undoubtedly are keeping many bright, independent, and talented people from running for office and defaults the electoral system to monied interests. American women, relatively few of whom are power brokers for Fortune 500 companies, have far less than a fair chance of becoming president. The same is true for racial minorities.

The maximum campaign contribution per voter, set at $1,000 until raised in 2001 to $2,000, ensures that a small minority will dominate the financing of elections. A record $2 billion was spent by federal candidates on the 2000 federal elections (50 percent more than the 1996 spending level). Of this, 55 percent went to Bush and Republican congressional candidates, including $646 million from corporations and CEOs "eager to underwrite the Republicans' hands-off approach to business" (Bates et al. 2001, 47) and who are able to deduct such political investments from their tax liability as a "cost of doing business" (Vidal 2001, x). Democrats were underwritten by the same corporations, but in smaller amounts among eight of the top ten industries.[7] In 2004, federal election candidate spending was expected to top $3 billion (again, a 50 percent increase over the previous presidential election year).

The study of Bates et al. (2001, 48) found that those federal candidates who raised the most money in 2001 won the White House plus 440 seats in Congress, losing only twenty-nine contests. In the case of George W. Bush, the candidate had already raised so much money by the first half of 1999 ($37 million), that he, along with Steve Forbes, was able to pass up federal matching funds and the spending restraints that such an option would have required. He ended up with almost $102 million in personal contributions, more than double what Bob Dole had raised in private contributions in his 1996 presidential bid. Of this amount, 80 percent came from contributors who gave more than $200 (Opensecrets 2001). He was expected to raise twice that much in his reelection bid.

George McGovern raised $15 million through direct mailing efforts in his 1972 presidential campaign (Johnson 2001, 155), but this came primarily from small donors. Since then, "one dollar one vote" has become institutionalized as the effective rule of political participation in American elections. Peter Kostmayer was a six-term Congress member from Pennsylvania, and by 1999, when running for the Senate, he found himself having to raise $50,000 per week to remain a contender. It wasn't enough (Kostmayer 2001). For the millionaires who dominate the Senate membership, such as Senate majority leader Bill Frist (R-TN), with blind trusts worth $31 million and the richest member of that body, this does not have to be a problem. For Senator Patrick Leahy (D-VT), with a combined cash account and growth portfolio of $30,000, it could be, especially if the national Republican leadership chooses to mount a challenge in that New England state (Fram 2003, A4).

In a 1997 fund-raising drive, the Republican Congressional Committee sent potential contributors a letter with a $1 greenback clearly visible through the plastic envelope and an enclosed note from Newt Gingrich that implored recipients to return the dollar and additional money to the party campaign organizers. However, the legion of small contributors is not the base of political support to whom the candidate is likely to be most solicitous. In money-driven contests, the steady winners include the large interest groups, such as the energy and pharmaceutical industries, which have the financial means to make money a decisive factor in regulating elections by separating the big players from the small, and the reliable and friendly candidates from the mavericks and change agents. Big money is a key element in perpetuating two centrist parties, marginalizing other parties and social movements, in the political elites' efforts to retain political legitimacy. (The financial nexus of political campaigns and consultants is discussed more thoroughly in chapter 6.)

In a money-driven political system, the largest corporations and their political and ideological allies have mastered the system of manipulating policy and electoral outcomes by effectively locking up the process with financial contributions and an inside-the-Beltway playbook. Were corporate contributions to candidates banned (in the present scheme of things, quite unthinkable), third and fourth party candidates would have a much better chance of widening the political spectrum. The fact that longtime consumer advocate Ralph Nader refused corporate contributions and did not have a financial portfolio like Ross Perot's severely limited his chances of being treated as a legitimate presidential candidate. With its benign neglect of the campaign contribution issue, the U.S. Federal Election Commission has only encouraged the commodification of the campaign process (that is, transforming its public character into profitable market exchange relationships), while other federal agencies have helped export the system to other countries, which is more fully discussed in chapters 4 and 5.

NOTES

1. David Butler and Austin Ranney write, for example, "The fundamental cause of the widespread 'Americanization' of electioneering [in the world], both in vocabulary and in technology, lies in the revolution in communications" (Butler and Ranney 1992, 280). James Carville, who served as a political consultant in Israeli elections, does not see himself as part of an "Americanization" effect: "They're not looking to me for advice on Israel. They're looking to me for advice on communications, on organization, on how to set things up, on how to respond" (Halimi 1999).

2. With the collapse of their communist parties, Eastern Europe became an irresistibly attractive opening for American political consultants. Among the entry points was the Czech Republic where Frank Greer assisted Czech President Vaclav

Havel in 1993 in that country's first open, multiparty election (Maxfield and Schlesinger 1997, 15).

3. For example, despite findings of voter alienation with corporate-financed elections in the study, Harvard political analyst Thomas Patterson had almost nothing critical to say about the money issue in his 2002 study of the "vanishing voter" (Patterson 2002).

4. Only 14 percent of the Senate and less than that (13.5 percent) in the House are women (2003). White men, with 32 percent of the national population, overwhelmingly dominate both bodies.

5. Professionalization implies a system of certification and regulation (with a regularly monitored code of conduct) by either or both a private association (of professionals) and government. Probably most members of the consulting industry would agree that none of these conditions pertain, and that, at best, an informal set of principles regulates the business behavior of consultants. Many consultants, operating both domestically and abroad, appear to write their own rules of conduct, and there exists no effective sanctioning body to restrain them. Membership in professional associations of consultants is entirely voluntary.

6. Countries with free political broadcasts on television and radio and banned paid political advertising include Belgium, Brazil, Czech Republic, France, Israel, Italy, Lebanon, the Netherlands, Norway, Portugal, Senegal, Sweden, Switzerland, Turkey, and the United Kingdom (Pinto-Duschinsky 2001, 22).

7. In one study, the industries that favored Republicans were finance, insurance, and real estate; manufacturing and retail services; health; energy; agribusiness; transportation; construction; and defense. Those favoring Democrats were communications and high tech; and lawyers and lobbyists (Bates et al. 2001, 48).

2

Managing the Electorate and the Public Sphere

> Like the effect of advertising upon the customer, the methods of political propaganda tend to increase the feeling of insignificance of the individual voter.
>
> —Erich Fromm, *Escape from Freedom*, 1941

PUBLIC OPINION, POLLING, PR, AND PROPAGANDA

In the new harsh and winning-by-any-means political environment, it is no longer taboo for consultants to acknowledge that their profession is about "managing public opinion," an oxymoron if ever there was one. Whereas the term *public opinion* is normally associated with democratic political systems, in more recent decades it has come to chiefly signify the use of professional polling. But as Justin Lewis notes, the

> conflation with public opinion with poll responses has been subject to considerable critical scrutiny, not least because it is the pollster rather than the public who will define the terms of the rather stilted, one-sided conversations that constitute polling interviews. Indeed, it could be argued that the dominant voice behind polls is not the public but the pollster, while the public's role in the enterprise is limited to acquiescence, evasion or refusal, with no control over the interpretation of those responses. (Lewis 2002, 79)

If voters are indeed not making political choices independent of pollsters and professional spinmasters' opinion management techniques, the notion of "government by the people" would appear to be extremely hollow. When the mass media acquiesce, as they generally do when the White House and/or Congress become fixated on a policy course, such as going to war in Iraq, pollsters usually find that the moral justifications, often phrases that are drummed into media audiences (e.g., "weapons of mass destruction"), can be quite effective, especially in the short run. Critics argue that if and when pollsters were to ask questions in ways that better address potential social outcomes, public opinion would register quite a different response. Critical poll designs are rarely undertaken, and when they are, they are infrequently referenced by the media and public officials.

Pierre Bourdieu insisted that the very notion of public opinion is fatuous, because, in his view, there is no publicly organized consensus about identifying the most relevant questions. There can be mobilized, elite-driven formulated opinion, he argued, but not public opinion in the sense that pollsters normally use the term. Most people do not themselves construct opinions on the issues that are pertinent to pollsters and the state, and what passes as public opinion polls on the whole are half-hearted attempts by respondents to accommodate the needs of the professional pollster. There is also a high degree of variation in people's responses to pollsters; some have strong or well-thought-out positions, others have only the vaguest familiarity with the question. The very act of polling, the presence of a pollster, and the peculiar form and content of the questioning act are interventions that interfere with the normal rhythms and routines of most people, which are bound to result in anomalous responses.

Polling questions are rarely extracted from the issues that arise from the experience and interest of voters themselves, but rather from well-organized interest groups of one kind or another (Bourdieu 1972 lecture, in Mattelart and Siegelaub 1979, 124–30). Communication theorist Joseph Klapper observed that new issues are those for which most people themselves have no preformed opinion and are thereby open to the influence of mass communications, against which they have no defense. Republican consultant Michael Murphy admitted that "We tell them [the voters] what they want to hear . . . . We take polls and find out that if we offer them chocolate ice cream, then they say they're for chocolate ice cream. So we only run on chocolate ice cream" (cited in Hill 2002, 163). Polling surveys thus become blunt instruments that news media, politicians, and policymakers can employ in depicting "public opinion" as a way of legitimizing their respective partisan interests. "And once the opinion is created," Klapper observed, "then it is this new opinion which becomes easy to reinforce and hard to change," especially "when the person has no other source of information on the topic to use as a touchstone" (cited in Schiller 1973, 166–67).

National politics derived from the opinion of the electorate would presume a form of (direct) democracy that has never existed in the United States or any other Western country and has only been imagined in anarchist texts or such works as *The Social Contract* by Rousseau, who first expressed the term *public opinion*. The nature of professional campaign work puts these specialists at odds with the idea of an active and politicized citizenry who genuinely and collectively formulate public opinion, inasmuch as their status as "professionals" casts them as brokers of the political system. Consulting as a business is driven not by ideals of participatory democracy as much as by the need to deliver victories for clients, for which they are well compensated and recognized. Guiding rather than soliciting the public pulse has been the concern of political elites since the time of the Founding Fathers. One of the principal authors of the Constitution, James Madison, believed in procedural democracy but one that defended the privileged political position of the landed classes, in order, as he put it, "to protect the minority of the opulent against the majority" (Chomsky 1997). For Madison, public opinion mattered much, but the public that concerned him was that of what he saw as the educated, virtuous elite, not the common people.

Modern consultants are far more solicitous of the masses than were the aristocratic early presidents, but their professional interests are more in line with those in positions of power. With respect to public opinion, it is critical for the maintenance of a low-intensity democracy like that of the United States that the public be able to voice its sentiments. But the range of expression is almost always within speech boundaries and a spectrum of political choices that do not challenge the legitimacy and sanctity of a private investor–based political economy. The modern institutions of mass media do not protect or encourage public opinion as much as replace it by discouraging a truly public sphere in which opinion is broadly engaged and debated without the constraints of commercial or political interests and technology and media intervention.

The modern state underwrites the study of collective psychology and public opinion formation. Indeed, public opinion as a field of study, in fact the entire academic field of communication studies, has deep roots in government-funded World War II propaganda research and operations undertaken by the Office of War Information (OWI). Several of the established OWI-era propaganda specialists went on to assume leadership positions in university communication departments and related fields as well as in the propaganda agencies of the U.S. government (including the successor of the OWI, the U.S. Information Agency) during the Cold War mobilization. The term *propaganda*,[1] which was widely used (mostly in a favorable tactical sense) in the late 1940s, fell into disfavor in the 1950s and was replaced by the more benign-sounding term *persuasion*. Propaganda, instead, came to be associated with marxist-inspired revolutionary movements and with how communist parties communicate to their publics.

Mind management has never developed to the expectations of its exponents or practitioners. Political consultants admit that they have a problem with controlling public opinion. Frank Luntz, a leading Republican Party consultant, ruefully acknowledged that "The public has turned against corporate America now [1996] more than at any time since the 1960s. . . . [T]he frustration and anger stretches well into the middle class and up through white collar and middle level management" (*PR Watch* 1997). To remedy this situation, the corporate community has welcomed political consultants to help them with their public relations, especially during the political off-season, and sometimes, what some consider crossing the line, acting as their lobbyists. According to one estimate, candidate campaigns make up 34 percent of political consultant income, ballot measures another 10 percent, and the rest, more than half, comes from "public affairs" work—lobbying, issue advocacy, and public relations (Nordlinger 2000, 26). Regardless of what political consultants may say, practically speaking, lobbying is simply another form of political campaigning.

Professionalization of politics is closely associated with the public relations field, and the leadership in this field is usually credited with the pioneering work of Edward Bernays. A nephew of Sigmund Freud and a strong advocate for the "engineering of consent" (see chapter 4), Bernays argued that the public relations professional "extracts from his clients' causes ideas which will capitalize certain fundamental instincts in the people he is trying to reach" (Friedenberg 1997, 16). In his view, it was an imperative of stable society that elites provide public instruction to citizens of lesser capabilities and understanding. During his long life, Bernays advised several presidents on their political campaigns, and at his pinnacle was touted by *Time* magazine as "U.S. Publicist Number One" (Denton and Woodward 1990, 49).

Public opinion and polling are inseparable from public relations, and both have long been heavily influenced by the needs of big business and mass media. Under the pressures of the Great Depression and the enlarged federal programs under Roosevelt's New Deal, corporations, particularly those from the National Association of Manufacturers (NAM), took up public relations as a core business strategy in the 1930s to ward off government regulation. It was not long before public relations experts became central to the process of conducting political campaigns as well. NAM led "a campaign to convert the American public to the economic goals, ideals, and program of business." The association's public relations budget went from $36,000 to almost $800,000 between 1934 and 1937, and its distribution system included radio, a press service for newspaper stories and editorials, a speakers bureau, direct mail, film strips, educational films, paid advertising, pamphlets, and publicity carried out in schools and factories. The pace of business-led propaganda accelerated during World War II (Fones-Wolf 1994, 25–29).

Public relations is also about how professional consultants package and sell themselves to their clients as victory brokers. The problem with the management of politics by professionals, according to two observers, is that "[f]or consultants to get business, they must continue to win elections. They are more likely, then, to accept only sure bets and once in battle, they may not recognize any limits to winning" (Denton and Woodward 1990, 68). In other words, issues and principles mean far less to the professionals than the results—by whatever means attainable. Their reputation, income, and professional future depend on it. Raymond Strother, head of the 2,000-member American Association of Political Consultants, says bluntly that the real goal of consulting firms is simply to "maximize profits," and "[a]ny consultant who says money doesn't affect the system is either naive or lying" (cited in Glasser 2000).

One of the first persons political campaign organizers typically hire is the pollster, but not because politicians wish to act as direct representatives of the people. In recent national elections, virtually every campaign issue was pretested with polls, and the 2000 election had more of them than any before. Polling is not a neutral technique for collecting and representing public opinion, however. The nature of the polling instrument is that it intersects with and helps form opinion around questions in which the pollsters (including those who fund polls) are interested. Some critical observers argue that, contrary to conventional explanation, public opinion research generally does not guide policy ideas; rather, policy decisions usually dictate public opinion research "in order to identify the language, arguments, and symbols most likely to persuade." The management of opinion enables campaign consultants to pursue niche marketing of candidates and for politicians to engage in "simulated responsiveness." Polling is seen by some as a tool "to deceive voters about the politician's true intentions and policies and to free themselves [politicians] to pursue their own partisan agendas that the majority of voters would reject if they were clearer about what the politicians actually were up to" (Hill 2002, 162; Jacobs and Shapiro 2000, 76).

Benjamin Ginsberg observes that "polling has [also] contributed to the domestication of opinion by helping to transform it from a politically potent, often disruptive force into a more docile, plebiscitary phenomenon" (Ginsberg 1986, 60). Polls can be highly manipulative devices for selectively capturing or even inciting a mood or disposition from respondents. The heavy reliance on polling by politicians and candidates has removed much of the personal aspects of politics that were more widely felt during the era when local ward leaders and precinct captains, the liaisons to existing and would-be officeholders, went door-to-door to hear people's concerns and garner their votes.

The role of political precinct activists, no strangers to their constituents, was to reinforce personal ties with voters of the neighborhoods, often acting as fixers for anything from distributing food to the poor to taking care of parking tickets to finding jobs for the unemployed and other forms of patronage (Kelley 1956, 207). Congressional representatives were expected periodically to make appearances at the political district level, whereas at present, aided by polling and other communication technologies, they are far more likely to speak through the mass media, their staffers, and pollsters (Selnow 1994, 171–74).

Polling thus helps to take the guesswork out of campaigning, so that politicians and their public relations teams can minimize the extent of politicians' public contact or the need to express extemporaneous ideas of their own. This was already emerging as a fact of political life in the 1950s. It is all the more true today, with far more sophisticated tools of election management available. Patrick Caddell, Jimmy Carter's polling specialist (later feted as the pollster of the 1980s "New Coke" ad campaign), said in a report to the president that "governing with public approval requires a continuing political campaign." He advised that the president could soothe the public mood on the strength of poll results and also should make use of celebrities and other surrogates to continually keep himself in the public limelight (cited in Bowman 2000, 63).

But what does "public opinion" actually say about what people think? Justin Lewis suggests three fallacies that arise from the attempt to treat public opinion polls as truthful representations. One is that pollsters record but do not interpret the meanings of the responses. Second, in the construction of public opinion, pollsters fail to acknowledge the messages conveyed to respondents in the polling instrument itself (by the newspaper or private polling organization, for example). And, third, the poll results do not capture the respondents' assumptions embedded in their answers to questions (Lewis 2001, 16). So-called public opinion polls often are little more than feedback mechanisms for measuring the effectiveness of framing, spinning, and elite propaganda, while supporting the legitimacy of state behavior and power relations.

Caddell's premise, that through polling the public decides the administration's policies—beyond being self-serving—is easily refuted in a number of ways. For one thing, polls are often taken at the height of a crisis or other reactive moment, which does not necessarily reflect the public mood over time, and often are employed to serve the partisan interests of a politician, his/her party, or an interest group. For another, the administration may choose not to follow the poll results, as was clearly the case prior to and during the Clinton impeachment hearings, when many poll results seemed to indicate that the majority of Americans did not regard the president's sexual "transgressions" as an impeachable offense. Third, polls are very selective in the kinds of questions that the public is asked to answer; the Gallup and Harris organizations are unlikely to ask Americans, for example, if they think corporations on the whole have too much power, whether the wealthy pay enough taxes, whether the criminal justice system discriminates against the poor, and if the present form of representative government seeks out and is responsive to the voices of ordinary citizens. Such questions might be considered too incendiary, regardless of what the public may actually think. And even if they were to include such questions, it is hard to conceive that the Congress, the higher courts, or the executive branch would act in accordance with opinion that in fundamental structural terms confronts elite governing assumptions.

The use of polling in politics is spreading to other countries. In Britain, which tends to follow (but occasionally leads) U.S. political behavior, it was becoming very clear to many close observers by the early 1970s that formal politics had become highly promotional in nature and the range of political debate was driven by the comparative advantages of technique, technology, and technicians. Labour Party candidates in particular have borrowed their electioneering style from their American counterparts, with "constant polling, use of focus groups, direct mail, telephone canvassing, and the targeting of voters . . . used now to an extent unprecedented in Britain" (Grose 1997). The *Times* (London) editorialized that the "most chilling aspect of modern elections is their impersonal quality." And it has reached the point where "[t]he elector is invited to vote not for a Member of Parliament, but for a Party; not for a Party but for its Leader; and not for its Leader but for a pre-packaged television presentation of what Market Research suggests the Leader should be" (cited in Mughan 2000, 141).

One of the standard tools of American professional political consulting is the focus group, which is "periodically conducted to test-market everything from the content of commercials to the selection of prepared lines in debates" (M. Green 2002b, 119), the results of which can be targeted to large or selective blocs of voters. Focus group research can be used to formulate messages that resonate both positively and negatively with voters, regardless of their accuracy. The "contract with America" slogan used by Newt Gingrich, when he was House Speaker, originated from focus group research (Johnson 2001, 106). MSNBC relied on conservative Republican pollster and advisor Frank Luntz to do its focus group research, and despite the obvious conflict of interest, the station refused to drop his contract.

Some observers worry that polling and focus group data are also abused in other ways. One of the problems noted is that candidates tend to direct their message not to their supporters or to the electorate as a whole but, rather, to the "swing voters," whose voting decisions may remain undecided almost to the last minute. It is said that Al Gore, like his predecessor and mentor Bill Clinton, was overly cautious in representing his broader ideas to the public, and relied heavily on focus groups to plan his campaign message. (The same was reported about John Kerry and George W. Bush in the 2004 presidential election.) One syndicated political pundit ruefully commented that Gore's bland liberalism and tepid social justice rhetoric were, at best, targeted to "a few focus-group chosen industries" (Frank Rich cited in McWilliams 2001, 184).

One might think that focus groups help democratize the political agenda. But the packet of questions put to participants and the responses they give is not about any urge to give voters a more active role and voice in politics. It's about constructing a winning candidate, with a winning message, and a winning personality. The energy exchange is mainly between the media consultants who design advertising pitches and the pollsters with their focus group data. In 1988, focus group research for George H. W. Bush yielded a conclusion that his presidential campaign should avoid using the word *Republican* (McWilliams 2001, 184). In 2000, Gore studiously ignored the word *Democrat*. The core strategy is mainly centered on controlling public relations and propaganda.[2]

The most forceful forms of propaganda are those that deal in half truths, the presentation of "facts," images, or icons stripped of context that manipulate the voting citizen in one way or another. Bush's campaign team in 1988 effectively used focus group techniques on likely Dukakis voters, playing on the test group's partial understanding of the Democratic candidate's political positions, to intentionally elicit negative reactions, and then incorporated the test results in hot-button political ads.[3] Campaign discourse becomes a highly scripted, choreographed, and stylized performance of the candidate acting under the direction and in accordance with the media practices and message constructions of hired consultants. Election results often are touted as evidence of the propaganda skills of the consultants, more than the informed voice of the voters.

Constant polling enables existing and potential candidates as well as officeholders to make a determination of whether to run (the "pre-decision poll"), whether to stay in the race (the "benchmark poll"), how well they are doing in the campaign or in the elected position from week to week (the "tracking poll"). The George W. Bush White House has a polling operation in Houston featuring a 185-station phone bank (J. Green 2002). Election polling is likely to be undertaken daily during at least the last ten weeks of the campaign, and at that point pollsters can devise questions and techniques that go well beyond the standard survey (Foster and Muste 1992, 29; Glasser 2000). This way of gathering information is less about improving the quality of leadership and making transparent to the public politicians' political values and objectives and more about how to craft messages ("crafted talk") to create an image of leadership and to market (spin) preselected policy ideas to the public.

Polling, especially by major polling organizations, is often more about creating opinions than soliciting them, as the crafting of the question is likely to cue the respondent to the "correct" answer as well as signify its importance as an issue. Major polling organizations such as Gallup, for example, frequently test poll positions in direct and immediate response to policy statements put out by the White House and prominent politicians. Polling also is more likely to reveal how effectively the candidate or officeholder is performing (how well the campaign or policy message is received) than what people actually think about the political issues or the system as a whole. Poll- and focus group–tested political language is often intended precisely to overcome the public's skepticism or resistance to partisan interest-group political agendas. Integrated with well-crafted speechwriting, polling is central to the scripted presidency or prime ministership. Polling has thus frequently become not the search for "public opinion" but rather Bernays's "engineering of consent," and the mass media have been complicit in legitimating its use and abuse. (See chapter 4.)

Bill Clinton is reported to have had such an insatiable appetite for polls that he never made an important decision, even about the choice of White House pets, without first having one conducted, heavily relying on its results as a gauge of the public mood. Dick Morris quipped that Clinton "polls as often as he breathes" (cited in Johnson 2001, 89) and claimed to have picked the president's vacation spots based on poll results (Bowman 2000, 67). But before and after him, both of the Bush presidents were well known to have been driven by polling information. For the younger Bush, the favored pollster, Jan van Lohuizen, and focus group specialist, Fred Steeper, were hired to spin policy ideas through the use of gut-level manipulative phrases that were not part of the mainstream vernacular. Bush's policies, it has been said, are less concerned with public opinion and more about "presentation" (J. Green 2002)—and his main brand of spinning is less about himself and more about his agenda. Both van Lohuizen and Steeper earlier worked for Bush's polling analyst and chief White House strategist Karl Rove.

The main problem with polling, as Gary Selnow (1994) notes, is that it becomes a substitute for dialogue. Candidates can collect data from samples of voters without ever conducting a local or national discussion about what the voters actually think about particular issues and policies in their own words. With the aid of advanced communications technologies, politics by polling, represented as a dialogue, is a simulation of discussion rather than an actual one. The discussion that does take place around issues is largely dominated by the mass media, usually very superficial and heavily driven by poll data (that is often incomplete), in which there is little space allocated for interaction, first, between voters and politicians; second, between voters and the press; and, third, among voters themselves.

THE TARGETED VOTER

Professionalized and technologically mediated elections depend heavily on a panoptic sorting of the electorate. This means that election messages, especially for national and state campaigns, are developed with the aid of computerized databases that sort probable voters' political and socioeconomic demographic data. With this information, campaign managers can begin to design cross-sectional focus groups to test various messages, campaign styles, keywords, and other elements that will find their way to the political ads and appearances that are run in various electronic and print media. The targeting of voters also relies on direct-mail pieces, brochures, websites, and other means of delivering the image and the message of their respective candidates.

Identity harvesting (through routine invasions of privacy) enables campaign consultants to develop complex and revealing polling analyses, consumer and census data profiles, and other intelligence, often proprietary, that surveils and "constructs" the voters and their issue orientations. According to Manuel Castells (2001, 176), during the 2000 election campaign, a U.S. company "created a database, named Aristotle, which, using data from different sources, provided political profiling of as many as 150 million citizens, selling these profiles to the highest bidder, usually the campaign offices of political candidates." In this sense, it is the politicians who are choosing the voters rather than the other way around. Campaigns are likely to devote far less attention to party loyalists than those at the margins, the so-called independent voters.

Central to the electioneering process is the pollster. Once a marginal player in the political campaign (e.g., Louis Harris in the 1960s), the pollster is now often a central strategist (e.g., Stanley Greenberg). Most polling surveillance is unknown to the voters themselves, even though information about them is being freely shared without their consent.[4] Lists of voter profiles are sold by database merchants, such as Atlantic List Company, which makes a business of collecting data on the buying habits of consumers. After careful surveillance of the voters, candidates and politicians are affectively packaged and "sold" back to citizens in exchange for their votes. "The selling depends, not on rational debate or real differences, but on concocting emotional bonds between the candidate and the audience" (Greider 1992, 271).

This commercial orientation of seeing the voter as a consumer, and consumer as voter, establishes integrating linkages between business and politics. A high-powered Anglo-American corporate consulting group, made up of Philip Gould, Stanley Greenberg, and James Carville, "is among the first to adapt political techniques to ensuring companies can modernise" (Gapper 1997, 7) and is part of a "dense network of cooperation" between British and American consultants (Plasser and Plasser 2002, 27). Almost every important political campaign organization in the United States employs electioneering specialists and communication-mediated techniques. American consultant Joseph Napolitan is said to have successfully convinced one Labour Party leader "to clean up his appearance, get a haircut, and put on a business suit in order to be more presentable to the British public" (Barnett and Goldstein 2002, 1). In Britain, a leaked memo in 2000 written by Gould called for the New Labour Party to become "more professional" in order "to reinvent the New Labour brand" (White 2000), and he openly acknowledged the influence of Clinton's war-room political tactics and, indeed, the "Clintonisation" of the Labour Party (Gould 1998, 176).

Consultants' skills and techniques employed "to change the climate of public opinion" were found to be particularly useful to companies engaged in major restructuring projects (Gapper 1997, 7). Additionally, their extensive methods and technologies of citizen surveillance, most actively applied in the commercial sales sector, have been adapted to a system of political management, mobilization, and control. (See chapter 3.) In political as in commodity sales pitches, the citizen (consumer) is appealed to as an individual, not as a member of the collective society. Selling candidates to targeted voters thus creates a highly individuated and partisan political climate in which politicians speak to the electorate largely through sound bites that their pollsters' data identify as safe, memorable, and marketable.

This mode of politics requires heavy investment in ICT applications drawn extensively from the business sector. As leader of the neoliberal world economy, the United States serves as a model for would-be leaders in other countries who share such an infatuation with technological and informational control that ICT accords to already powerful institutions. In Britain, the New Labour Party under Tony Blair's dominion also enthusiastically endorses the formulaic applications of sophisticated ICT in the electoral process. The Tories, on the other hand, are said to favor a newspaper-clipping and television-monitoring service approach (Harriman 2001), but also use a software package for identifying and targeting voters and their preferences, which they call, not surprisingly, the Blue Chip system.

Labour's party headquarters, the Millbank Tower, imported the Excalibur computer system that a California party leader, Robert Mulholland, previously had introduced to the Democratic Party. The software allows its users to track at blinding speed the records of politicians, especially the most embarrassing details, as part of its opposition research and a rapid rebuttal system similar to the Clinton 1992 war room. An advisor to Labour noted, however, that although the technology cost £500,000, it proved to be "a complete shambles" and "the Attack Task Force often found it more convenient to use the paper files hanging on the wall than to trawl through the computer" (Gould 1998, 302–3). Nonetheless, the Excalibur Computer Corporation, which produces the system, also claims to have sold it to the British Ministry of Defense and the government's top intelligence branches (Harriman 2001).

Along with new high-tech software that can moonlight either for political or military purposes, there is a range of techniques employed in elections that borrows heavily from the commercial advertising and public relations fields. The well-tested means of segmenting consumers by values, attitudes, and lifestyles, a process known as psychographics, can be used to break up, target, and massage the electorate along specified issues, images, and catch phrases. The intent is to reduce the friction between voters and candidates, which is referred to as "high interest, low backlash" communication (Friedenberg 1997, 100). This contributes to a demassified but regulated political atmosphere in which it becomes difficult to identify a public consensus around broad issues. The "public" is reduced to a plethora of "demographics." Campaign managers will take no chances in possibly polluting well-researched sections of voters with information about the candidate's positions on issues other than those for which they have been profiled and which otherwise might turn them off. A good database is like an arsenal of smart bombs: it has demographic coordinates and is intended to never miss its target.

Direct mail is often the medium of choice for such targeted voter strategies, a technique that is seen by an Australian observer as "more about personalised propaganda than about providing real information on policies" and which "allows the manipulation of individual political sensitivities and may impede the development of national outlooks" (Beresford 1998, 30). In such a carefully crafted surveillance system, voters tend not to learn a great deal about issues that do not directly or subjectively interest them. Political outlooks become disaggregated and narrowly partisan. Together with the television industry's general disinclination to inform and educate viewers, this helps to explain why American voters who were polled two days before the 2000 election could not answer basic questions about the candidates' positions on core issues (Taylor 2002, 13).

Single-issue voters will thereby have a difficult time making connections between political positions of the candidates and seeing the "big picture." This strategy for organizing majorities would seem to better work for Republicans who might want to separate job, health, and Social Security concerns, which are traditional Democratic Party platform issues, from other defined problems, such as abortion, taxes, and crime. Religious morality and flag issues are constructed with particularly strong emotional and irrational appeals to primordial identities. Clinton, with the advice of his political consultant Dick Morris and in consultation with his "New Democrat" colleagues, identified and incorporated both sets of issues, which helped earn him the "slick Willie" sobriquet. Several of his campaign team (see chapter 3) were so pleased with their voter management techniques that they began to think more about their global applications.

MEDIACRACY?

Lance Bennett has argued that power in America is most often discussed in personalistic rather than structural terms, which reinforces as much as it is influenced by the power of the highly concentrated and conglomerated mass media. The biggest ideas in politics are reduced to transitory, winner-take-all communication strategies. This involves the use of polling and other methods of capturing, creating, and exploiting short-term moods and memories of the electorate. Advertising replaces news as the main conduit of political information. The horse-race style of coverage becomes the main framework that newsrooms use to assess the strength of competing candidates, and leaders in the various political races are measured by poll rankings and the candidates' respective financial resources. Bennett found that in 1992 only 67 of 1,024 network election news stories featured candidate statements of longer than twenty seconds (Bennett 1996, 126–28, 131). The average political soundbite length has since been reduced to single digit. Political education is reduced to the lowest common denominator.

From April through October 1996, the two major parties' candidates transmitted 752,891 television political commercials (Johnson 2001, 117). Factoring in inflation, political advertising on television across the country increased fivefold from 1980 to 2000 (Wayne 2003, 96). With increased spending limits permitted under the 2002 campaign finance "reform" bill, television has gotten even richer from its election season customers. And inasmuch as news corporations are exempt from spending limits on political coverage, interest groups like the National Rifle Association are looking to buy TV and radio stations in order to have a pulpit for expressing their policy and candidate preferences, largely free of restriction.[5]

The mass media, particularly in the United States, have become central to the political process in several ways. First, they are the main source of news information for the American public, and politicians, policymakers, and others who need to communicate with the public must go through these channels in order for their message to be heard. Political communication is a joint and reciprocal project between the communicating individual and the media. The mass media, in turn, are primarily commercial enterprises that depend on advertising revenue, including political advertising, and thus have a stake in legitimating high-finance electoral campaigns. Because the rates media enterprises charge advertisers are determined by circulation and the social class (and disposable income) of readers, listeners, or viewers, political and other news coverage must have sufficient commercial and mass marketing appeal to deliver the audience (or "demographic") to their patrons. The largest share of "news" in a newspaper is actually advertising. In broadcasting as well, although its share of airtime is about a third, news (and other) programming is much more directly influenced by advertising through the structuring, pace, and content of the presentation (commercial breaks, time allocation per sequence, action-orientation, topical choices, etc.). Political communicators learn to work within this discipline and to adopt the media shorthand of sound-bite journalism.

Second, media enterprises are among the largest transnational corporations in the world and have a compelling need to protect their investments and stockholders as players in a high-stakes economy. Record-breaking industrial-financial conglomerations have been led during the past twenty years by the telecommunications, electronics, and mass media mergers and acquisitions (among them, AOL/Time Warner/Turner Broadcasting, ABC/Capital Cities/ Disney, Westinghouse/CBS/Viacom/ Infinity Broadcasting/Paramount/ Blockbuster, AT&T/TCI, GE/RCA, News Corporation/Fox/UPN). The media empires have powerful conservative agendas of their own to pursue. Even a majority (61 percent) of investigative reporters acknowledge that corporate media owners impose themselves on news coverage decisions, according to a Pew Center for the People and the Press poll in 2000, and 41 percent of reporters could give specific personal examples of decisions or demands to change their stories on behalf of the news organization (cited in Hartmann 2002, 229). Owners have a need to manage and construct the larger ideological frame of news in ways that protect their business and financial interests and cast the public gaze toward safe subjects that induce consumption moods (mainly through entertainment). As campaign advertising is a very large part of media revenues, preserving this commercial form of political communication is very important to the industry.

Third, the mass media not only report politics in a certain way but are required to become players in the political process in pursuit of protection and favorable legislation. Toward these ends, the mass media engage in politics through a large and active lobbying presence in the federal and state capitals. They are also major contributors to federal and state political campaigns. In an election system that relies so heavily on private sector finance, the media are able to establish a quid pro quo with politicians and legislators that limits regulation of their privileged position. As an example, the National Association of Broadcasters (NAB) has successfully fended off free airtime provisions that would allow the major as well as minor parties and candidates to gain easier access to the airwaves. According to one study on their legislative behavior, media corporation lobbyists have fought vigorously in opposition to FCC restrictions on press and broadcasting conglomeration, as well as in support of tobacco and alcohol advertising in print and broadcasting, respectively. Media lobbyists also have lobbied aggressively against campaign finance reform, as a soft-money loophole has enabled many associations and political action committees to spend vast amounts of money on political advertisements on radio and television with little scrutiny from the Federal Election Commission. Even with soft-money controls, hard-money spending in the media has continued to flow in record amounts.

The same study pointed out that:

- From 1993 to mid-2000, media corporations gave $73 million to federal candidates and the two major parties;
- Both Al Gore and George W. Bush received over $1 million in media contributions during the 2000 campaign;
- From 1996 to mid-2000, the fifty largest media corporations and four of their trade associations spent $111.3 million to lobby Congress and the White House;
- In 1999 alone, 284 media lobbyists spent $31.4 million, of which Time Warner and Disney respectively spent $4.1 million and $3.3 million;
- From 1997 to mid-2000, media corporations, led by News Corporation, the NAB, and the National Cable and Television Association, spent $455,000 to take 118 members of Congress and their staffs on trips for lobbying purposes, and from 1995 to mid-2000, the media industry spent $1.5 million on lobbying trips for FCC members;
- From 1996 to mid-2000, NAB lobbyists, of whom more than a third previously had been on congressional staffs, the FCC, and the Federal Trade Commission, spent $19.42 million. (Gallavan, Rebholz, and Sanderson 2000, 1–2, 9, 11)

One outspoken veteran media consultant of both Canadian and U.S. elections, Hal Evry, sees elections as television-driven marketing extravaganzas:

It's simply a marketing job. Research is the tool that lets us find out what's in the consumer's mind—in this case, the voter's mind. . . . Party support is a mirage. . . . What has the real effect today is television. . . . If you appear to be all things to all people, get on television and don't say anything but make it sound good, you can get three out of four to like what they read into you. (cited in *New Internationalist* 1985)

No U.S. president was more attentive to his TV image and better able to work the medium than Ronald Reagan. As a primarily visual medium, television was seen by the Reagan camp as an ideal instrument to project image, particularly since Reagan, his "great communicator" moniker notwithstanding, had great difficulty performing in unscripted and impromptu conversations with news journalists. Presidential aide Michael Deaver, who had an advertising background, was brought in to help craft the Reagan portrait. Media consultant and television producer Mark Goode made sure "that nothing was left to chance and every public appearance was fully orchestrated" (Denton and Woodward 1990, 55–56). Richard Wirthlin directed all of Reagan's opinion surveys during his two administrative terms, did analyses of the Congress and the electorate, and played a central role in running the White House communications strategy (*Wirthlin Worldwide* 2001).

The mass media industry's attachment to entertaining spectacles (which made the former actor Ronald Reagan so compelling) has greatly influenced how politics and politicians are covered and, by many accounts, has seriously lowered the standard of political discourse in the United States. The media also frequently run with sensational political claims without prior verification. When George Bush Senior and the Republicans made repeated claims in the 1992 campaign that Clinton had instigated 128 tax increases as governor of Arkansas, the press reported the charge repeatedly without verifying its accuracy (Selnow 1994, 3). Whether factual or not, the refusal to hold to a stricter measure of evidence suggested that the media were more interested in creating spectacle than documenting relevant public information. Little media attention was given to the fact that Bush's son, then governor of Texas, supported raising taxes in Texas, notably when a sales tax hike was proposed to finance a new stadium for the Texas Rangers. Bush Junior happened to be a team owner, and the governor's approval ultimately provided a $200 million public subsidy to the privately owned baseball franchise (J. Green 2002; Lewis 2000a).

Sound-bite journalism reflects the headline and competitive orientation of commercial television news. A single nugget from a candidate's speech, which is in effect coproduced by the campaign team and media outlets, is designed for evening news or late newspaper edition formats. Media advisors and speechwriters prepare comments to accommodate news broadcasters' preferences by crafting messages with words and images that reduce complex realities into rhetorical phrases that they think will resonate with the media and the public. "The meat of a speech has become less important than its sizzle, because only the sizzle makes the seven o'clock news" (Selnow 1994, 142). It is the market orientation of the media rather than thoughtful articulations of governing ideas and long-range outlines of political objectives that drive the campaign rhetoric and message style. Hugh Heclo, a professor of government, finds that the best metaphor for political campaigns is that of "a commercial sales campaign between competing companies" (Heclo 2000, 13).

The mass media's prolonged obsession with Bill Clinton's sexual behavior set a new standard for coverage of politicians. Gary Hart had earlier been driven out of presidential contention (1988) after the media surveyed his personal life and exposed an extramarital affair, although he briefly considered a second try in 2004. The ending of the fairness doctrine by the Reagan administration in the 1980s, which was intended to ensure balanced reporting, led to a wave of no-holds-barred radio talk show politics, overwhelmingly conservative and Republican, encouraging sensational, scandalous, and testosterone-driven opinions about political events and personalities. One observer described talk radio as "ambush radio" and about as fair as World Wrestling Entertainment (Epps 2004, B1–B2).

Radio talk show celebrities such as conservatives Rush Limbaugh, Michael Reagan, and Oliver North, joined by other conservatives on cable news stations, are continuously in the campaign mode railing against Democrats and liberals and can mobilize millions of voters to show up at the polls for Republican candidates. FCC chair Michael Powell (son of Secretary of State Colin Powell) pushed to open up the upper limits on the number of stations a single network can own, clearly to the benefit of conservative conglomerates like Clear Channel, which controls more than 200, and moved to lift restrictions on cross-ownership of radio by TV and newspapers in the same market (Epps 2004, B2). Democrats are far less influential in talk radio or talk TV, in part because the few liberal talk show hosts who exist tend to eschew the popular visceral style of their conservative counterparts, including those on the Democratic Party–leaning "Air America" network, created in 2004. Greens and other minority party candidates are almost voiceless in the media. Political dialogue informed by well-articulated ideas seems to have little place in broadcasting.

The system of campaigning also feeds into "mutually assured destruction" of political rivals. One of the behind-the-scenes methods employed by campaigns is called "opposition research," the use of which grew rapidly in the 1990s (Sabato and Simpson 1996, 155). Opposition research is frequently little more than investigation of scandal on political opponents, often about their marital or extramarital lives. In fact, it's often performed by private investigators, and its use encourages personal surveillance and intrusion on privacy. One Louisianan specialist who does such double duty says, "There's not a garbage pail I won't get in, not an angle I won't aim a hidden camera. . . . I take cases from Republicans, Democrats, conservatives, liberals. It's all information" (cited in Hill 2002, 143). Candidates, especially those running for high office, including Bill Clinton in 1992, sometimes undertake a corollary to opposition research called "vulnerability research," which involves hiring a firm to uncover as much muck on themselves as can be found and preparing a counterstrategy for dealing with it when it becomes public. The mass media are certain to amplify such revelations if their management thinks they will attract audiences. In general, the media's political gaze, whatever form it takes, is mainly toward presidents and prime ministers and much less toward other party leaders, cabinet members, and parties as a whole, or to officials' linkages to elite interest groups—which collectively is where most legislative activity and policy development actually occur. One study argued that in the British case, this narrow focus can be explained more by deliberate campaign management than by the intent of media executives and is a trend that has increased over time (Mughan 2000). The British electorate likely senses that their elections and public involvement are being seriously compromised, as membership in the major parties has declined precipitously. Moreover, turnout for the parliamentary elections in 1997, 71 percent, to that point was one of the lowest in British history. That year, the London mayoral election brought out only 34 percent of the voters. In 2001, it was worse: the parliamentary election turnout was 59 percent, the worst in Europe. The 1999 European Parliament election was still worse: only 23 percent of the electorate showed up at the polls (Norris 2001, 177). In the controversial presidential election in France in 2002, the turnout was 72 percent, its lowest in almost forty years, even if impressive by U.S. standards. In Russia, a widely observed decline in voter interest corresponds with the increased use of media, technology, campaign professionals, and dirty tricks (Plasser and Plasser 2002, 248).

European parliamentary elections have felt the influence of television, particularly in the way that TV producers and directors seek out key individuals whom they think can explain the political process and agenda. Complex aspects of policymaking do not play well in a commercial visual medium, which is dedicated more to entertainment than to education. The neoliberal pressures that led to the increased privatization of television in Britain and Europe added value to the entertainment objective—and it was inevitable that political dialogue would be affected by it. Rupert Murdoch's vast media holdings in Britain and its conservative slant unquestionably was a major factor in influencing the British electorate to vote for Margaret Thatcher in 1979. And despite having never held office previously and without an established political party, Silvio Berlusconi, the largest media mogul in Italy, employed his vast media network to help capture the prime ministership in 1994 and again in 2000 (even while under a criminal investigation for graft). Regarding a remote Western enclave, one observer found that "New Zealand elections since the advent of television in the 1960s have increasingly taken on the style of American presidential campaigns in which rival leaders and their teams tour the country and vie for mass media exposure" (Les Cleveland, cited in Mughan 2000, 3).

The deep association of television with politics notwithstanding, it is too easy to attribute changes in societal relations as a direct result of technology per se. Robert Putnam errs in this direction in citing television as the source of the problem of declining civic participation in the United States (Putnam 1995) without considering that the development of commercial television is itself an epiphenomenon of a more extensive system of production and societal organization. In its American incarnation, TV has been developed since its earliest years mainly with the needs of the advertising and marketing industries and the white suburban household in the minds of its corporate progenitors. By the 1960s, the medium was becoming a more creative form as well as an effective instrument of propaganda and could be employed by political groups to organize public consumption of political images and messages. (This is discussed at greater length in chapter 5.)

The key point here is that the structure of political discourse in America, whether presented over television or other media, is heavily laden with the embedded and unrelenting logic of the market. In the market, the relationship between producer and consumer is highly abstract, and the relationship between politician and voter is taking on a similar abstraction. Media and ICT do not cause these occurrences, but they are employed in ways that distance politicians from voters. Gary Selnow says, with a certain degree of technological determinist syntax, that it's "mostly rubber-glove campaigning. Candidates don't touch voters directly; they send their messages through broadcasts, print and direct mail. These technologies separate and isolate the voters from the candidates" (Selnow 1994, 6).

ICT is often used to shrink distance in higher-level production relationships, that is, between top-level management within and between companies and countries, and increases distance between higher- and lower-level economic and political relationships (corporate management and workers, political organizations and citizens). This is also clear in the case of the military establishment, which uses ICT as part of its chain of command within the officer corps of the branch services and in the distancing of the military as a whole from the enemy (the electronic battlefield). In adversarial labor-industry relations, ICT is used to physically and socially segregate workers from management, from the local to the continental divide. Similarly, it's the desire of political candidates to protect themselves from the close scrutiny of the voters that makes the flexible uses of advanced ICT so compelling—one reason why political campaigns were among its early and most enthusiastic adopters.

SPATIAL, TECHNO-PROFESSIONAL, AND POLITICAL ECONOMIC CONVERGENCES

In the rapid shift in the use of computers for record keeping, data processing, and public and private decision making, an accounting of the overall social costs of these changes has lagged far behind. To promote oneself as technologically adept, especially in the uses of ICT, is to add cachet to one's professional respectability. And there is almost always a presumption of sophistication and progress inferred from anything associated with the milieux of technological innovation, whether it's a PowerPoint presentation or the rapid tabulation and projection of voter results (despite the fiasco of the 2000 presidential vote count). The attention given to technology and the skills that go with it tend to dominate how politicians, consultants, and the media conceive and talk about the electoral process.

This is not a new phenomenon. The mix of science fiction and real achievements that became manifest during the 1950s in ways of thinking about electronic technologies, including television and the computer, found applications in the political arena. A crowning symbolic achievement occurred with the use of UNIVAC, an early computer system built by Remington-Rand originally for the Census Bureau. In 1952, CBS-TV News, anchored by Walter Cronkite, featured it as a wondrous instrument able to calculate and project the winner of the Eisenhower-Stevenson presidential election. In fact, CBS had set up a very conspicuous mock-up of a futuristic-looking UNIVAC (aided by an invisible telephone feed from Philadelphia) to wow viewers into believing that they were witnessing the real thing. The UNIVAC "brain" had made an impressive national television debut (Winston 1986, 169).

Since that time, reverence for technology has only increased. Parents and their children formed long cues to tour NBC-TV in Rockefeller Center to learn how it was that television could bring moving pictures into the home. The Smithsonian Arts & Industries museum continues to be a pantheon of the genealogy and heroes of technological progress. Technological enthusiasm has no less captured the imagination of the politician's world. House Speaker

Newt Gingrich jumped on the bandwagon in 1995 with the writing of a fore-word to one of futurologists Alvin and Heidi Toffler's literary paeans to the digital age, *Creating a New Civilization: The Politics of the Third Wave*. But the most trenchant assertion of technological determinism was captured in Margaret Thatcher's often quoted erudition, "there is no alternative."

Although digital management of information has become central to the po-litical campaign and the public spectacle it creates, it is still a relative new-comer compared to television, which, as two authors categorically claim, "has done more than anything else to transform electioneering" (Butler and Ranney 1992, 281). What any viewer can clearly see, however, is that televi-sion news has been augmented by computer-generated graphics and scrolling texts of news and entertainment items, sports and stock market tickers, weather and time reports, and station logos. If fast-paced moving images on the tube weren't enough to distract viewers from reflection, the latest screen formats make thinking virtually impossible. And, moreover, the television re-ports that ultimately appear rely heavily on Internet sourcing, electronic data-bases, satellite and microwave feeds, computer-generated graphs and graph-ics, and a host of other digitally based applications that have converged on the news-viewing audience.

Another aspect of political convergence is geographic. Attracted to neolib-eralism's new global thresholds, American and other Western political con-sultants have introduced their electioneering skills to many parts of the world where previously they were resisted. The consultants' capacity to organize elections has little to do with understanding of locations, histories, and cul-tures. American political strategists typically have little knowledge about and no language proficiency in the non-English countries where they work. In their profession, the basic assumption, as in conservative economics, engi-neering, law, and neoliberalism in general, is that political or cultural knowl-edge is not as relevant as expertise in technique and technology. Sidney Blu-menthal, a journalist and observer of electoral behavior, more recently a consultant, commented, "Professional techniques can be used for any purpose in different places under different circumstances. . . . Techniques can be used on behalf of any agenda, any candidate" (quoted in Halimi 1999).

The techniques of polling, political advertising, opposition research, tele-marketing, and other means of conducting modern elections through surveil-lance are rapidly spreading to other countries. Philip Noble, one of the lead-ing international consultants, says, "Campaigns are becoming globalized just like everything else. You have a similar media environment, you have similar tools and techniques, and you have similar domestic political issues" (quoted in Schrader 1999, A17). With the convergence and concentration of methods and styles, political communication across national borders also tends to take on common characteristics. In the 1990s, Tony Blair sounded very much like Bill Clinton, both in his style and underlying assumptions about market priorities. The political rhetoric of his 2001 election opponent, William Hague, played to the core themes of American Republicans. The way of staging elections in different countries, especially in the West, has become less politically and culturally specific and more homogenous.

This enables political strategists such as Mark Mellman or Stanley Greenberg to casually cross borders to run elections along lines similar to those employed in the United States. Following the lead of his American counterparts, French media consultant Jacques Séguéla argues that campaign funds would be better spent on political advertising news clips than on public meetings (Halimi 1999). James Carville and Paul Begala portray themselves as liberals at home, but this did not impose ideological constraints on them in 1993 when they worked, together with Carville's wife, Mary Matalin, for the rightist campaign of Greek premier Constantine Mitsotakis. The successful Socialist candidate, Andreas Papandreou, had the services of Chris Spirou, an American chair of the New Hampshire Democratic Party (Maxfield and Schlesinger 1997, 15). But, as many political consultants will admit, campaigning is more about money than political principles.

With American-style electoral contests going on in almost every time zone around the world, there has been an explosion of interest and entry in consulting, with plenty of work to go around. And consultants need not restrict themselves to political candidate campaigns. As specialists in multiple aspects of political canvassing and persuasion, they have become increasingly important in issue advocacy, making themselves especially valuable as expert resources in the growing wave of ballot initiatives and referenda. The rapid growth of ballot initiatives and referenda in many states, California the first among them, has the clear fingerprints of the political consultants.

Beyond the ballot, consultants are also becoming a critical asset to corporations that hire them to clean up their images before the public. For those consultants not farming their skills abroad, political off-season is a time when the corporate world beckons their expertise. Many of the celebrity political consultants boast of having Fortune 500 companies among their clients. Corporations use them as hired guns to find out what the public does not like about them and can thereby adjust their public relations messages to alter public perceptions—and public policy. These convergences of private and public sector livelihoods mean a lack of separation of corporations and the state, a far more constitutionally threatening development than, for example, the recent tendencies toward federal support of organized religions.

The nexus of business and government ensures a consolidation of the business agenda, permanent campaigns, and endless employment for consulting services. Many policymakers and regulators anticipate life after government as employees of the corporate sector and are well served to prepare their portfolios and business-friendly credentials while still in public service. The telecommunications industry is filled with former FCC commissioners and staff members. Members of Congress and the executive branch are finding lucrative opportunities as lobbyists in a range of industries, including those that had business on the table of committees and subcommittees on which the politicians previously served.

Monsanto, for example, has been called a "retirement home" for members of the Clinton administration. Several of Clinton's trade and environmental protection administrators, ambassadors, and Social Security and treasury officials left the administration to join the Monsanto board. Monsanto's CEO, Robert Shapiro, was an advisor to Clinton on trade policy, which led the president to promote the corporation's interest in trying to get British prime minister Tony Blair, a willing accomplice, to accept genetically modified (GM) food production in Britain. On the British side of the isle, Philip Gould, confidant and pollster for Blair and friend and partner of Clinton pollster Stanley Greenberg (whom he quotes liberally throughout his memoir, *The Unfinished Revolution*), interviewed British MPs and civil servants on behalf of his client, Monsanto. Concurrently, the British supermarket tycoon Lord Sainbury, who sells unlabeled genetically modified food, was made science advisor to the prime minister and given the charge to organize a public relations campaign on behalf of GM products (Cohen 1999, 27). (The close linkages of U.S. and British politics and their respective "middlemen" are further discussed in chapter 5.)

COMMUNICATION TECHNOLOGIES, POLITICAL CONTROL, AND THE PUBLIC SPHERE

Consultants are distinguished by a set of technical skills that are indispensable to their occupation. Since the 1960s, the use of computers, telecommunications, electronic media, polling, and public relations have come to define the meaning of professionalization of political campaigns. These technologies and subindustries have "opened the door of opportunity to orchestrate, amplify, and inject the presumptive voices of the American people," whereby politicians and candidates "know about the public without having any real human relationship with the people in particular" (Heclo 2000, 25–26). Elections are seamlessly woven into the new industrial forms of production in which skilled but contingent (underemployed) professionals engage in part as "symbolic analysts," develop products that are regularly recustomized as new information is garnered concerning public taste, habits, values, attitudes, and lifestyles.

In politics, the products are politicians, who are (re)constructed as artifacts of polling and image making. The election industry has drawn in specialists who treat politics as a permanent money trough of public relations. The Clinton strategists in 1992 took this principle to new heights in their war-room strategy, which enabled them not only to collect information about voters and opposition candidates but also to respond quickly to political attacks on their candidate—if possible, quickly enough to get their response on that evening's TV news. Candidates not able to employ telecommunications and other digital technologies for voter profiling, political advertising, rapid response, and news management are effectively shut out of contention.

There is also a host of ways in which techniques and technologies are used to physically make over candidates. Focus groups provide electronic responses that help determine the candidate's wardrobe or hairstyle. Digitally generated techniques can touch up the candidate's image by hiding certain features and thereby making her/him look more attractive. Digital imaging can also distort the appearance of opponents by highlighting certain features, such as darkening the complexion, exaggerating the look of fatigue, capturing a pose that looks awkward, and so forth. A study undertaken at the University of Oklahoma during the 1996 U.S. presidential election found that 28 percent of the political commercials studied had misused technology in some way to alter the images or messages of candidates (cited in Johnson 2001, 136).

Even in a poor country like India, the political parties, especially the Congress Party, are bringing advanced ICT applications into the election process. The 2004 national parliamentary election was marked by the extensive use of telemarketing (including cell phone messaging), campaign websites, and e-mail in a country where the vast majority of the people are without telephones, let alone computers, and a large percentage do not even have electricity. That year, the country also moved to an all-electronic voting system. This represents a major threat of disenfranchisement for the millions of Indians who are illiterate. And given the growing reports of political corruption in India, it was likely to raise fears about voting machine irregularities and ballot tampering.

Are new technologies being employed in ways that contribute to a more vibrant public sphere? Does their use compensate for the loss of community in modern life, or are they associated with a kind of withdrawal and cocooning into narcissistic individualism that "encourages inertia as a destroyer of sociability and civic virtues" (Chambat 2000, 270)? It would be misdirected to blame apparent voter disinterest in the political system simply on technology, inasmuch as technological applications are nothing more than the designs and range of possibilities that people and institutions program into them. The larger concern is the corporate takeover of politics that, aided by technology, has industrialized its character and turned elections into what economists call rent-seeking activities,[6] in which major political and economic stakeholders prevail. The next chapter looks more extensively at the work of the political consultants and the armory of technological weapons at their disposal for constructing and destroying political candidates.

NOTES

1. Stripped of ideological associations, the term *propaganda* has three essential characteristics: it is intentional communication aimed at a targeted audience; it has persuasive aspects associated with instrumental purposes, whether they be for political (e.g., campaigns), commercial (advertising), or public relations (e.g., preserving corporate reputations) objectives; and it typically is centralized and unidirectional as opposed to interactive (Snow 1998, 21).

2. One of the more blatant uses of propaganda of the George W. Bush administration was its distribution of a government video news release of a staged news report (using an actor posing as a reporter) on the occasion of Bush's signing of the 2003 Medicare reform package, including a new prescription drug benefit for seniors. Some forty news stations aired the report, despite its inauthenticity, without revealing to viewers that the patently propagandistic "report" was created by the administration to boost the president's popularity (Moyers 2004b).

3. The most notorious of the anti-Dukakis political ads was one that featured "Willie" Horton (an African American who committed a rape while on furlough from a Massachusetts prison). George Bush's son Jeb ran a similar ad in 1994 against Lawton Chiles in an effort to unseat the incumbent governor of Florida. In the latter case, the attack ad, used in a direct-mail letter sent to thousands of potential voters, cited a woman murdered by a parolee as a way of discrediting Chiles's record on crime. Chiles's campaign retaliated with push-polling telephone messages to some 75,000 Florida voters (Swint 1998, 125).

4. A simple database might consist of name, address, telephone number, occupation, income, party affiliation, and religious membership.

5. Federal finance law does not permit interest groups that receive corporate or union finances to broadcast political ads the month before primaries and two months before a general election if federal candidates are named, candidates' districts are targeted, or if the messages are paid for with corporate or union money. The rules do not apply to radio, film, or television (Theimer 2003, A4).

6. Rent seeking in politics usually refers to lobbying, that is, payments made to secure political favors, and Washington, D.C., is the capital of political capital in this

sense. The flip side of this is rent extraction, which refers to the ways that politicians actively draw financial support from corporate interests in exchange for favorable policy consideration. This term suggests that corporations in defense of their self-interests are coerced into participating politically. In my view, the relationship is symbiotic, both politicians and corporate CEOs mutually benefit from a system insulated from the demands of the public majority.

3

Campaign Professionals and the Tools of Their Trade

The very need of reaching large numbers of people at one time and in the shortest possible time tends towards the utilizations of symbols which stand in the minds of the public for the abstract idea the technician wishes to convey.

—Edward Bernays (cited in Ewen 1996, 172)

In the past the man has been first; in the future the system must be first.

—Frederick Winslow Taylor (1911)

This chapter discusses the work and techniques of political professionals and provides synopses of some of the leading or celebrated consultants, recent and current, engaged in national and international electioneering. Related to their formal political activity are the close associations many leading consultants maintain with the Fortune 500 business community. This suggests that modern American politics has become to a large extent an artifact of the increasing industrialization, corporatization, and engineering of everyday life in the United States. The campaign professional occupation is becoming almost indistinguishable from that of corporate public relations, as "strategists who are ideological enemies in politics put their differences aside to work together on large-scale corporate campaigns" (Mitchell 1998). This is also evident in the ideological flexibility that political consultants entertain when working for foreign clients. Money, it appears, puts almost all political consultants in the same political party, the capitalist party. To give fuller meaning to professionalization and its implications for citizen participation in the electoral process and civil society, this chapter also describes the arsenal of strategic tools of the political consulting trade, with particular attention given to the central role of television in the political campaign.

Political consultants play a crucial part in state legitimation. Their job is not only to win elections, which is what makes them marketable to other politicians and corporate patrons, but also to build public interest or at least consent around specific politicians, parties, and hegemonic ideas. The most important of the hegemonic ideas is that the electoral process itself is a legitimate means by which citizens engage in a meaningful exercise of democratic enfranchisement and register their political preferences. Arguments that rely on the "professionalization" thesis to explain changes and choices in democratic participation miss the central relationship of professionalization and contests of power to the dynamic role of the market in the production of politics. How professional can these "professionals" be when there is neither a formal body of knowledge to certify them as such nor a certifying administrative process of conferring professional status other than self-declaration? Political professionals do not even have enforceable codes of conduct.

Professionalization arguments also fail to recognize the *hyperindustrialization* that has taken over most spheres of public life, including organized politics. The concept of hyperindustrialization is more fully explained and developed in chapter 5. In general, however, I use the term to describe the enlarged industrial context in which the formal political process operates. In any state, politics is lodged within a political economy, which refers to the intersection of public policy with resource control, development, and allocation. Political economy is best understood in its historical and global dimensions. The present international division of labor, which determines who works where and with what compensation, is an outgrowth of a long trajectory of colonialism and interstate relations, and has a lot to do with the professionalization of politics in the United States and elsewhere. Without going into the complex background of the international division of labor that historically established Western domination of trade and global politics, it is reasonable to assume that without the hegemonic power relations that govern the production and distribution of media and information systems throughout the world, the current possibilities of technology-based professionalization would be infeasible.[1]

Without reference to political economy or the industrial characteristics of electioneering, professionalization becomes a discourse about the inevitability, natural outcome, and progress of Western technique and technology and the opportunity for its benevolent transfer to the rest of the world. It forms an understanding of political change not within the governance of empowered interests but rather the political process. Professionalization tends to ignore questions about empowerment in society and how it is organized and whether uses of power are compatible with the preservation of the public interest. Such a discourse helps to shield corporate and other elites from public awareness of their investment and active political involvement in electoral outcomes. Critical understanding requires insight into the embedded politics and political economy of professionalization.

CONSULTANTS AND THE MONEY CHASE

The professionals have turned political communication into a routine capital- and technology-intensive "rationalization of persuasion" (Mancini 1999, 235). Traditional modes of authoritative, face-to-face political communication, with its highly stylized and commanding oratory and debate performance, are largely a thing of the past. Politicians now address citizens through a system of communications that is highly mediated by a complex network of industrial manufacturers, software designers, broadcasters, and others with customized applications of electronic media, advertising, and information management. It's an industry based on "[t]echnology, technocrats, and techniques [that] require considerable capital investments" as a condition of operation (Mancini 1999, 236).

The main trade journal of the industry, *Campaigns & Elections*, lists among the specialties and specialists in professional campaigning: database management, fund-raising software, website development, media purchasing, focus group analysts, satellite services, video production and duplication, telemarketing, legal compliance attorneys, and media consultants. GeoVoter, a national database firm, offers candidates campaign-targeting software based on personalized demographics; Campaign Connections advertises its direct mail, strategic planning, and both paid and free media services for sale; CampaignOffice.com sells website creation capabilities and online fund-raising expertise; and DG Systems provides satellite-based audio and video production and distribution services for rapid response and targeted political advertising throughout the country.[2]

The person usually credited with having masterminded massive direct-mail fund-raising solicitation is Richard Viguerie, who focused on the targeting of thousands of individuals to help fund political campaigns for Republicans. In the 1960s, Viguerie began to take advantage of federal laws requiring lists of donors of more than $50 in election contributions and organized a team to aggregate these names and target them for future campaign support (Friedenberg 1997, 104–5). In doing so, Viguerie and others who followed in his footsteps were able to effectively overcome the intended limitations in campaign finance reform legislation in the 1970s. Viguerie inspired new generations of direct-mail specialists who have little or no connection to the candidates for whom they work (Witcover 1999, 73).

With campaign professionals formally at the controls, local party organizers and the phalanx of loyal political volunteers, though still needed, are bypassed as the critical elements in the planning of election strategies and tactics. Political consultants are beholden not to political parties but only to their candidates, their allies and patrons in the election industry and the media, and themselves. Among the larger consulting firms, such as Burson-Marsteller, it is not unusual to find its partners working for different party candidates. In 1969, Joseph Napolitan, who worked almost exclusively with Democrats (but in other countries with little partiality), became a partner in Public Affairs Analysts with Republican consultant F. Clifton White, who had served as campaign manager for archconservative Barry Goldwater in 1964. Commenting on this seemingly strange alliance and trumping of principle, Napolitan explained it simply as, "We are diametrically opposed politically, but we share the same techniques" (cited in Blumenthal 1982, 156).[3]

Today, he wouldn't have to apologize for it. Richard Wirthlin and Mark Mellman, supposedly loyalists to the two dominant parties, collaborated in studying the public's attitudes toward the tax system. Former Democratic Party strategist Charles Sewell now works on behalf of the conservative group Americans for Fair Taxation. Since the early 1980s, many political consultants have sought business outside of campaigning in the off-season, and corporations have used them as influence peddlers to gain access to Congress (Mitchell 1998). Contemporary elections are enormous spending bonanzas, increasingly indifferent to party labels or ideology, and operate on a simple but deceptive premise: "It's the consultants, stupid!"

The expanded influence of political communication specialists in the United States corresponds with decreased levels of political participation.[4] Some political consultants, in fact, will readily acknowledge their *preference* for smaller election turnouts, as predictability (and therefore their credibility) is greater with the participation of the more reliable and targeted voters. In the early 1980s, a Republican political strategist said as much: "I don't want everyone to vote. Our leverage in the election quite candidly goes up as the voting population goes down" (quoted in Bennett 1996, 50). Indeed, as the sitting but not always erudite president Richard Nixon said (in the "Nixon tapes"), "the smartest thing the [Founders] did was to limit the voters in this country. Out of 3½ to 4 million people, 200,000 voted. And that was true for a helluva long time, and the republic would have never survived if all the dummies had voted along with the intelligent people" (cited in Hill 2002, 278).

One study also finds that electoral strategies are actually built around low turnouts "where the name of the game is to drive down your opponent's vote total rather than to build up your own" (Taylor 2002, 14). Edward Rollins, who ran Ronald Reagan's 1984 campaign, boasted to the press that during the 1993 New Jersey gubernatorial race, when he worked for Republican candidate Christine Todd Whitman, he had paid off African American ministers to discourage their congregations from voting. He later retracted the claim, but the point about strategy remained. It was likely a consultant who, on behalf of Jesse Helm's Senate reelection campaign against black challenger Harvey Gantt, persuaded the North Carolina Republican Party to send 125,000 postcards to registered voters in the state's predominantly black precincts informing them that they were ineligible to vote. Helms won the election and happily paid a $25,000 fine for violating federal election laws (Hill 2002, 159).

Poor election turnouts and other measures of low-level participation that are at least partially attributed to campaign tactics distinguish the United States from other democracies. Political campaigns' use of attack ads or negative advertising against opponents is by design an effort to suppress the vote on the other side. And it works (Ansolabehere and Iyengar 1995). According to one longtime political consultant (now retired): "In 90 percent of the cases, the consultant, especially one working for an incumbent, wants to suppress the turnout, because of the better chance you have of getting your people out, being successful, more than the person who hasn't got a constituency base that they've dealt with for the last 5, 10, 15 years. Which is why it's so difficult to beat a congressman" (Galizio 2002). Nonvoters are indeed the largest single bloc, far larger than the numbers who vote for either of the two dominant political parties. It might be more accurate to treat such turnouts as evidence of "no confidence." To do so would provide reason to demand new elections or a radical restructuring of the electoral process, one that could bring forward what the electorate would see as legitimate candidates that truly represent their demands and interests.[5]

The two dominant parties, in fact, pay little attention to mobilizing the electorate and addressing the fact of low voter participation, the Republicans fearing the probable identification of new, especially poorer, voters with Democrats; the Democrats afraid of the class realignment that workers and people of color would demand in terms of the party's issues and ideological platform.[6] As the two major political parties largely coalesce where transnational corporate interests are concerned (e.g., the World Trade Organization, NAFTA, deregulation, the use of military power, etc.), the need for symbolic conflict becomes all the more important as a way of maintaining the mythos of electoral choice. In electoral contests, personality, "character," and "leadership" emphases tend to take center stage. In Israel, where U.S. consultants have had much political influence, a political scientist noted in 1996 that with the change to direct election of the prime minister, "Both Labour and Likud are focusing more on personalities than before and less on parties" (quoted in Battersby 1996, 7). The experience led the Israeli government to subsequently rescind the change.

One of the central features that has characterized the growth of the political consulting business in the past twenty years and its indifference to broad political concerns is the growing technical specialization in the industry. The general consultant of the prewar and early postwar years has given rise to an army of specialists in database management, media buying, polling, focus group organization, telemarketing, opposition research, and other areas. Consultants themselves see the candidates as largely disengaged from both the tactical and content aspects of the political campaign. In fact, almost half (48 percent) of consultants rate candidates as fair or poor in quality but, nonetheless, the overwhelming majority (82 percent) of them believe that consultants themselves can make them win elections with the right message—and adequate money. More than 40 percent boast they "can sell voters on a weak campaigner." Not surprisingly, consultants, especially Republicans, consistently oppose campaign finance reform (Pew Research Center 1998).

One of the legends of the political consulting industry, Richard Wirthlin, spoke plainly his view of the less-than-democratic character of the electoral system. In a party document not intended for public access, he asserted that "American democracy is less a form of government than a romantic preference for a particular value structure" (*New Internationalist* 1985). Wirthlin seems to share the skeptical view, but in his case profiting from it, that elections are merely symbolic events staged to satisfy the public's "romantic" urge to feel connected to the political process. In line with the rationale offered by Bernays and others (see chapter 4), the political process is in Wirthlin's view less about connecting existing public values with candidates as much as constructing both; that is, it's about the "engineering of consent." Less sanguine, political scientist Lance Bennett finds that such a system of marketing politics "has dealt a possibly fatal blow to the health of political parties in America" (Bennett 1996, 151).

Political consultants also have a professional interest in pursuing ambiguity and symbolic manipulation, as opposed to voter education and party and candidate accountability, in the campaign process (Petracca 1989, 13). On their own, candidates do not necessarily wish to evade clear responses on issues; rather, they are compelled by the structural imperatives of professionally run campaigns to employ loose, catchall phrases that broadly generalize approaches to governance.[7] Mark Petracca found that, second only to fundraising, the most important priorities for candidates from the consultant's perspective are the advertising strategy and voter profiling and management, definitely not nuanced articulations of complex issues and policy approaches. It is more important to steer the voter toward desired reactions than to encourage rational voting thought processes and, least of all, grassroots organizing (Petracca 1989, 13). One study found that politicians tend to veer slightly away from party or ideological agendas when elections are imminent in order to get last-minute legislation passed and appeal to swing voters (Jacobs and Shapiro 2000, 43–44).

The use of professionals in campaigns has significantly raised the length and costs of the campaign, especially in the United States where political advertising was first used, and the willingness of corporations and politicians to turn politics into multibillion-dollar patron-client relationships has attracted more consultants into the field. The number of political consultants tripled in the 1990s, and "their involvement in political campaigns, once confined to high-profile races, has spread infectiously to down-ballot races, ballot initiatives, and local elections" (Hill 2002, 146). This development, in fact, does not sit well with knowledgeable voters. Consultants' reputations tend to rank low among the section of the public familiar with their role in politics. Even some politicians express strong misgivings about the system. Reflecting on the contemporary state of political affairs in 1999, former president Gerald Ford dismally described elections as "candidates without ideas, hiring consultants without convictions, to run campaigns without content" (cited in Hill 2002, 147).

While many regard political advertising as technically sophisticated, others see its content as largely banal, often painfully unsophisticated and crude, and the cause of much of the revulsion that the public feels toward politics, politicians, and government. Regardless of their value, the American Association of Political Consultants honors themselves each year with "Pollie" awards for the best political ads. Describing the permeation of advertising in public life, Harvard economist John Kenneth Galbraith, author of the 1967 classic *The New Industrial State*, commented, "Every corner of the public psyche is canvassed by some of the nation's most talented citizens to see if the desire for some merchantable product can be cultivated. No similar process operates in behalf of the nonmerchantable services of the state" (quoted in Denton and Woodward 1990, 167). When a candidate has a multimillion-dollar war chest, this simply means he or she has funds to support advisors, pollsters, fund-raisers, speechwriters, media consultants, opposition researchers, telemarketers, focus groups, direct-mail specialists, and other professionals and can be a player in the television advertising markets (Johnson 2001, 32). (See table 3.1.)

Table 3.1.   Political Advertising on Television, June 1–November 7, 2000 (and 1996)

Ads for:	George W. Bush	Robert Dole (1996)	
Bush Campaign	$39,210,195	Dole campaign	$33,000,000
Republican Party	$44,744,774	Republican Party	$25,000,000
Groups	$2,113,756	Groups	n/a
Total	$86,068,725	Total	n/a
Ads for:	Albert Gore	Bill Clinton (1996)	
Gore Campaign	$27,906,724	Clinton campaign	$38,000,000
Democratic Party	$35,150,025	Democratic Party	$23,000,000
Groups	$14,004,163	Groups	n/a
Total	$77,060,912	Total	n/a

Source: Brennan Center for Justice 2001

TELEVISION AND THE BUYING OF THE PRESIDENCY

The political professionals, the media, the technical specialists, and the politicians are mutually constituted through the dispersal of corporate largesse. Electioneering players create synergies to maximize their individual and collective power over the electoral system. Cooperating at the level of the commanding heights enables political elites to maintain social and physical distance from the broad public, engaging the electorate mainly through symbolic politics to create the illusion of a popular mandate to rule. Of all the technologies deployed for political purposes, none is more useful to this idea of democracy and mode of governance than television. Former FCC chair Reed Hundt noted that "TV and newspapers are the gatekeepers of public perception and can make a politician popular or unpopular. . . . Politicians know that in their bones; the only ones who don't are the one who don't get elected" (cited in Croteau and Hoynes 2001, 199). Probably no politician better blended into the world of television fantasy than Ronald Reagan, a man who often seemed incapable of distinguishing between image and reality.

It is not only the great diffusion of television in American (and other countries') households that makes it such a powerful medium for transmitting news and political information to the public; the style and aesthetics of commercial television formats also influence how these news and informational messages are constructed. Political advertising on television is very closely designed by its commercial counterpart, and it often involves the very same advertising firms and creative talent, especially at higher level campaigns (Senate, president). High-powered advertising executives set the pace for election styling down below. Successful commercials breed imitation of product ads in campaign advertising at a very generic level (pacing, mood creation, imagery, and the like). Some mirror specific commercial ads themselves. MTV commercials are often used as a prototype in campaign advertising.

Hollywood actually influences politics and political campaigns on a number of levels. As commercial television has much to do with popular taste, it sets a certain standard for how campaigns can package their candidates and influence voter preferences. Sometimes even Hollywood long-form film producers and directors get involved in political campaigns, writing and producing commercials for candidates (Galizio 2002). It should not be so puzzling, therefore, that people like Ronald Reagan and more recently Arnold Schwarzenegger are treated as credible politicians and why the mass media ooze with delight and attention over their campaigns. The mass media are largely engaged in entertainment and advertising, and showbiz, camera-ready politicians provide endless opportunities for coverage in ways that people in the industry best understand.

The first televised appearance of a president occurred in 1939 at the World's Fair when Franklin Roosevelt's words and images were transmitted to an estimated 100,000 viewers, and the following year Americans witnessed for the first time a televised political convention (Jamieson 1996, 34). In 1948, the existence of a coaxial cable linking the Philadelphia convention site of the Republicans and Democrats to New York and Washington, D.C., was a strategic move on the part of the two major parties to bring the event to citizens in states representing 168 electoral votes (Barnouw 1968, 257).[8] Seeking to influence voters, the Truman-Dewey presidential race that year was the first time candidates bought television time (Jamieson 1996, 34). Television advertising represented a significant step toward outsourcing campaign expertise to nonparty professionals, although Truman still trekked 31,000 miles in campaign stops across the country. The age of television politics truly took off with his successor (Moyers 2004a).

In 1952, Republican presidential candidate Dwight Eisenhower, former commander of the Allied forces in Europe in World War II, and his campaign staff hired Madison Avenue firms Batten, Barton, Dustine, and Osborn (BBD&O), Young & Rubicam, and the Ted Bates advertising agency, and commissioned Disney animation and an Irving Berlin jingle as part of the television spectacle. All this staging helped Ike defeat a more articulate but less telegenic Adlai Stevenson—the reluctant candidate of the Democrats. Stevenson complained that the Eisenhower campaign was being promoted "in precisely the way they sell soup, ammoniated toothpaste, hair tonic, or bubble gum" (quoted in Witcover 1999, 53). He was not far off the mark, as Eisenhower's campaign did hire ad man Rosser Reeves to run a series of TV spots for the candidate, aided by the polling firm of George Gallup, the group that had falsely projected Thomas E. Dewey as the presidential election victor in 1948. Reeves had gained celebrity status in the industry for having come up with the long-running slogan for M&Ms, "Melts in your mouth, not in your hands." But Stevenson, lacking the name recognition of the war hero Eisenhower, also resorted to bringing advertising specialists into his campaign, including the Baltimore agency of Joseph Katz, which ran eighteen television and radio simulcasts (Kelley 1956, 163). For both candidates, television in particular was a critical medium of political persuasion.

An important moment in television politics occurred when Eisenhower's running mate, Senator Richard Nixon, with the help of BBD&O, purchased a thirty-minute spot, which became known as the Checkers speech, to respond to media allegations of corruption against him. With the help of television producer Ted Rogers, who was then well known for a number of TV program successes (including a children's favorite, *The Lone Ranger*), the vice presidential nominee presented himself in a way that calmed public criticism toward him. Although Eisenhower and Nixon were elected in 1952 and again in 1956, widespread concerns about Nixon's integrity never fully subsided. As a senator, he had been an active investigator in the House Un-American Activities Committee, employing an aggressive political style rife with red-baiting tactics that first got him elected to Congress as a representative from California.[9] Running at the head of the Republican ticket in the 1960 presidential campaign, Nixon hired the advertising firm J. Walter Thompson as well as H. R. Haldeman, who had worked there, as his advisor to polish up his coarse image.[10] By that time, political consulting and television advertising were already the main staples for producing the candidate's public persona (Kelley 1956, 180; Witcover 1999, 54–55).

Prior to the television age, the two major political parties were still choosing their presidential candidates in "smoke-filled rooms," and party conventions held a lot of meaning and suspense. One author observes,

> In the pre-television era, campaigns were characterized by great land armies of volunteers, canvassing, leafleting, organizing meetings, and cajoling the faithful to turn out at elections. They were labour-intensive, low technology affairs, with decision-making centres dispersed across the network of full-time regional and constituency agents. By contrast the modern campaign is capital intensive, relying on a much smaller base of volunteers, much tighter central direction of campaign operations, increased reliance on non-party experts from media and marketing, far less face-to-face communication with voters and increased targeting of floating voters. (Scammell 1999, 720)

The shift to the state-by-state primary and caucus system gave voters more exposure to presidential candidates and somewhat more of a voice in choosing the party nominee (although party activists still dominate the selection), but the process quickly turned into a media carnival. Candidates were required to barnstorm the country in search of convincing victories, significant financing, delegate votes, and the serious attention of the mass media. Television coverage helped to nationalize presidential campaigns through news coverage and spot advertising. Nixon spent $61 million and McGovern $30 million in their 1972 presidential campaigns, much of it going to television advertising. In 1984, Jesse Helms spent more than $13 million and Jay Rockefeller almost $8 million in their respective Senate races in North Carolina and West Virginia. From his vast cash reservoir, Perot spent $35 million on television ads alone in a losing 1992 presidential effort, but winning the honor of "Adman of the Year" by *Advertising Age* (Bennett 1996, 60).

Television advertising costs have escalated with each increasing phase of monopolization of the medium. (See McChesney [1999] for a discussion of media monopoly and democracy.) Although there are at least four major networks and their affiliated stations contending for the advertising dollar (previously there were only three), the broadcast giants have also swallowed up the television competition, namely cable. Viacom (CBS) leads the rest in the control of the cable stations, and between that conglomerate and Disney (ABC), General Electric (NBC), and Fox and their owned and affiliated stations, there are few outlets where political campaigns can lay down their advertising dollar. As the G. W. Bush administration clearly favored the principle of increasing the audience share and number of stations a single television corporation can control and also opposed the principle of requiring free TV airtime for federal candidates, it can be assumed that the Republicans see monopoly working to their electoral advantage.

The amount of campaign dollars that flows to broadcast media has escalated to all-time highs. By 1996, political advertising had contributed about $400 million in national, state, and local elections.[11] That year, incumbent John Kerry (D-MA) poured $5 million into radio and television ads, more than half his $9.6 million campaign pool raised since 1991, to defeat Republican Massachusetts governor William Weld for the Senate (Common Cause 1997). In 1992, Clinton and Bush spent 60 percent of their campaign budgets on television ads (Clark 1996, 868). Close races are particularly attractive to television media, because it means that candidates will empty their coffers on advertising to get a victory. As central Washington, D.C., consultant Bob Squier once commented, "You'll find people in my business tend to use the word 'viewer' and 'voter' almost interchangeably" (cited in Shea and Burton 2001, 12). The 2000 election campaigns were estimated to pay out $1 billion in political commercials, according to Paine Webber, and

Campaigns & Elections estimated $14 billion for the 2000–2004 election cycle. The 2004 campaign topped 2000 threefold.

Among all categories of paid advertising on television, political ads rank third (10 percent airtime), behind only automobiles (25 percent) and retailing (15 percent) (Morgan 2000; Wayne 2000, A1). Most federal-level campaigns can expect to spend two-thirds of their funds on TV and radio advertising. Actual costs of airing such ads are only 10 percent of the price that TV stations collect (Moyers 2004a). The rest is profit for the television industry. See table 3.2.

Because it is so profitable, TV stations have a perverse incentive to reduce news coverage of campaigns in order to force candidates to invest more money in political advertising. The business logic is flawless, with the result that news coverage of candidates declined by 28 percent from 1988 to 2000, despite the latter being tightest presidential race in forty years (M. Green 2002b, 287). Inflation adjusted, the amount of money spent on television political ads jumped over 400 percent from 1980 to 2000, with the heaviest spending concentrations in big cities and swing states (Taylor 2002, 7). It should not be surprising, therefore, that the media focus a great deal of their "horse-race" campaign news on how much of a war chest each candidate has raised prior to, during, and immediately following the primaries. And it is ob-

Table 3.2. Political Advertising TV Spending and Population: Top 12 States, 2000

State	Revenue (thousands)	Revenue Rank	Pop. Rank
CA	$126,949	1	1
NY	$ 91,406	2	2
PA	$ 71,397	3	5
FL	$ 58,604	4	4
MI	$ 51,884	5	8
OH	$ 41,976	6	7
WA	$ 35,311	7	18
MO	$ 34,962	8	15
NC	$ 23,363	9	10
MN	$ 19,666	10	20
TX	$ 17,447	11	3
IL	$ 16,101	12	6

Source: Adapted from Alliance for Better Campaigns, 2001

Note on outliers: WA: Seattle was the number 5 urban market in political spending, and the state is a major high-tech center; MO: St. Louis was the number 8 urban market in political spending, and Missouri was a closely contested election; MN: Minneapolis was the number 9 urban market in political spending, and Minnesota was a closely contested election; TX: Texas was a weakly contested election; IL: Illinois was a weakly contested election.

vious that in big-money campaigns, advertising paces the style of coverage, though in a real horse race, the amount of money spent on a particular horse is not presumed to determine the winner. The type of media coverage of the election is closer to resembling the stock market than a horse race.

When a *New York Times* front-page story on the Democratic Party's 2004 competing presidential candidates, for example, uncritically reports "Dean's Surge in Fund-Raising Forces Rivals to Reassess Him" (Nagourney and Janofsky 2003, A1), the embedded message is that the "dialing for dollars" campaign is a legitimate basis on which to assess the quality of a prospective head of state. The entire story, by two of the *Times*'s top political correspondents, discusses the strategies and relative advantages of the candidates in efforts to outfund their rivals. There is no question raised about what this does to the quality of political leadership or its implications for democratic discourse and participation—as if an influential newspaper such as the *Times* has no obligation to pursue such a line of inquiry. As if to justify this form of political reporting, the authors write that "the candidates' success at drawing contributions helps build early impressions about their viability among Democratic delegates, elected officials, union leaders and, inevitably journalists, whose reports on fund-raising help create those critical impressions" (A1).

Like corporate advertising, the selling of candidates for elected office favors rapid-fire, often subliminal, images, short sound bites (down to less than eight seconds in 2000),[12] and staged events (Postman and Powers 1992, 82), and panders to photo opportunities, character stereotypes, and political attacks. Political advertising draws inspiration from television's pacing, which encourages exceedingly short voter attention spans. Of all political advertising in the top seventy-five markets during the 2000 election, over 97 percent were thirty seconds or less, and even of the "issue ads," more than 90 percent were thirty seconds (Holman and McLoughlin 2002, 33–34). In Germany, party political broadcasts are usually 2.5 minutes; in France, 4 minutes; and in Britain, though not often used, 10 minutes (Norris 2000, 152). Without a framework and with far too little time, information, or substance on which voters can make rational choices, the short spot political ads that mark U.S. elections typically resort to phrases that stick in the voters' consciousness (such as "Read my lips, no new taxes"). This is a technique obviously borrowed from product slogans, although it's now professional consultants not advertising agencies, as in Eisenhower's time, who make the tactical decisions on promoting candidates.

With television coverage eating up the largest share of campaign spending, media consultants for political campaigns are in on the pork barrel, typically pocketing a 15 percent commission for each ad placed with a TV station—the same percentage paid for direct-mail houses, phone bank operations, printers, and other campaign media businesses (Witcover 1999, 26). Television, with its associated costs (see table 3.3), not only shuts out candidates without deep pockets or corporate backers; it also forces candidates to speak the grammar and idiom of the visual medium, which reduces issue articulation to the level that commercial media deem appropriate for "effective" message construction and transmission. In this way, the television industry helps set the terms and limits of the discourse.

In Britain, to date, TV (and radio) spots for political advertising are not permitted, political parties "receive no campaign or organizational state finance," and limitations are set on local spending by individual candidates (Farrell 1998, 173–74). British campaign periods are brief; the one in 1997, lasting six weeks, was the longest to that time. On the continent, all television spot advertising in political campaigns was banned until quite recently. Countries now permitting political TV advertising include France, Germany, Italy, Austria, and Sweden (Farrell 1996, 173). France does not allow any advertising during the last three months of the campaign. Israel permits it only during the three weeks before election day.

If a major portion of election news coverage shifts to cable TV and the Internet, which many Americans still cannot afford, this only means that political information, such as that on C-Span, will be parceled under a system of political education by subscription. The big five media conglomerates (including the largest four TV networks) that presently control twenty of the twenty-five major cable stations will control even more of the public attention to politics. Neither Congress nor the FCC is likely to require the media to take more responsibility for voter education. Not only do media reporters fail to actively discuss the issues (which, they typically argue, the voters find boring) but they usually refuse to investigate the issue claims made by politi-

Table 3.3. Top U.S. Senate Campaign Broadcast Ad Spenders, 2000

Candidate	State	Total Spent	Broadcast Spending	Percentage Spent on Broadcast Ads
Jon Corzine (D)	NJ	$63,202,492	$39,999,560	63
Rick Lazio (R)	NY	$43,038,453	$20,935,067	49
Hillary Clinton (D)	NY	$29,595,761	$16,530,095	56
Spencer Abraham (R)	MI	$14,415,920	$ 7,961,319	55
Mark Dayton (D)	MN	$11,957,115	$ 7,722,091	65
Maria Cantwell (D)	WA	$11,538,133	$ 7,007,000	61
Rick Santorum (R)	PA	$12,826,761	$ 6,290,145	49
George Allen (R)	VA	$ 9,894,904	$ 5,650,709	57
John Ashcroft (R)	MO	$ 9,742,579	$ 5,568,434	57
Dianne Feinstein (D)	CA	$11,604,749	$ 5,126,440	44

Source: M. Green 2002b, 109

cians, preferring instead to report on their personal conflicts. If, as the media industry often insists, the public loves sensation, why doesn't it investigate the lies and distortions told by politicians? (Senator X caught in the act of lying!) Television can help anoint politicians, but it cannot guarantee a candidate's chance of victory. Dan Quayle, the often-ridiculed vice president of George Bush Sr., could not resist the image-building possibilities of broadcast advertising as a way of informally initiating a 1996 run for the presidency. But even his appearance in a Frito-Lay potato chip commercial during the 1994 football Super Bowl (parodying his celebrated inability to spell *potato* during an embarrassing 1992 media campaign event) could not revitalize his political life.

Political consultants usually will admit that they cannot work magic with a politician who has no charisma or personal appeal. But it was not until the late 1970s that political management became a serious science in an effort to take the risk out of campaigning and turn politicians into human chameleons who could adapt themselves to different groups of patrons and voters and win pluralities. Backed by campaign expertise and modern audience-profiling techniques, broadcast and public appearances could be choreographed in various elaborate ways, using sound bites, backdrops, or seating arrangements beneath the podium, to construct events as symbols of political momentum. There have been a number of particularly creative individuals involved in the staging of elections, a few of whom are discussed in the following section. What is impressive about this list of high-profile consultants is not only their importance in organizing elections in the United States and increasingly around the world but their credentials as agents of brand management for Fortune 500 companies. Their corporate ties and links to one another have served both their career advancement and their indispensability, within a highly interdependent system of politics, industry, and finance, in the capture of the political and legislative process.

A LINEUP OF POLITICAL PROFESSIONALS

Richard Wirthlin

One of the pioneers in postwar modern electioneering is Richard Wirthlin. Building on his earlier research on product marketing, Wirthlin helped start a company in 1969 with Vincent Breglio, Decision Making Information, Inc., that deployed market simulation models for political objectives. Working with Ronald Reagan in the 1970s and 1980s, along with other Republicans (including George Bush Sr.), as aide and chief pollster, Wirthlin became a leading political marketing analyst. Breglio went on to work for Alexander

Haig's 1988 presidential nomination campaign.[13] A psychographic study of strong Reagan voters that Wirthlin undertook in 1979 found that their profiles indicated that they "obtained high scores on the scales for respect for authority, individualism, authoritarianism, and a low score on egalitarianism" (Denton and Woodward 1990, 90). These findings are consistent with those of the liberal social theorist George Lakoff (1996).

Wirthlin is known as the person who popularized the use of hand-held "perception analyzer" (dial meter) instruments for focus groups. His "Political Information System" database and working team targeted "up-to-the-minute attitudinal survey work, fixed demographic information, historical voting patterns for every county in the country, on-going assessment of political party strength in each state, and subjective analysis" (Nelson 1989, 74–75). Under this system of political surveillance, "daily and weekly gathering of polling data became the basis for every decision and public statement or action" (Perry 1984, 169). The cost of organizing elections on this basis also helps weed out less well-heeled and independent candidates, reducing the number who might otherwise attempt to seek office without big corporate financial backing. The structure of the electoral processes thus deeply discourages potential leaders with messages and values that are not easily accommodated within the style, lexicon, and cost demands of getting and staying elected.

Wirthlin met Reagan in 1968 while doing polling for Arizona senator Barry Goldwater, who recommended the young pollster to the future governor of California. Although Wirthlin Worldwide declares that 90 percent of its clients are business enterprises and only 10 percent political, Wirthlin gained national prominence as Reagan's chief strategist and pollster, and his ties to the both the Reagan and George H. W. Bush administrations favorably positioned him for lucrative private sector opportunities. With a doctorate from the University of California, Berkeley, Wirthlin is widely regarded as one of the pioneering figures in the fields of political and corporate survey research and communications strategy. His polls helped convince Reagan to put off a plan to cut Social Security (J. Green 2002). He also polled for issue advocacy groups, including antiabortion groups, that backed the administration. Beyond working for Reagan, Wirthlin has been a much-valued pollster for the Republican National Committee and has run campaigns for Republicans at virtually all levels of government (*US Newswire* 2000).

Wirthlin is also a force internationally. His Sydney, Australia, office was used as the official polling and strategy center for conservative Prime Minister John Howard (Aslam 1999; Gagliardi 1999, 17). In 1998, when the International Monetary Fund (IMF) needed to craft a response to the scathing criticism coming from many quarters about its role in the financial crises in

Russia, Brazil, and several Asian countries, it tapped into its $24 million "external relations budget" to hire Wirthlin Worldwide, in operation since 1969, with branch offices in Brussels, London, and Hong Kong. Public relations experts variously estimated the cost to the IMF to be somewhere between $100,000 and $1 million to have Wirthlin's company gauge public opinion about the Fund through in-depth interviews with 400 key individuals in eighteen countries (Aslam 1999).

Why would the IMF seek out Wirthlin Worldwide to shore up its reputation? It is perhaps for the same reason that Citizens for a Free Kuwait, a coalition of wealthy Kuwaiti citizens and government officials (including the Kuwaiti ambassador to the United States) had in hiring Wirthlin and public relations giant Hill and Knowlton in 1990 to drum up political support for U.S. involvement in what was to become the Persian Gulf War. In that effort, Wirthlin's company employed focus groups, perception analyzers, and international public opinion polling to measure attitudes and assist in the formulation of a persuasive communications strategy (Carlisle 1993; Aslam 1999). Since 1969, Richard Wirthlin and Wirthlin Worldwide have helped elect a U.S. president and an Australian prime minister and assisted a host of transnational corporations in "brand management" and "strategic communications." Among Wirthlin's corporate and federal government clients over the past three and one-half decades have been DuPont, Mobil, Citibank, Coca-Cola, Chase Manhattan Bank, Dow Jones, Mercedes-Benz, Boeing, ConAgra, American Express, the Internal Revenue Service, the U.S. Postal Service, the U.S. Air Force, and the office of the U.S. secretary of defense (Wirthlin Worldwide 2001; Gagliardi 1999; *Meetings & Conventions* 2000; *Los Angeles Times* 2001). In fact, Wirthlin Worldwide's website claims that over two-thirds of the top 100 Fortune 500 companies have been the agency's clients (Wirthlin Worldwide 2001). Wirthlin Worldwide revenues in 1999 were $33.5 million, with 19.3 percent or $6.5 million generated outside the United States (*Marketing News* 2000).

Wirthlin advertises his firm's specialties as image and reputation enhancement, brand equity and positioning, advertising strategy and assessment, issues management, building employee commitment, customer satisfaction and loyalty, new product development, crisis management, and political campaign strategy. In 1998, Wirthlin was commissioned by, among others, Chrysler Corporation and Daimler-Benz AG to assess public opinion on corporate mergers. His lead researcher on the project, Dee Allsop, a onetime journalist now working for the company, found that 76 percent of respondents thought mergers were good for stockholders, but only 45 percent thought they were good for consumers (Stoffer 1998). The corporate consortium of Welfare to Work, a nonprofit corporate-government entity representing such transnationals as Monsanto, Bank of America, Citigroup, and Manpower, Inc., hired Wirthlin in 1999 to gauge attitudes toward perceived results of the major welfare legislation of the late 1990s (Welfare to Work 2001; Tait 1999). The goal, of course, was not to align corporate regulation with public opinion but to help business organize public perceptions.

In a 1999 interview, Wirthlin said that after his Reagan White House years his aim was to engage less in politics and instead "focus on what I viewed as a more stable revenue flow" (Gagliardi 1999, 17). His resume is a testament to the ruling synergies that consultants help to create between business and politics.[14]

Karl Rove

Prior to becoming senior White House advisor, Karl Rove was chief strategist for George W. Bush's 2000 presidential campaign. Rove rapidly moved from hired campaign consultant to senior policy advisor and the chief operative within the president's inner circle, in charge of the Office for Strategic Initiatives for long-term political planning. He is sometimes compared in his zeal to his Democratic Party counterpart, James Carville, although Rove had considerable more influence in policy advising than Carville ever had in the Clinton administration (losing White House favor after the first term). In 2003, Rove was under suspicion for leaking to a conservative news reporter the name of a CIA officer, who happened to be married to a diplomat and Democrat who had been critical of the Bush administration's policy in Iraq. Further suspicion was drawn to the White House's own investigation of the leak incident, because Rove had been a paid consultant in three earlier political campaigns of the attorney general, John Ashcroft (Bumiller and Lichtblau 2003, A1, A22).

Rove is often called the "brains" inside the younger Bush White House, the president's Machiavelli, and is said to view William McKinley's advisor, Mark Hanna (see chapter 1), as his inspiration. Rove indeed compared the Bush success in 2000 to that of McKinley's victory in 1896, anticipating a long string of Republican White House triumphs thereafter (Baker 2003, 43). One of Rove's functions is helping the president spin policy language in ways intended to lower the public's resistance to federal reductions in social spending. When Bush referred to Social Security as "retirement security" or "wealth-generating private accounts" (supporting the privatization of the government-run system) and urged other poll-tested conservative pitch phrases, such as "school choice" (vouchers), "death taxes" (estate taxes), and "education recession" (critique of public-funded schooling), it was Rove's tactics at work (J. Green 2002). Rove also was one of the central planners of the 2002 off-year elections in which the Republicans gained control over both congressional chambers and mastermind of the 2004 campaign.

Rove's rise to prominence began when he was elected chair of the College Republicans organization in 1973, aided by another conservative upstart, Lee Atwater[15] (Carney and Duffy 1999). Rove dropped out of college and left his native Utah for Houston in 1977, when he began working for the Bush family. In Houston, he became executive director of the Fund for Limited Government, a political action committee run by former Republican stalwart James Baker, on behalf of the elder Bush (Dubose 2001). He would later run both of George W. Bush's successful gubernatorial campaigns. With a penchant for pet names, Bush Junior affectionately refers to Rove alternately as "Boy Genius" or "Turdblossom" (*Economist* 2002).

Rove also started up a direct-mail business in Austin, Praxis List Company, run under his political consulting firm. His aggressive direct-mail fundraising, candidate recruitment, and take-no-prisoners campaign tactics helped convert Texas's statewide elected offices from largely Democratic to heavily Republican. His list of victorious clients, aside from the Bush family, includes U.S. Senate candidates Texans Phil Gramm and Kay Bailey Hutchinson and nearly half the state's Republican officeholders (Dubose 2001). Karl Rove & Co. consulting has made millions working for other Republicans in some twenty-three states and for foreign politicians, including Sweden's rightist Moderate Party (formerly called Conservative Party), as well as for numerous corporate clients. He was a "paid political intelligence operative" for Philip Morris from 1991–1996 and until moving into the White House, his financial portfolio included over $100,000 in equity in at least six different corporations, Enron, Intel, General Electric, Johnson & Johnson, Pfizer, and Cisco, all of which maintained strategic personal contacts with the Bush consultant (Baldauf 1999, 1; Dreyfuss 1999; Lardner 2001).

James Carville

One of the most colorful political consultants in the 1990s was James Carville. By the time he began working for the Clinton election in 1992, he was already widely known among his peers as a high-powered spin doctor and political "attack dog" and the top political consultant in the field, managing more elections than anyone in the history of the profession. What is rather remarkable is that Carville, an unnoteworthy lawyer from Louisiana, was already in his forties when he began to make a name for himself, in a field that caters largely to younger, well-traveled men, and he did not venture overseas until age forty-five (Hockstader 1999). His reputation and celebrity status soared when he and George Stephanopoulus ran the Clinton presidential campaign's war room in

1992. He is also different from most of his peers in his intensely expressed loyalty to Democratic Party liberalism. Also remarkable is that his wife, Mary Matalin, is said to be just as intensely loyal to Republican conservativism and serves as a political advisor to George W. Bush. Political difference of opinion apparently can be overlooked where teamwork brings serious financial returns, as in their shared experience in giving political advice in the 1993 Greek national election. Together, the couple was estimated by the *Forbes* 1999 list of top money-making political, legal, and financial experts to have raked in $3.4 million (Brown 1999).

Following his withdrawal as a strategist for Clinton after the president's first term, Carville began spending more time doing corporate and international consulting. His political clients have included prime minister candidates Ehud Barak of Israel, Tony Blair of Britain, and the conservative Constantine Mitsotakis of Greece. In Latin America, Carville worked for the presidential campaigns of Francisco Labastida of Mexico, Fernando Enrique Cardoso of Brazil, Carlos Flores of Honduras, Jamil Mohuad of Ecuador, Eduardo Duhalde of Argentina, and São Paulo mayoral candidate Celso Pitta. Along with many in his field, Carville moonlights as a consultant and pitchman for major corporations, such as the software developer MS2 Inc. in Silicon Valley, and is not above doing commercials for Alka Seltzer and Nike sneakers (Petersen 2000). And like other leading political professionals, Carville has no problem moving between lucrative public and private sector opportunities. His work bridges the two, which challenges the idea of "conflict of interest." Of late, Carville has been most visible as a cohost of CNN's *Crossfire*.

Mary Matalin

Rising within the Republican fold under the tutelage of Richard Bond, George H. W. Bush's political director for the 1988 presidential campaign (Harbrecht 1990) Mary Matalin has been a stalwart party loyalist despite being married to Democratic Party consultant James Carville. This apparently represents no serious barrier in today's flexible "third way" politics.[16] Matalin negotiated a deal to keep religious right leader Pat Robertson and conservative Jack Kemp close to party ranks following their own failed bids at securing the 1988 Republican presidential nomination and helped organize the Bush campaign in Michigan that year. Matalin also was put in charge of "Victory '88," the Republican National Committee's get-out-the-vote operation (Harbrecht 1990). For these efforts, she was placed in the number two spot working under then party chair Lee Atwater, the man who organized the notorious and racially tinged 1988 Bush presidential ad campaign against

Michael Dukakis. Following Atwater's death, Matalin became political director for Bush's unsuccessful 1992 campaign. More recently, she was asked to be George W. Bush's political assistant and a counselor to his vice president, Richard Cheney

Matalin has otherwise been a media personality, hosting CNN's *Crossfire* program (before her husband took over), coauthoring with Carville a book about their courtship and political life that pocketed them nearly a million-dollar advance from Simon & Schuster and Random House together with a movie contract, and taken in fat paychecks on the lecture circuit (Schimdt and Mintz 2001). The duo headlined a luncheon at the 1999 American Correctional Association's (ACA) annual winter conference in Nashville, Tennessee (Tischler 1999), an umbrella organization that represents the interests of over 20,000 members of the U.S. prison-industrial complex, including private and military prison facilities and prisons (ACA 2001). They also spoke at the 1999 Informex, which claims to be the "world's leading custom chemical, intermediate and outsourcing trade show." Their audience included many of the leading corporate players in this sector: Dupont, Union Carbide, Hoffman-LaRoche, Cyanamid Corporation, Amoco, and 3M Company (Shiley 1999). Their other speaking engagements included the annual Retail Management Conference of the Securities Industry Association (SIA) in Washington, D.C., an organization established in 1972 to represent over 700 securities firms involved in $358 billion worth of investment banking, brokerage, and mutual fund management interests (SIA 2001). In 1993, the twosome teamed up with liberal consultant Paul Begala in Greece to work for the failed reelection of Mitsotakis. Though she remains a Republican loyalist, Matalin's successful partnership with an avowed New Democrat shows that when it comes to their big business attitudes and the allure of money, like the two-party system there is little to separate them.

Stanley Greenberg

Another close associate of Carville is Stanley Greenberg, who is regarded as one of the top political pollsters in the United States. Greenberg holds a doctorate from Harvard University. His political reputation is left-of-center, and his international clients have included Britain's prime minister Tony Blair (for whom he still provides public opinion polling services) and the Labour Party in Britain, the Labour Party of Israel, Francesco Rutelli (unsuccessful candidate for prime minister of Italy), Gerhard Schröder, and, on behalf of the National Endowment for Democracy (NED), Nelson Mandela.[17] (See chapter 4 on the NED.) At home, he has been a consultant for Democrats Al Gore,

Chris Dodd, Joseph Lieberman, Jeff Bingham, Jim Florio, Walter Mondale, and John Kerry, and for the Democratic National Committee.

Working closely with Carville, Greenberg was central to Bill Clinton's 1992 election campaign but left when Clinton's health care plan had to be abandoned, for which Greenberg took partial blame. Greenberg consults for many large corporate clients, including Boeing, British Petroleum, British Airways, United Airlines, Monsanto, Ameritech, MCI, Unistar, the Organization for International Investment, and the Business Roundtable. His firm, Greenberg Research, worked for "America Leads on Trade," a coalition of corporate participants, including the Business Roundtable, the National Association of Manufacturers, the U.S. Chamber of Commerce, and some 550 other companies and trade associations seeking to promote fast-track authority for the president in 1997 (Greenberg Research 2001b; Stone 1997). And despite his reputation as left leaning, Greenberg is fully a player in the world of the Fortune 500 and the neoliberal New Democrats (of the Democratic Leadership Council). In Britain, Greenberg was commissioned by the genetic engineering firm Monsanto "to find out why its public relations was not working" there (Monbiot 2000, 266).

Philip Gould

On the British side of the Atlantic, political consultants have become just as central to electioneering as their American counterparts. Once described by the *Times* (London) as "Tony Blair's pet pollster," Philip Gould, who holds a master's degree in political theory from the London School of Economics, is most closely associated with the focus group that helped generate Blair's and the New Labour Party's adopted "third way" motto. Before he became associated with politics, Gould was a founder and partner in an advertising agency, Brignull Lebas Gould Limited, and went on to work as senior manager in global advertising firms DDB and Interpublic (Greenberg Research 2001a). His clients have included Coca-Cola, Time Inc., and Express Newspapers. With his advertising background and keen interest in politics, Gould was recruited in the late 1980s by Peter Mandelson, Labour's director of campaigns and communications, and put to work on the Shadow Communications Agency. Gould convinced the party elite to allow sympathizers working in public relations and advertising to assist the party in its bid to gain power (Mcelvoy 2000).

Gould became very much influenced in his political thinking by the experience he had as a guest of Bill Clinton's war-room strategists in Little Rock for four weeks of the 1992 presidential campaign and returned during the 1996 campaign as a guest of the Clinton administration. He then joined forces in 1997 with Carville and Greenberg to form the international consulting and corporate communications and strategy enterprise GGC-NOP. In the 1997 British parliamentary elections, the Blair campaign, with Gould closely involved, had a strategy and response center—in homage to Clinton also called the "war room." Being trusted pollsters and advisors to Blair and the Labour Party undoubtedly helped GGC-NOP win British government contracts worth over £250,000 immediately following the 1997 election (Gerard 2001).

Gould has also taken his services abroad, advising the unsuccessful campaigns of Nicaragua's Sandinistas in 1990, the Jamaican Labor Party in 1993, and the pro-European Union campaigners in Norway's 1994 referendum, in addition to working for the governments of Sweden, the Netherlands, Greece, and Denmark (Milne 1996; Greenberg Research 2001a). Borrowing the "line of the day" media-management orientation of White House communication directors, Gould wrote in his book, *The Unfinished Revolution*: "In a campaign you must always seek to gain and keep momentum . . . [which] means dominating the news agenda, entering the news cycle at the earliest possible time, and repeatedly re-entering it, with stories and initiatives that ensure that subsequent news coverage is set on your terms" (cited in Barnett and Gaber 2001). Gould has been a good student of his American mentors.

Dick Morris

One of the more controversial national/international consultants is Dick Morris. Before he worked with the Clinton campaign in 1996, Morris was a self-declared Republican, having previously worked for archconservatives Mississippi Senator Trent Lott and North Carolina Senator Jesse Helms. He didn't switch parties, he merely worked both sides of the aisle, and Clinton, driven by political opportunism, decided to employ him to beat the Republicans at their own game. Following Morris's advice, Clinton adopted the strategy of triangulation, which essentially meant preempting conservative issues with a more centrist twist (e.g., tax cuts, "tough on crime" measures, voluntary school prayer, welfare reform). Morris advised Clinton at the outset of the Monica Lewinsky scandal but was forced to resign following a media sex scandal of his own in which he was linked with a Washington, D.C., prostitute. He has since reinvented himself as an online political consultant via his website vote.com, which has helped him find both national and international political and business clients.

Morris was an attractive campaign advisor to Clinton, a politician all too willing for political expediency's sake to shift from social democratic to centrist positions. The coining of the term "third way" is attributed to Morris (Halimi 1999). In consulting circles, Morris has the reputation of disregarding the political values of his candidate and being concerned only with what works tactically and strategically. One political scientist sees Morris as being uniquely skilled at rapidly moving cash flows into polls and political advertising (Witcover 1999, 45–46). Abroad, Morris worked on the Blair and Schröder campaigns and faced off against Carville for campaign supremacy in Mexico, Honduras, and Argentina (*Business and Finance* 2002). In 2004, he signed on as a consultant for Lia Roberts, an American, native-born Romanian, and former chair of the Nevada Republican Party, who decided to return to her home country to run for president and "bring investment from the U.S. and jobs to help the [Romanian] middle class" (Richardson 2004). Working the election for Romania's Social Democratic Party were Greenberg, Carville, and Robert Shrum.

Arthur Finkelstein

One of Arthur Finkelstein's credits is that he engineered a U.S. Senate victory in New York for an unknown Long Island town supervisor, Alfonse D'Amato, a Republican, over longtime incumbent Democrat Jacob Javits. Finkelstein's strategy was to use attack ads to call attention to the seventy-six-year-old Javits's failing health, a result of Lou Gehrig's disease, which gave the consultant a ruthless reputation among his peers. He also demonized Javits as an uncompromising "liberal," a tactic he would repeat in D'Amato's unsuccessful 1998 senatorial race against Charles Schumer. This kind of sustained and directed key word ("liberal") attack has been Finkelstein's signature as a campaign strategist. During a heated 1992 senatorial campaign, when D'Amato was momentarily trailing in the polls, Finkelstein advised the incumbent to accuse Robert Abrams of trying to link him to Mussolini. Finkelstein followed up this advice with a thirty-second television spot showing archival footage of the Italian dictator and the narrator decrying Abrams for pandering to religious and ethnic fears. A backlash resulted against Abrams and secured the Senate seat for D'Amato.[18]

Working on behalf of Jesse Helms, Finkelstein pilloried his opponent in 1984, Governor Jim Hunt, for supporting a national holiday in honor of Martin Luther King. Finkelstein has had rather odd associations with archconservative clients like Jesse Helms and strong ties to the Christian Right. His intellectual dedication to people such as Ayn Rand and F. Clifton White and early political devotion to Barry Goldwater is based on a shared fanatical hatred of communism, trumping other loyalties and identities that he may or may not have—as a Brooklyn-raised, gay Jew (Rodrick 1996). Finkelstein has pushed a right-wing lexicon on the Republican Party, turning the word *liberal* into a disreputable epithet to suggest something out of kilter with popular sentiments, whereas *conservative* is treated as a moral standard. (In most Western democracies, ironically, "liberal" parties are normally associated with the conservative side of the political spectrum, whereas the left is typically identified as some variant of socialism.) More recently, Finkelstein worked as a pollster on the 2002 George Pataki and Mitt Romney gubernatorial campaigns in New York and Massachusetts.

Frank Luntz

The political slogan "contract with America," used by the national Republican Party in 1994 came out of focus group research conducted by party consultant Frank Luntz and the spin-doctoring mastery of Arthur Finkelstein. The result of this rhetorical offensive was to bring to political center stage the persona of Newt Gingrich and help his party capture a House majority that year and the speakership for himself.[19] Luntz's other clients have included New York mayor Rudolph Giuliani (who himself became a high-priced consultant at the end of his mayoral term); Giuliani's successor, Michael Bloomberg; Italy's prime minister, Silvio Berlusconi; Britain's Conservative Party; the 1992 third party presidential candidate Ross Perot; the presidential fringe candidate Pat Buchanan; and George W. Bush. According to Luntz's lecture circuit agency, the pollster as of 1998 had "written and supervised more than 400 surveys for political and corporate clients in ten countries since founding his company [Luntz Research Companies] in 1992" (Harry Walker Agency 1998).

Though Luntz is well known as a leading political pollster and consultant for Republican candidates, his polling efforts of late have been on behalf of Fortune 500 and other big corporate clients and lobbying and trade associations. He also has worked with the Chamber of Commerce, the National Association of Manufacturers, the National Federation of Independent Business, and Hugh Hefner's Playboy Enterprises. In 1998, Luntz was hired by the former chair of the Republican National Committee and concurrent president of the American Gaming Association, Frank Fahrenkopf (Batt 1998). In support of gaming initiatives, Luntz put together focus groups to test reactions to arguments put forward by gambling opponents. He presented his findings to the gaming association's board of directors at Caesars Palace and apparently hit the jackpot with Vegas stalwart Steve Wynn, chair of Mirage Resorts, Inc., who decided to retain the services of Luntz for consumer marketing research (Batt 1998). Luntz's corporate accounts were so profitable to that point that he announced plans to leave electoral politics to concentrate solely on business clients (Batt 1998; Harry Walker Agency 1998). In fact, he has remained active, though less so, in politics.

Like Stanley Greenberg, Luntz was educated at prestigious universities: BA at the University of Pennsylvania and PhD at Oxford University. In high school, he was state chair of the Teenage Republicans and mentored under longtime Republican consultant Arthur Finkelstein. Trained by Richard Wirthlin, Luntz subsequently became best known for his use of focus groups to discover themes, measure public responses, and craft corporate and political messages. A pocket-size pamphlet he put together for the Republicans, "Right Words," and a 406-page binder called "A Conversation with America 2000" provide speech texts on a variety of subjects.

Borrowing discursive tactics from Finkelstein, Luntz coached candidates to say "opportunity scholarships" rather than "vouchers," "climate change" instead of "global warming," and "tax relief" rather than "tax cuts" (Lemann 2000). The National Center for Policy Analysis, the Enterprise Prison Institute (headed by former Reagan Attorney General Edwin Meese), the Criminal Justice Policy Foundation, and the Workman's Fund, which represent conservative policy interest groups and private prison operators, sought to capitalize on America's expanding "prison-industrial complex" and hired Luntz to conduct a poll on public attitudes toward the use of prison labor. Luntz also has worked closely with transnational pharmaceutical companies, major health maintenance organizations, and leading health care trade associations, and conducted focus groups with the United Seniors Association, a right-wing alternative organization to the AARP.

Luntz's focus groups helped him write a memo to House Republicans instructing them how to frame Medicare cuts as attempts to "save Medicare," even as the party was seeking ways to cut $270 billion from the Medicare program (Lieberman, excerpted in TomPaine.common sense 2001). He advised Republicans to substitute the term "streamlining" for "privatizing" education, although privatizing is semiotically recommended for pitching prison policy. He also suggested that when discussing corporate subjects, party spokespersons should not mention stockholders or money but rather pitch images of a future "in terms of people, ideas and visions" (Corn 1996). Following the 9/11 events, Luntz prepared a memorandum for Senate Republicans as part of a campaign to recapture that chamber, which called for the broad circulation of the brand slam "Daschle Democrats," together with the associated term, "obstructionist." Despite his highly partisan political background, MSNBC saw fit in 2003 to have him host a TV show called *America's Voices*.

Mark Mellman

A graduate of Ivy League universities and president and CEO of the successful Democratic polling and consulting firm, the Mellman Group, Mark Mellman has become one of the most active and sought-after opinion pollsters in the United States. He chooses to work exclusively for Democratic Party candidates and those ballot initiatives and issues supported by the party. He has worked with a number of leading Democratic candidates, including Senate majority leader Tom Daschle and House minority leader Richard Gephardt, as well as the Democratic National Committee and various senatorial and congressional committees. In the 2004 campaign, he polled for Democratic candidate John Kerry. According to Mellman's website, his international clients have included the Leningrad and Moscow Soviet Democratic blocs; FMI Indonesia (an engineering firm); the former president of Colombia, César Gaviria; the Spanish Socialist Party; and Rukh, a right-of-center political movement in the Ukraine. His website also lists as clients the World Bank, Radio Marti, and Univision (Mellman Group 2003).

Mellman sells his company's political expertise and business strategy advice to a number of major corporate clients—industries ranging from military aircraft to chocolate milk. These include Bell Atlantic, Aetna, Bankers Trust, Oracle, Genentech, Massmutual, United Airlines, GE Mortgage, GTE, Janus Mutual Funds, Sallie Mae, Kodak, Nestle, Dr Pepper/7 UP, PepsiCo, and a number of health care industry companies. Mellman also has been a frequent guest on the political talk show circuit and a consultant to corporate media owners CBS News, PBS, and CNN. He's also been a contributor to the popular Beltway political chronicle *The Hotline* (Mellman Group 2003). In 2000, Mellman released a study undertaken by his firm on the growing problem of drug smuggling in Colombia, which was commissioned by defense contractor Lockheed Martin. *Newsweek* revealed that what Mellman did not mention in his report is that his sponsor was not a disinterested party in the study's findings, inasmuch as the company produces radar-equipped planes sold to the U.S. government for drug interdiction (Erickson 2000).

Phil Noble

In 1994, Phil Noble ended a brief political career after losing a race for lieutenant governor of South Carolina. Following the defeat, Noble returned to his occupation as a political consultant and pollster and has since become a specialist in opposition research, online consulting, and electronic political fundraising, creating in 1996 PoliticsOnline for these purposes (PoliticsOnline 2001). Noble boasts that his "Instant Online Fundraiser" will "do for campaign finance what the machine gun did for bank robberies" (Raney 1998). This tool is available to almost any client, regardless of party affiliation (though most of his U.S. political clients are Democrats),[20] seeking to raise funds over the Internet. In this regard, Noble can be considered a political mercenary. His firm, with offices in the United States and Sweden, takes a 10 percent cut of each donor's credit card contribution (Raney 1998).

On his PoliticsOnline website, Noble claims that his firm has been involved in more than 300 corporate and public affairs projects and political contests in and outside the United States, including twenty campaigns to elect heads of state in North and South America, Europe, Asia, and Africa (PoliticsOnline 2001). In much of the world, political clients are often cautious to publicize their ties to American consultants, but Noble's website trumpets legions of international clients and "client countries" across the political spectrum (PN&A 2001). His client base lists the presidential campaigns in El Salvador (Francisco Flores), Costa Rica (José Méndez Mata), and Nicaragua (Haraldo Montealegre); Chief Moshood Abiola of Nigeria; the British Labour Party; Canada's Conservative Party; Labor Party of Malta; Moderate Party of Estonia; Socialist Party of Cyprus; National Party of New Zealand; Liberal Party of British Columbia (Canada); and African National Congress, as well as the Yes to Europe Referendum campaign in Sweden. His firm also conducts multiparty training seminars in a number of countries, especially in East Europe, and various other business relationships in both the developed and developing countries (PN&A 2001). In 1997, the American Association of Political Consultants feted him as its "international consultant of the year" (PoliticsOnline 2001).

THE INDUSTRIALIZATION OF ELECTORAL MANAGEMENT

This section examines the U.S. election industry within the globalizing neoliberal economic framework. The principal concern here is on the organizing tactics of professional consultants, their uses of new information and communications technologies (ICT) in the election process, and the implications of both on participatory democracy, nationally and internationally. How does the current emphasis on free-trade economics link to the decline of the popular political engagement and the widely perceived weakening of the public sphere? What changes in the election process can be traced to the restructuring of the global economic system and the digital technological mode of industrial, cultural, and political production? These questions are approached by examining the activities of election professionals in the United States and the store of communications instruments and techniques they carry into election forays at home and abroad.

The American-style election has become a global tour de force, full of staging, technique, and a carefully crafted political star system—not unlike the advertising blitz and premiere of a Hollywood blockbuster. Electioneering is just another development of an ongoing industrialization, technologization, and globalization of commodity and cultural production in everyday life. With beachheads already established in much of the world, the transnationalization of politics is enacted through export of U.S. political expertise, communications technologies, electronic data and public relations, and the commodifying of electoral techniques. Political transnationalization has escaped the attention of a public largely unaware of the planning, mechanics, and electronics of the electoral process, how the political spectacle is constructed (Edelman 1988), and the roles played by consultants, opposition researchers, pollsters, fundraisers, media specialists, get-out-the-vote organizers, and other campaign managers and operatives (Thurber and Dulio 1999, 28). The public is even less informed about the linkages between communications specialists and the most powerful interest groups and political bankrollers.

One of the critical changes in electoral processes, particularly in the United States but increasingly in other countries, is the shift from party-centered to candidate-centered politics.[21] Another is the growing technification of campaign management and control. A third is the drift from an issue-oriented to a star system–based symbolic politics. A growing convergence of public relations, advertising, and political consulting in the United States has merged with the organized corporate interests that dominate campaign funding. Political consulting has become a growth industry. By 1996, the domestic consulting business already was taking in over $1 billion in election-year billings alone (Clark 1996, 867; *Wilson Quarterly* 2000, 119). By the late 1990s, the industry was raking in $6 billion in overall (elections and other consulting opportunities) domestic billings (Plasser 2000, 40), with some 7,000 full-time professionals servicing some 50,000 national, state, and local campaigns per year. One group of consultants involved in Clinton's 1995–1996 reelection, including Dick Morris, was paid $60 million by the Clinton-Gore campaign and another $40 million by the Democratic National Committee (Witcover 1999, 26).

The typical profile of the consultant is white (94.12 percent), male (81.8 percent), fortyish (average age is 45.9 years) with average incomes in 1999 of about $122,200, although more than half have family incomes above $150,000, and one-third make more than $200,000 (Thurber and Dulio 1999, 28; Pew Research Center 1998), statistics that have only increased over time. Those who work on the major campaigns at home and abroad make considerably more. In the 1999 Israeli elections, each of the foreign consultants made between $300,000 and $600,000 (Stevenson 2000b). Dick Morris bragged that while working for Clinton in 1996 he made a million dollars (Shea and Burton 2001, 8).

Not all consultants make that kind of money, of course. It used to be that consultants first entered the business with strong partisan interests on the side of a political candidate or party, but that is changing. According to one retired political professional, "There are very few consultants that are in that situation these days." Political consulting has become more of a business and less a matter of the consultant strongly believing in the party for which he or she happens to be working. In most cases, he says, the idealism consultants may have had when they entered politics usually disappears once they begin to take on work with corporations (Galizio 2002).

With a clientele base delinked from capricious economic cycles, there is plenty of political and corporate consulting work to go around. The reason is that no regime of power or business group can ignore the electoral and public relations process as a fundamental matter of protecting its stakes in the system. The key requirement in electoral strategy is funds solicitation. Applying Ferguson's "investment theory" approach (discussed in chapter 1), this means that major corporate and wealthy donors see the electoral process as a way of getting a generous return on their campaign contributions. In responding to this demand, the ubiquitous political pollsters and other political functionaries "accustomed to assisting candidates on the campaign trail, spend their afternoons and evenings convening focus groups, testing advertisements for products, helping to craft commercial spots, or searching for just the right wording for public relations materials" (Novotny 2000, 12).

Once the election season is underway, the larger consulting groups run concurrent multiple campaigns, and sometimes their partners work for candidates on both sides of the party divide. The same is true for major lobbying firms. But consultants generally do not rely solely on political campaign work for their fame or their fortune. Since the 1980s, there has been continuous shuttling of major consulting firms between political candidates to corporate and trade association clients (Johnson 2000, 45). These linkages have the effect of building corporate-consultant-political networks. During campaign downtime, the candidate, other campaign organizers, or elected officials connected to the campaign will throw the consultants business in corporate consulting or lobbying, which will keep them employed throughout the year. As one veteran campaign consultant, Michael Galizio, explained, "That, more and more, has been the picture of the way things have developed, because the consultants want to make the maximum amount of money. You can't make the maximum amount of money if you're [only] working for a Congress member" (Galizio 2002).

According to Galizio, the number of consultants doing corporate work in off-season

> has grown in leaps and bounds in the last ten years. It is phenomenal what's happened, because everybody saw there was a huge amount of money to be made if you can parlay the relationships that you have with elected officials into con-

tacts with corporations who need the eyes and the ears of those various elected officials. It's an age-old thing. Lobbyists have done it via building relationships through campaign contributions. Others have done it through raising money for individuals. You may work for a major public relations firm in Washington, and you spend a lot of your life raising money for candidate x, y, or z, because you know that those candidates if successful as Congress members can be very helpful to your corporate clients. That's much, much bigger than it ever was. (Galizio 2002)

Consultants also increasingly work for powerful interest groups and various government agencies. Straddling politics, public policy, and industry dissolves the distinction between political advisor and industry or government public relations functionary or lobbyist. It also breaks down differences between work done on behalf of government and corporate clients, and creates a seamless web of interrelationships between the public and private sectors, with profound implications for even the relative autonomy of the public policy process. It is the protection of public interests that is likely to lose out in these elaborate liaisons.

In 2003, the cozy relationship between politicians, consultants, and lobbyists became evident in California, when the press in that state reported that two legislators who had hired Richard Ross as a political consultant were supporting bills to benefit Indian tribes for whom Ross had served as a lobbyist. Ross's double-dipping was seen to represent a logical nexus in the "high-stakes relationship between California's interest groups and lawmakers." At the federal level, a lobbying organization, the Committee for Justice, with such clients as Citigroup, R. J. Reynolds Tobacco, and Microsoft, actively worked to promote George W. Bush's judicial nominees even as two-thirds of the lobbyists had clients with cases pending in courts where those same judges, if confirmed, would serve. Two other members of the lobbying group are linked to companies that are defendants in cases involving federal lawsuits (*Desert Sun* 2003). (The revolving door of consultants, lobbyists, politicians, and corporations is further discussed in chapter 6.)

THE MODERN TOOLS OF THE TRADE

The rapid pace of innovation in the electronics and telecommunications sectors has been a boon to professionalization. This last section of the chapter describes the main technologies that have been employed in the election process. The uses of electronic media and processing equipment have altered the way professionals and voters relate to the political process and have enabled new forms of control over the information that reaches the public. In the United States, the state primaries still provide many citizens the opportunity, though quite brief, to see and hear candidates for federal office. For the most part, however, candidates and politicians have become more isolated from public view. The professionalization and capture of the electoral process by global corporations has much to do with why this has occurred. The modern tools of the trade consist of the following.

Broadcast Television

This is still the principal chosen medium by well-financed political candidates. Television overall absorbed 83.5 percent of political advertising funds in 1998 (Morgan 2000).[22] Media consultants with extensive experience in creating and placing television advertisements command substantial fees, and those in the top tier reject many potential clients. This omnipresent visual medium offers a penetration rate of 98 percent of U.S. households. The decreasing audiences of the major broadcast networks has resulted in more ad revenue for and attention given to cable television and specialized programming. However, the main broadcast networks have come to own and dominate the programming on the cable side.

The Pew Research Center for the People and the Press found that 75 percent of Americans say they consider television their main source of campaign news (Aday 2003), although, in fact, the time allocated for network campaign news coverage in the both the United States and the United Kingdom has been steadily declining. In the United States, radio and television talk show hosts have increasingly replaced news organizations as the popular source of political information. In Europe, television is steadily displacing newspapers as the chief source of news for most people. It may be the case, as some have predicted, that television may not remain the preeminent medium of political persuasion in the future; however, in the foreseeable period, no other instrument of news and information is likely to draw as much public attention and the campaign investment dollar.

Cable and Satellite Television

Adopting the lessons from product marketing, political professionals use strategic media buying to target television spots to selected voter segments, such as the "undecided" group. The rapid change in production and distribution processes along with narrower voter demographics permit specific target-group appeals. Cable television took in 3 percent to 6 percent of the average campaign media budget in 1996, and this percentage is likely to increase significantly. The vast majority of congressional races now include cable in their media mix. Broadcast TV is often seen as inaccessible and too expensive, whereas cable stations have been willing to provide lower rates, major discount packages, and other incentives to campaign advertisers, including the availability of subscriber lists (Friedenberg 1997, 184–87). An added value of satellite broadcasting was found by the Clinton campaign in 1992 when his team intercepted Bush political ads and was able in a very timely way to issue "instant" rejoinders as soon as they were aired, giving the appearance of spontaneity (Selnow 1994, 3).

Microwave TV

Microwave multipoint multichannel distribution service (MMDS) delivers video signals using microwave transmission. Campaigns can create events, press conferences, or messages and distribute them to news stations and local markets. A hidden code can be placed in the signal to track its subsequent use by local news stations. This is yet another technology that permits the wide distribution of campaign-controlled messages with relatively little effort or expense.

Digitally Distributed Advertising

This refers to television spots converted into digital files that can be transmitted over a satellite network for national network distribution and airing. Its technological convergence capabilities are useful in rapid-response television advertising in the twenty-four-hour news cycle. In addition, the technology permits campaigns to tailor distinct messages to particular regions and demographic groups. Once digital television reception becomes pervasive, direct political advertising could be carried out in a more systematic voter-profiled, customized, household-targeted fashion.

Direct-Mail Videos

These are short, slickly produced videocassette pieces, often sent to local opinion leaders and interest groups. Still another way to circumvent media scrutiny and appeal directly to voters, videos offer complete editorial control and the possibility of grassroots distribution.

Radio Advertising

This mode of advertising goes back to the 1920s and today operates on a smaller scale than television but at a much lower cost. Radio's early use of jingles and highly stylized speech set the pattern for television forms of commercial and political advertising. Closely related to political radio advertising is the service that partisan talk show hosts perform in publicizing candidates and ridiculing their opponents. There is a broad swath of radio stations across the United States that caters to blaring nationally syndicated right-wing politics (led by such personalities as Bill O'Reilly, Michael Savage, Rush Limbaugh, and Laura Ingraham), joined in 2004 by "Air America," a liberal version of the same aggressive style.

Polaris

Political monitoring of opposition campaigns relies on technologies originally designed for nuclear warfare. One company, National Media Inc., introduced Polaris (political advertising reporting and intelligence system), which is similar in design to the nuclear submarine system from which it drew it acronym. The political monitoring system is able to detect a sound "fingerprint" created by a political advertisement, which, once encoded, can be sensed as it is transmitted by satellite to cable and broadcast stations. Previously developed for commercial advertisers, this technology can be a valuable tool in evaluating how the opposition campaign is using political advertising, in what markets, with what frequency, on what stations, during what programs, and the type of audience and share of it that it is reaching (Friedenberg 1997, 180–83).

Polling/Tracking Surveys

Polling, the "radar" of politics, has become primarily telephone-based, largely replacing face-to-face interviewing as a matter of cost, speed, and convenience, though not necessarily accuracy. Tracking polls are surveys of targeted voter groups throughout the campaign. Polling includes but is not limited to public perception, attitude benchmark, tracking (following the voter group's response over time and in response to particular events), and campaign communication evaluation polling, all of which are central to the creation and adaptation of a campaign's message. Pollsters are often the first political professionals hired in the campaign, and they typically absorb 5 percent to 10 percent of campaign expenditures. Among the major tracking poll specialists are the Tarrance Group for the Republicans and Lake Research for the Democrats. The Tarrance Group is said to stay open "twenty-four hours a day for the last six weeks of the campaign cycle, a kind of 7-Eleven convenience story polling" operation (Hill 2002, 150).

Polling data segments the electorate and convinces candidate organizations to avoid districts and regions with little prospect for big vote tallies. Phones and computers deliver a night's harvest of responses to polling professionals with results delivered to campaign headquarters the following morning. Canadians call this "rolling polling." There is also a "dirty tricks" style of "polling" called the "push poll," in which organized party "pollsters" call potential voters, usually in the last week of the campaign, to ask if a negative characteristic of an opposing candidate would affect their choice at the voting booth, thereby insinuating a reason not to vote for that candidate.[23] It is not, in fact, a poll at all but, instead, an effort to discredit the political opponent. The main purpose of push-polling is to suppress opponent voter turnout.

Focus Groups

These are selected groups representing specific demographic voter profiles that are deemed important to the campaign. Focus groups are often used to test potential campaign messages and themes prior to the creation and distribution of canned television advertisements. In some cases, the candidates watch focus groups from behind one-way mirrors to learn how to stylize their campaign pitches and organize platform issues. Focus groups usually consist of eight to twelve participants and may be tested in several voting areas before a political message is publicly aired. It is conceivable that with the advent of widespread digital television reception, focus groups could be conducted via transmission to individual households, a "convenience" that could make their use, together with polling, far more extensive and inclusive than at present.

The origin of focus groups goes back to the making of propaganda and training films for American troops, Frank Capra being one of the best-known directors in this effort. Capra was assisted by academic sociologists, including Robert K. Merton of Columbia University. These experiments in mind management became part of the techniques employed in postwar commercial marketing. Writing about the 1992 national election, one reporter, Elizabeth Kolbert, expected that voters "will not see a single ad that has not been tested before a focus group, nor are they likely to see even a minor shift in strategy that has not been played out before a one-way mirror" (Kolbert 1992, 21). As a result, political campaign communication is far more preedited than ever before.

Perception Analyzer

A perception analyzer (or dial meter) is a computer-based system for analysis of a campaign message through immediate feedback from a handheld dial and ratings meter. These are often employed in focus groups by commercial as well as political entities seeking to gauge the visceral response to a verbal or visual stimulus. Campaign consultants can administer this instrument on focus groups to test-market themes, key words, images, and ultimately political commercials in a confidential setting.

Telemarketing

This is another political information system borrowed from the field of advertising. It includes computer-generated high-volume "predictive dialing" of targeted, preselected households for direct, unmediated voter contact. The system of predictive dialing software (also called computer-assisted telephone interviewing) enables telemarketers to automatically dial a list of people appearing on a computer screen, filtering out busy signals, telephone messages that the line is not in service, and answering machines—to respond only to a live "hello." A computer automatically connects a contact with an available telemarketer who can then begin reading the standardized pitch or questionnaire, or it can leave a prerecorded message. The greater cost efficiency of this system over others is that it maximizes the use and productivity of the telemarketer in terms of completed calls per unit of time and reduces agent idle time.[24] Some firms boast up to 100,000 calls per hour for get-out-the-vote, polling, voter identification, and messaging—with multilingual and "accent neutral" call delivery. It also stores information on responses for future uses and can target specific demographic areas of interest to a political organization or candidate. Some of these uses include voter contact, fund-raising, polling, and mobilizing support for certain issues (Conrad 1994, 25–26).

Dialed Surveys

Through sophisticated automated dialers in large call centers, computerized phone programs reach thousands of either randomly selected or registered voters with campaign-tailored messages and questions that are supposed to be more statistically based than those used in ordinary telemarketing. After cross-referencing data purchased from a voter file company, dialed surveys permit campaigns to acquire additional voter information on candidate and issue preference, which can be used for future communications to the targeted voter list.

Direct Mail/Direct Marketing

These are targeted mailings based on customized databases employing the latest computer-based graphic design technology. Richard Viguerie started direct-mail operations in 1965 on behalf of conservative candidates and causes, building up a list of millions of names of reliable ideological and party donors. Direct-mail professionals point to their ability to circumvent the media filter, focus the voter's attention on hot-button issues, and mobilize targeted segments of the electorate through "narrowcasting." If all elections, from local to federal, are counted, direct mail is the biggest cost item in the campaign process (Johnson 2001, 155).

Voice Broadcasting

Some claim that it is much cheaper and more effective to send out the prerecorded voice of the candidate or a well-known politician or celebrity, perhaps that of Bill Clinton or Charlton Heston, to thousands of residential telephone answering machines with an endorsement for an office seeker than it is to send direct mail. This technique is intended to give a "personal touch" to campaign communication and is often done just before the polling date.

Electronic Messaging

This includes targeted electronic mail and Internet fax messaging, including electronic filtering, auto-response, and web-page tracking technologies. The specific uses of Internet technology offer campaigns another option for communicating directly, without media filters, with voters as well as to the media. Consultants can also collect data on voters through their Internet use and create profiles that would aid in their direct-mail efforts, invasions of privacy notwithstanding. The "power fax" enables campaigns to communicate with hundreds of media outlets of all kinds and for journalists to "research" election stories without moving from their desks, while "spamming" refers to mass mailings to potential voters by e-mail or fax. Instant responses from opposition candidates, also by fax, allow journalists to construct a highly packaged "debate," with the most minimum effort on the part of the press (Selnow 1994, 123–24).

The Internet could have a long-term, profound impact on voter behavior, and many political consultants are counting on it, especially following the recent controls imposed on the use of soft-money spending in federal elections. Web-based fund-raising is not restricted under the 2002 campaign finance provisions. (See chapter 6.) If voting were to be permitted over the Internet, in the absence of radical campaign reform, one could expect there to be a vast amount of online informational manipulation, not to mention a computerized record of each voter's preferences. It is also a threat to the independence of voters that consultants and lobbyists can target voters with customized messages based on information taken from their Internet correspondence. Even without electronic voting, the potential for spamming Internet lines with political messages, rumors, or disinformation close to polling dates could be a viable tactic in discrediting opposition and ensuring elections for favored candidates. There is also the threat of sabotage of the voting process itself.

Campaign Software

Computer software is now available to assist in almost every facet of campaigning, from fund-raising and volunteer list management to media-buying and campaign expenditure accounting ledgers. The collection and processing of large volumes of data, including Federal Election Commission filings, is used in multiple aspects of campaign management.

Databases

Databases include computer, CD-ROM, and software lists containing multi-leveled demographic and voter analysis. Databases are used in the service of campaign consultants to build organized lists of names, phone numbers, and addresses within a voting district, as well as "enhanced voter data" on a range of demographic information that can provide individual profiles of occupation, educational background, property assessment, voting history, magazine subscriptions, organizational memberships, religious affiliations, race and ethnicity, and social and political views, including party registration. This allows for sophisticated targeting and direct marketing to the voter set up by information warehouses such as Aristotle Industries and GeoVoter.

In one of its ads, GeoVoter boasts that "When people say the NRA has an unfair political advantage, they're absolutely right. The NRA has GeoVoter!" (Hill 2002, 158). Most of the data, including voter registration lists, is available for a small fee from government agencies and private firms. Millions of voter profiles can be compiled on compact disks and sold to users who select information from the CDs based on various criteria (Graff 1992, 25–27). One mailing list firm, "I Rent America" (!), claims to have 220 million names on its computer lists (Hill 2002, 157). The once widely assumed sanctity of the voting booth is now a quaint political concept.

Bar Coding

This technology is useful for campaigns to track the response rate for mailers and fund-raising letters. Bar coding allows for easy data collection and tracking of political constituencies.

Geographic Information Systems (GIS) Mapping

Employed for everything from media buying, get-out-the-vote campaigns, and reconnaissance of the electoral district, geo-related computer programs visually illustrate patterns and relationships from an array of demographic and other politically useful data. Census data combined with geographic-base map data generated by a system called Topologically Integrated Geographic Encoding and Referencing (TIGER) and packaged with election history and household data are being used to create detailed political maps of voter districts and individual voter profiles. These databases are continually updated with new information. Election teams send targeted individuals computer-generated customized letters with standardized crafted paragraphs, complete with authentic-looking signatures, that emphasize those issues of the candidate that are assumed to appeal to the voter (Graff 1992, 26). Political mapping allows the war room to better visualize the "battlefield" and plan the strategic attack.

Computerized Retrieval of Candidate Speeches

One of the activities of the research team is to locate speeches made by the opposition candidate. Computer-stored files of speeches can be a gold mine for dredging up statements and promises from the past that appear to contradict present behavior and can be used in political advertising with devastating effects. This is part of what is known as opposition research.

Websites and the Internet

Websites represent a 24/7 interactive advertising medium used to track visitors, solicit money (including online credit card contributions) and volunteers, and disseminate campaign information to voters and reporters. At the end of 1999, it was reported that there were thirty companies with websites for political marketing, including election campaigns, lobbying, and public policy communications, in a new industry already worth $2.5 billion a year (McManus 1999, 76). Viewed by some as the newest frontier of political campaign communication, online politicking increasingly allows campaigns to track voters and gather personal information from even casual visitors to the site. Senator John McCain reportedly raised $5.5 million during his 2000 presidential campaign (Shea and Burton 2001, 9), and the use of this medium for fund-raising escalated rapidly in the 2003–2004 election cycle, although it was far less effective in reaching voters than television.

Whether the presence of the Internet will enable a new form of "electronic democracy" is yet to be determined—but it will not be determined merely by the availability of this new interactive medium. Much will depend on the degree of access to different socioeconomic groups, and which groups organize the uses of the Internet as a political tool. There is no assurance by any means, given the domination by commercial and entertainment interests, that this instrument of communication will widely increase the appeal of political discourse and the level of critical social interaction.

Voting Machines

The shift to electronic voting machines presents very serious problems in authenticating voter preferences, especially given the fact that private companies run the vote counts in a system that is largely unregulated. Although election industry officials assure the public that electronic voting systems are secure from tampering, other technical observers have found that this is not the case and that votes can be changed with virtually no one knowing about it, including election supervisors. The leading companies that manufacture the machines insist that their operating systems are trade secrets, but critics say it is very difficult to detect errors in vote tallies. Accenture, formerly Andersen Consulting (a division of the discredited accounting firm, Arthur Andersen), won the contract to conduct the online U.S. military vote count in the 2004 federal election.

Diebold Election Systems, the second-largest and fastest growing company in the industry, has sold electronic voting machines to thirty-seven states. In what some see as an egregious breach of security, the company put 40,000 of its files on an open website—information that "amounted to a virtual handbook for vote-tampering: They contained diagrams of remote communications setups, passwords, encryption keys, source code, user manuals, testing protocols, and simulators, as well as files loaded with votes and voting machine software" (Harris 2003). Swarthmore college students posted the information to dozens of websites to demonstrate the ease with which hackers potentially could disrupt proper vote counting.

Of equally deep concern, it was also reported in the press that the chief executive of Diebold, Walden O'Dell, announced in an August 2003 fund-raising letter to Ohio Republicans that he is "committed to helping Ohio deliver its electoral votes to the president next year." O'Dell attended a strategy meeting at George W. Bush's ranch in Crawford, Texas, with other Republican high rollers and then helped organize a $1,000-a-plate event for the Ohio Republicans' federal campaign fund, of which he is himself one of Bush's "Rangers" (contributors of $200,000 or more). Earlier, he organized a fundraiser for Dick Cheney that pulled in $600,000. Democrats brought a court challenge to block his company from tallying votes for the 2004 election. Bev

Harris, a writer whose website brought this problem to public attention and led to scrutiny of voting machines by a number of states, argues that the voting process, controlled by private companies, has become "secretive and proprietary," and removed from the eyes of voters (*Buzzflash* 2003; Smyth 2003). (Canada, by comparison, still uses pencil-and-paper ballot in elections, and its polling officials are able to tabulate the national vote in a matter of hours.)

Harris points out that the largest of these companies, Election Systems and Software (ESS), is owned by the campaign finance director, Michael McCarthy, for Senator Charles Hagel (R-NE). Hagel held stock in ESS and its parent company and was CEO and chair of the voting machine company that counted the votes in his last election. Both companies, and others in the industry, are filled with past and present close associates and fund-raisers for Bush and Cheney. Two of the top six companies are foreign owned, and one of the six, VoteHere, is chaired by Admiral Bill Owens, a big Cheney supporter, and has Robert Gates, former CIA director and head of the George Bush School of Business, on its board (*Buzzflash* 2003; Smyth 2003). With these and other links to the Bush administration, too numerous to discuss here, it is easy to draw antidemocratic if not conspiratorial conclusions about the control over the election-counting process in the United States, a system that may be or become only technically different from the practice of voter fraud in some countries and the history of electoral theft in America's own past.

NOTES

1. The international division of labor, and its historical antecedents, is also responsible for the fact that most of the TVs, computer and telecommunication equipment, and digital software used in the West is produced in Third World countries.

2. The types of mailing lists that are rented to campaigns can enable quite specific targeting for political contributions or voter information: contributors to handgun control, the names of millionaires or multimillionaires, senior citizens state-by-state, subscribers to certain kinds of magazines, "Born-Again Doctors Who Vote, Check-Writing Evangelical Activists, Texas Christian Activists, and California Evangelical Political Givers . . . American High Income Donors, Conservative Wealthy Arts Donors, Spanish-Speaking Donors, and Cream of the Crop Jewish Donors" (Hill 2002, 157–58).

3. In 1964, the Lyndon Johnson campaign created the infamous "Daisy" TV political ad in which a little girl plucking a daisy is featured in the forefront as a nuclear bomb goes off in the distance. The ad, produced by the agency Doyle Dane Bernbach (which was then known for its Volkswagen advertising), was part of a fear strategy

Johnson and his team used that portrayed Goldwater as a trigger-happy politician ready to use nuclear weapons to resolve international conflicts (Rutherford 2000, 31).

4. Robert Putnam discusses the decline of civic and political participation as not just election cycle activity but also membership in civic organizations (Putnam 1995).

5. The "instant runoff" is one idea, which provides that voters choose two candidates for office: the first is their candidate of conscience, and the second is their automatic fallback choice if the first does not win the election. This procedure encourages the participation of third and additional party candidates, who otherwise have no practical chance of winning in the winner-take-all system of voting in the United States. It also induces citizens who don't believe in either of the dominant two parties to participate in elections. In such a system, voters could vote for third party candidates without fear of "wasting their votes." The winning candidate would always have a majority, not simply a plurality, of the votes cast.

6. Although congressional Democrats pushed through a Motor Voter Act in 1993, they deleted key portions that would have eased the registration of poor voters, including sign-up opportunities at welfare offices (Ginsberg and Shefter 1999, 22).

7. After presidential candidate Howard Dean received national media backlash in September 2003 for speaking directly to the need for a two-state solution between Israel and Palestine and the requirement for the United States to act sufficiently neutral to help bring this about, he learned to stay away from further straightforward comments of this sort.

8. More than a century earlier, the Democrats in Congress funded the first long-distance telegraph line, between Washington, D.C., and Baltimore—the site of the 1844 Democratic Party convention.

9. Also part of the Republican attack team was Wisconsin senator Joseph McCarthy, who in a nationally televised speech referred to Stevenson's "aid to the Communist cause" and made numerous allegations of the candidate's and his staff's subversive (i.e., Communist Party) associations (Kelley 1956, 192).

10. During his presidential tenure (1968–1974), Nixon also had the services of two other J. Walter Thompson admen, Dwight Chapin and Ronald Ziegler.

11. Broadcast television alone took in more than $30 billion in overall ad revenues in 1996, much of which originated from the same sources that funded the political campaigns that year.

12. One study found that sound bites on the Public Broadcasting System's coverage of the 2000 election averaged fifty-two seconds (Farnsworth and Lichter 2003, 154).

13. Another highly touted campaign strategist for Reagan and the elder Bush was Sig Rogich, who served a similar role for Bush as Michael Deaver had done for Reagan. A Nevada-based advertising executive, Rogich's previous clients included Frank Sinatra (whom he helped obtain a gambling license) and Donald Trump. He also served as a boxing commissioner, a director at Bally's Casino, and a media advisor to help clean up the image of the Stardust Hotel, then linked to organized crime. Rogich was brought to the 1988 Bush campaign to design attack ads against Dukakis, which included the infamous Willie Horton and prison release political commercials. He also served as a major fund-raiser for the younger Bush.

14. Among Wirthlin's more recent corporate clients is Boeing Co., for which he conducted an assessment on public attitudes on the safety of flying after the 9/11 attack (*Los Angeles Times* 2001). His firm's public opinion surveys have been done for many other corporations, including American Express, which wanted to understand worker attitudes toward their bosses (*Meetings & Conventions* 2000). The Information Technology Association of America (ITAA), an umbrella trade association representing the $740-billion information technology industry (ITAA 2001), hired the Wirthlin group to do a study on consumer attitudes concerning online purchasing (*Multimedia News* 1998).

15. Atwater later became both the celebrated and notorious mastermind behind the elder George Bush's 1988 presidential campaign ads featuring Willie Horton and challenging the Democrat Michael Dukakis's loyalty to the stars and stripes.

16. Third way politics refers to a middle road between the strict laissez-faire ideology that guides the conservative parties in the United States and the United Kingdom and the welfare state politics of the New Deal and postwar Democrats. It embraces globalization in the economic sphere, reduction of state social spending, less regulation in policymaking, and more of a public-private partnership approach.

17. Another American consultant, Bill Clinton's advisor Frank Greer, worked with Nelson Mandela during South Africa's first open elections in 1994 (Maxfield and Schlesinger 1997, 15).

18. A defensive Abrams actually had accused D'Amato of using "fascist" tactics against him, which Finkelstein turned around with a counteraccusation (spin) that Abrams was linking his client to Mussolini and causing immeasurable damage to the D'Amato family (Rodrick 1996).

19. With the Senate also changing hands, it was the first time in forty years that the Republicans controlled both chambers.

20. He was once quoted as saying, "There's no greater pleasure I get out of life than taking some self-righteous Republican and wrapping his ass around his ears" (Tu 1993).

21. Doris Kearns Goodwin, a scholar and regular analyst on PBS's *News Hour with Jim Lehrer*, observed, following the last of the Gore-Bush debates on October 17, 2000, that both candidates spoke about policy only in first-person terms, what *they* would do, never acknowledging the legacies of their respective parties. This is but one indication of the decline in the status of political parties and how candidates relate to them and the emphasis given to the person, personality, and "character" of the candidates.

22. Radio's share was 10.2 percent, newspapers 4.6 percent, billboard/outdoor 1.5 percent, and magazines 0.2 percent (Morgan 2000).

23. In 1996, it was reported that Robert Dole's presidential campaign team secretly hired a telemarketing firm in New York City to use a push poll in Iowa and New Hampshire to attack a rival for the Republican nomination, Steve Forbes. Dole denied involvement, but the press subsequently revealed that his campaign was behind it (Swint 1998, 123). In 1950, Richard Nixon's U.S. Senate campaign workers in California employed a kind of push poll, telephoning thousands of prospective voters and asking if they knew his Democratic opponent, Helen Gahagan Douglas, was a Communist, a

tactic that helped earn the future president the nickname "Tricky Dick." In 2000, the Bush primary campaign in South Carolina telephoned people to ask if they would vote for John McCain if they knew that that he had fathered a black child out of wedlock (or, a variation, if they knew his wife was a drug addict).

24. Under the automated predictive dialing system, the telemarketer is expected to achieve forty-five minutes of talk time per hour. Similar to call monitoring used in airlines and telephone companies, predictive dialing also captures such information as agent productivity, average call length, rate of calls abandoned for lack of sufficient agents, live answer rates, rate of successful closes (pledges), etc. (Desmone 1999, 40).

4

Postwar Electoral Interventions

> We have 50 percent of the world's wealth, but only 6.3 percent of the its
> population. In this situation we cannot fail to be the object of envy and re-
> sentment. Our real task in the coming period is to devise a pattern of rela-
> tionships which will allow us to maintain this position of disparity.
>
> —George F. Kennan, State Department Director of Policy and
> Planning, 1948 (cited in Robinson 1994, 45)

One of the remarkable shifts in recent world politics is the open involvement
of foreign consultants and public and private agencies in the management of
elections, including, even more remarkably, political campaigns in countries
that just a few years earlier were under Communist Party control. Just after
World War II, many clandestine electoral interventions were secretly undertaken by the Central Intelligence Agency (CIA) as part of U.S. Cold War
strategy to prevent left-wing and nationalist leaders and parties from gaining
power in targeted countries. But what were once undercover political operations are now done in the open by private professional political management
teams, primarily American, brought in on behalf of both conservative and liberal candidates and parties to help them capture or retain the reins of government. Political globalization, a corollary of neoliberal economic globalization, is one of the less talked about aspects of world politics.

In some countries, the invitation of foreign advisors is still regarded as controversial and not publicized. Candidates tainted by association with American
power brokers can sometimes be discredited as unpatriotic. Indeed, the work
of American political consultants is important to U.S. global policy objectives.
They not only contribute to electoral victories abroad but also help to solidify
linkages between U.S. and foreign state and economic power interests. This

chapter discusses the earlier period of CIA electoral intervention as a context for understanding the global implications of the work of more recent international political professionals, and the National Endowment for Democracy.

Electoral management has long had links to systems of state propaganda. Dedicated political persuasion is often associated with repressive regimes that employ specialists in crafting and cultivating "great leader" images, official ideologies, and public submission—Nazi practices in this area being only the most stark example. Woodrow Wilson's Committee on Public Information (or Creel Commission) was organized by public relations and propaganda experts, including Ivy Lee and Edward Bernays, in a effort to win over an isolationist American public to the need to send troops to war-ravaged Europe. The Creel Commission was called "the costliest propaganda campaign" to that day (WNYC 2003).

Ivy Lee, although considered the founder of the public relations field, had a much shorter and less stellar career than Bernays. His clients included several of the leading robber barons of his day, including E. H. Harriman and J. P. Morgan. Lee is known for having advised tycoon John D. Rockefeller Sr. to change his public image by handing out dimes to street children. In 1914, Lee was hired as a public relations advisor for John D. Rockefeller Jr., following the billionaire family's ruthless union-busting actions that led to the Ludlow massacre of strikers at a Rockefeller-owned coal mine of Colorado. Unperturbed, Lee later provided the family with public relations assistance for their mining operations in West Virginia (Stauber and Rampton 1995, 19–22).

Lee scorned what he derisively called "the divine right of the multitude" and considered himself "a physician for corporate bodies" (Ewen 1996, 75–76). In the 1930s, Lee worked his way up to counseling the Nazi regime in Germany on how to influence American public opinion. One of Lee's German clients was I. G. Farben, the chemical company that manufactured the Zyklon-B poison gas used to exterminate concentration camp prisoners. Lee, who died in 1934 soon after testifying before a hostile U.S. Congress on his relations with the Nazi regime, did not live to see the full results of his fascist client's research and development.

His colleague Bernays, a nephew of Sigmund Freud, went on to have a much longer career in political public relations. After World War I, Bernays's next major political initiative was to become an advisor to Calvin Coolidge, for whom he helped turn a dour countenance into a presidential election victory in 1924. Defending elite notions of social and ideological control, Bernays argued in his 1928 book, *Propaganda*, that symbolic uses of language and images constituted "the currency of propaganda," and that "[t]he conscious and intelligent manipulation of the organized habits and opinions of the masses is an important element in democratic society" (Blumenthal 1982, 34–36). He also wrote that "If we understand the mechanism and motives of the group mind, it is now possible to control and regiment the masses according to our will without their knowing it." His writings were well received in the United States and were also said to be among the favorites of Nazi propaganda minister Joseph Goebbels (Stauber and Rampton 1995, 23–24).

Bernays's résumé in commercial and political persuasion listed many of the wealthiest corporations in the country as clients, and it also had a few foreign policy credits. One of his charges was to help organize a propaganda campaign in the 1950s against Guatemala's reformist and democratically elected president Jacobo Arbenz, on behalf of his client, the United Fruit Company. The company, with vast landholdings throughout Central America, detested Arbenz's efforts to tax its banana exports and institute a land reform program for landless peasants, which would have meant nationalizing United Fruit plantations. Together, Bernays and the company instigated U.S. intervention in Guatemala, which led to a 1954 CIA-organized military coup, whose officers engaged in a wave of violence, torture, and terror against real and imagined opponents (Chomsky 1989, 29; Lewis 1991, 183).[1] Guatemala was one of the early postwar targets of political consultants in the service of covert foreign policy objectives.

Contemporary public relations firms that have actively contributed to U.S. foreign policy, such as Hill and Knowlton, owe a lot to the pioneering efforts of people such as Lee and Bernays. On retainer to the Kuwaiti emirate during the Persian Gulf War of 1990–1991, H&K operations in that part of the world constituted to that point the largest foreign-funded campaign aimed at steering American public opinion. The firm was found to have duped the U.S. Congress and American public with manipulated news stories and fabricated tales of Iraqi atrocities.[2] Its research arm was Richard Wirthlin's polling firm, which reportedly received $1.1 million for research and poll results for the Kuwaitis (Stauber and Rampton 1995, 169–70). The Republican lobbying group Black, Manafort, Stone, and Kelly (BMSK), a subsidiary of Burson-Marsteller, has taken on many foreign clients, including U.S.-backed Angolan anticommunist rebel leader Jonas Savimbi and his UNITA movement. BMSK was paid $600,000 a year to provide "favorable media coverage for UNITA and secured further political support and aid from U.S. politicians and lending agencies" (Gozan 1993).

Parent Burson-Marsteller (BM) was acquired in 1979 by the Young and Rubicam advertising conglomerate, which itself became part of the worldwide WPP advertising and public relations group in 2000. BM was contracted by the Nigerian government and Royal Dutch/Shell at the time of the genocidal Biafran war and was later called back to do public relations for that government. Its lobbying subsidiary, BMSK, was paid more than $1 million in image-recovery efforts during the 1990s. BM also played a similar role for the Indonesian government in 1996 at the time of that country's assaults on East Timor. BM's other clients have included the Argentine military junta leader General Jorge Videla, whose regime was responsible for 35,000 "disappeared" citizens; Romanian dictator Nicolae Ceaucescu; the Saudi Arabian government; and the single-party-run Singaporean government. Saudi Arabia hired BM to protect its image following the September 11 air attacks in New York and Washington, D.C., carried out largely by Saudis. BM's reputation is also built on the strength of its long list of Fortune 500 clients, many of whom are also engaged with some of the most active American international political consultants (see chapter 3), which—like the work of the CIA—is generally hidden from public view (*Corporate Watch* 2002). Management of public opinion has continually been a key ideological function in state and corporate domination of societies.

POSTWAR REALIGNMENTS

The frequent early postwar use of covert intervention in foreign elections is often seen as the result of hostile postwar global power realignments, led by the world's two superpowers, the United States and the USSR. The arms race, the ideological struggle for world power, especially targeting the newly emerging Third World nations, and nuclear brinkmanship were all part of the tense and mutually hostile international environment of the Cold War. For the United States, the early postwar era was one of unparalleled economic expansion; hegemonic political, military, and cultural influence; and a national confidence, some would say an arrogant superpower complex, that frequently expressed itself in rogue state behavior and rhetoric. Underlying this confidence was a pace of internal economic development, technological innovation, manufacturing, growth, and exports that was unprecedented in human history. The United States in the two decades after World War II dominated the world's output of steel, iron, automobiles, petrochemicals, electronics, media, commercial and military aircraft, weaponry, and many other industrial products. By the 1990s, 51 of the world's largest 100 economic entities were transnational corporations (the other 49 being nation-states), of which most were based in the United States.

On the political front, the United States organized a series of worldwide diplomatic and strategic military alliances that aimed to contain the Soviet Union and its allies and to protect a capitalist international division of labor built upon a legacy of 500 years of Western (now including Japan in its orbit) colonial rule. The postwar Western economies, in ruins in all cases but the United States, were revived with the efforts of U.S.-inspired organizations and programs, including the World Bank, International Monetary Fund, General Agreement on Tariffs and Trade (GATT) (recently superseded by the World Trade Organization), and the Marshall Plan. Led by the United States and the other G-7 (now G-8) countries, there has been a coordinated half-century of expansion and integration of world markets. Throughout the postwar period, the United States took it upon itself to police the world against perceived threats that nationalist and socialist movements represented to a U.S.-led world market system.

The end of fascist rule in Europe and Asia was in no small part the result of the organized resistance of various socialist and communist forces, which stood to gain politically once the Japanese and Germans were defeated. Standing against this possibility, U.S. leaders, starting with Truman, were determined to create an intelligence apparatus that would destabilize and defeat serious challenges to U.S. hegemony. There was certainly nothing new about U.S. intervention in world affairs. Between 1798 and 2001, there were over 200 separate acts of direct U.S. military intervention (103 *before* 1895), challenging the political sovereignty of many countries. This does not count the continuing attacks on Native American nations within the North American continent that colonized their territories. And it didn't end with decolonization after World War II. As the nineteenth-century conservative prime minister of Britain Benjamin Disraeli once counseled, "Colonies do not cease to be colonies [just] because they are independent."

Covert interference in foreign countries' national elections is largely a post–World War II development. Although usually couched in a rhetoric of democracy assistance, the United States frequently supported, condoned, and sponsored often extremely repressive dictatorial regimes, and such actions were usually justified within the discourse of "political realism." The Cold War provided an ideological pretext for defending authoritarian rule where allied interests were involved. A "political realist" and architect of early postwar (anticommunist) containment policy and considered a moderate in his Cold War views, George Kennan, cited above, also advised the U.S. government in 1948 that "We should cease to talk about the raising of the living standards, human rights, and democratization. The day is not far off when we are going to have to deal in straight power concepts. The less we are then hampered by idealistic slogans, the better" (cited in Robinson 1996, 1).

Current U.S. intervention in the political affairs of other countries is carried out by a number of different agencies, both governmental and nongovernmental, which have constructed the larger political economic environment in which international political consultants operate. And yet, there is a fundamental and long-standing principle of international law of "the right of a people to settle its own affairs without the intervention of foreign powers" (John Rawls, cited in Damrosch 1989, 1), which is enshrined, among other places, in the United Nations Charter. The Organization of American States, for example, declared that "No State or group has the right to intervene, directly or indirectly, for any reason whatever, in the internal or external affairs of any other state" (Damrosch 1989, 7). Despite this, major (and sometimes minor) powers have in the past and continue to frequently interfere in the political activities of other countries. The United States has held as a matter of right the prerogative of manipulating through financing or other support mechanisms the electoral outcomes in foreign countries. Yet, when the Clinton administration came under attack, mainly from Republican Congress members, for accepting alleged financial payments from Chinese government sources to his reelection campaign, the Democratic National Committee was obligated to return $2.8 million in illegal or improper contributions raised by two Asian Americans (Pinto-Duschinsky 2001, 7). Such payments, especially from a communist party, are considered as subversive of the American political system.

Unleashed by virtue of its power from honoring self-determination principles in its own foreign policy behavior, the United States helped install or defend many antidemocratic regimes. A short list includes Marcos; Suharto; Pinochet; Mobuto; Somoza; Trujillo; Batista; Diem; Chiang; the Shah; the royal Saudi family; the South Korean, South Vietnam, Pakistan, Nigerian, Guatemalan, Salvadoran, and Thai military dictatorships; the juntas and paramilitaries in Greece, Brazil, Haiti, Honduras, Argentina, Colombia, Mexico, and Uruguay; and the apartheid regimes in South Africa. William Robinson, whose list is more extensive and detailed, concluded that "Despite all the rhetoric on 'electoral democracy' and emphasis on 'free and fair elections,' the United States is only concerned with assuring procedurally clean elections when the circumstances or results favor U.S. interests" (Robinson 1996, 111). Countries not incorporated into or resistant to the U.S.-dominated market economy have been excoriated or attacked. Until the administration of George W. Bush, which made antiterrorism the emblem of its foreign policy, it was Cuba, China, and the former Soviet Union that received the strongest hostile attention of the government and mass media. Rhetoric concerning "human rights" violations was often invoked to justify aggressive policies toward these socialist countries, even as more repressive regimes were given far less attention—or else treated as U.S. allies. It is not hard to find a pattern in the selective interpretation of human rights violations, which mainly has to do with the degree to which open markets and untrammeled access by foreign capital are provided by countries of interest to the United States.

The collapse of the Soviet Union enabled the United States to expand its sphere of influence into formerly socialist East Europe, Central Asia, and Russia. In the 1990s, American political consultants followed the gold rush of free marketers to the region to participate in "democracy-building" efforts and to introduce U.S.-style electioneering. Facilitating this global flow of political "expertise," the U.S. Agency for International Development (USAID) adopted in 1991 a "democracy initiative" conditionality for extending grants and loans to various "developing" countries (an act similarly adopted by the European Union two years earlier) (Hoogvelt 1997, 173). One organization involved in these proclaimed objectives, the Washington, D.C.-based International Foundation for Election Systems (IFES), notes how the "end of the Cold War in 1989 created opportunities . . . to respond to an overwhelming demand for technical non-partisan expertise in democracy and governance." IFES claims to have field offices in thirty-five countries with a cadre of 1,500 consultants (IFES 2003), including big campaign consulting names like Stanley Greenberg. Some IFES consultants are able turn the democracy-assistance work into contract opportunities with foreign political candidates (Maggs 2000). Joseph Napolitan, founder of the American Association of Political Consultants, is on the IFES board, along with other well-known American campaign specialists.

These kinds of projects are reminiscent of the "nation building" and political "modernization" efforts that the United States pursued in postcolonial and newly independent Third World countries in the 1950s and 1960s. What occurred in many of these modernization programs, as in Latin America, the Caribbean, and Southeast Asia, were severe economic downturns, a collapse of Western-style political institutions, and a wave of military takeovers that relied heavily on U.S. assistance, training, and political support. This left a lasting legacy of distrust in much of the Third World of U.S. motives for engaging in the internal affairs of the formerly colonized areas. With the exception of a very few less industrialized economies, such as Singapore, South Korea, Taiwan, Hong Kong, and China, none of the other Third World countries experienced consistent growth or the economic "takeoff" stage anticipated in American modernization theory.

Instead, a series of radical nationalist and revolutionary movements spread throughout much of the Third World in the 1960s and 1970s. Many Third World economists, intellectuals, and revolutionaries challenged the core assumptions of American development theory and proposed alternatives: either "dependency theory," which rested on more historically conscious, industrially and structurally self-reliant approaches to political and economic progress, or explicitly state-driven socialist ideas about development. A "new international economic order" (NIEO) and nonalignment movement became the mantra of several Third World leaders and intellectuals, who resisted U.S. pressures to align their countries with the U.S.-led global military structure (for example, the Southeast Asia Treaty Organization or bilateral military base agreements) and economic institutions (World Bank, International Monetary Fund, GATT, USAID). American "free trade" rhetoric appeared to many Third World leaders (Nehru, Sukarno, Nkrumah, Nasser, Lumumba, Ben Bella, Sihanouk, Chou, Ho, Castro, and others) as a rationale for U.S. corporate domination of their economies and resources.

By the 1970s, the death or overthrow of most of these leaders, a series of military coups, China and the USSR's rapprochement with the United States, the rifts between the socialist countries, and the continuing stagnation or decline of most Third World economies led to a weakening of nationalist and socialist polemic, a new trend toward debt assumption, and increased technological dependency. Internal conflicts and the end of Soviet and Chinese support to several socialist Third World countries further eroded the force of the NIEO and nonalignment. Third World states militarized in the 1970s began to adopt more parliamentary approaches in the 1980s and 1990s. In Eastern Europe and the Soviet Union, economic decline and the attraction of more democratic political forms accelerated the collapse of the various communist parties. This opened a vast new opportunity for political globalization.

THE CIA BRAND OF ELECTIONEERING

Prior to the collapse of the Soviet system, the CIA was one of the principal instruments of U.S. Cold War policy. With the strategic global economic advantage enjoyed by the United States after 1945, political elites in Washington, D.C., presumed to take the lead in world military, political, and economic matters. One of the apparatuses to emerge from the Cold War, the CIA, successor to the wartime Office of Strategic Services, was created in 1947. Its mission was to collect and collate intelligence on other countries through espionage, research, and other means in order to advise the National Security Council and other government foreign policy agencies and committees. Beyond its information gathering and spying activities, the CIA took on a more active and covert engagement in and sponsorship of propaganda along with political and economic interference against enemy states, political movements, and targeted individuals. These efforts included the use of dirty tricks and other clandestine practices, counterinsurgency, organized violence, sabotage, support for police and military repression, and assassination to carry out its objectives.

Over the years, the CIA has had many assets in its global arsenal: human, financial, technological, and institutional. One of its front organizations in the

1950s was the Congress of Cultural Freedom, a left-leaning but anticommunist group that operated with secret CIA funding and sponsored conferences, seminars, various cultural and political events, and a host of periodicals throughout the world. Among the CIA-subsidized media organs were the West German news agency DENA, the international writers association PEN, some French newspapers, the International Federation of Journalists, a London-based news service Forum World Features, and the publishing empire of Axel Springer, owner of *Der Spiegel*. By the 1980s, Springer had become the biggest press mogul in Europe. The agency also helped publish hundreds of books and ran several shortwave stations beamed at Eastern Europe and the Soviet Union, the most familiar of which were Radio Free Europe and Radio Liberty (Blum 1995, 104–5, 118).

Advertising and public relations served as good backgrounds for CIA recruits. People such as Edward Bernays contributed their public relations expertise to the operation of CIA covert activities. But perhaps the CIA's most important assets directly in its service were the over 400 American journalists working overseas, who regularly functioned as the agency's most effective eyes and ears. This group does not include hundreds of other reporters, American and foreign, who occasionally worked for or traded information with the spy organization. Press people who actively participated in the CIA's worldwide covert activities network included *New York Times* columnist C. L. Sulzberger, together with his uncle, *Times'* publisher Arthur Hays Sulzberger, and executives William Paley of CBS television, James Copley of Copley News Service, Barry Bingham Sr. of the *Louisville Courier-Journal*, and Henry Luce of *Time* magazine. Other media organizations that secretly worked with the CIA included Associated Press, United Press International, the Hearst and Scripps-Howard news chains, the *Miami Herald*, *New York Herald-Tribune*, *Newsweek, Saturday Evening Post*, Britain's Reuters, and the CBS TV, ABC TV, NBC TV, and Mutual Broadcasting System networks (Bernstein 1977, 57; Overbeck 1999).

The CIA's work was assisted by "more than 50 newspapers, news services, radio stations, periodicals, book publishers and other communication entities, most of which were overseas," along with countless foreign news organizations and reporters. The *New York Times* alone provided cover for some ten CIA operatives between 1950 and 1966. For much of the press corps, the CIA's work was seen as a common cause. Such affiliations were also useful to some people's career paths, notwithstanding the compromise of journalistic integrity that such choices represented. In this massive network of propaganda, American readers were ultimately the principal objective of the "blowback" stories and disinformation that the CIA regularly planted in foreign publications starting in the late 1940s (Bernstein 1977; Lee and Solomon 1990, 114–17).

Working under CIA chief Allen Dulles (brother of the then-Secretary of State, John Foster Dulles), Air Force Lt. Col. Edward Lansdale (the prototype for the character Alden Pyle in Graham Greene's *The Quiet American*) parlayed an advertising background into psychological warfare assignments for the agency against communist movements in the Philippines, Vietnam, and Cuba. Lansdale's CIA activities in those three countries were among the more flagrant and widely reported but certainly not the only covert actions undertaken by the Eisenhower and Kennedy administrations. In the Philippines, Lansdale was sent as an operative to help supervise national defense secretary Ramon Magsaysay in the early 1950s. The first objective was to defeat the revolutionary Huk movement. The next, in 1953, was to propel Magsaysay into the presidency as "America's boy" in Manila in order to protect U.S. interests in that country, especially its trade and investment privileges and its largest overseas naval and air force installations. To help secure the political victory, the CIA created a National Press Club to draw attention to the election, secretly ran stories in the local press, paid off local journalists, and ran a "national" poll-watching agency, Namfrel, to monitor the election (Bonner 1987, 41; Smith 1976, 242–46).

Lansdale was aided in this effort by David Sternberg, a CIA operative posing as a journalist with the *Christian Science Monitor*. Gabe Kaplan was the agency's person in charge of setting up Namfrel. American syndicated newspaper columnist Joseph Alsop went to the Philippines in 1953 at the behest of the CIA to assist the agency in various assignments and to help sway the election in Magsaysay's favor. "I'm proud they [the CIA] asked me and proud to have done it" as a matter of "duty to his country," he asserted (Bernstein 1977, 57).[3] Henry Luce, a dedicated anticommunist, lent his influential *Time* magazine to the CIA's cause and put Magsaysay on its cover, calling the Philippine official the best hope for the "U.S. experiment in transplanting democracy" (Bonner 1987, 41, 110).

Dirty tricks were used extensively. The presidential and congressional elections involved the CIA's "extensive disinformation campaigns, heavy financing of candidates, writing their speeches, drugging the drinks of one of the opponents . . . plotting the assassination of another candidate," bringing in American speechwriters, and pouring in at least $1 million in addition to soliciting contributions from the American Chamber of Commerce, the local Coca-Cola franchise, and other local and foreign financial interests. In the event that Magsaysay were to lose the election, the United States had a coup backup plan. It didn't seem to matter to the United States that under Philippine national law, "No foreigner shall aid any candidate directly or indirectly or take part in or influence in any manner any election" (Blum 2000, 170–71; Constantino and Constantino 1978, 308).

With the CIA victory in the Philippines in pocket, Lansdale was next sent to Vietnam to organize an election for another U.S.-sponsored candidate, Ngo Dinh Diem, and he brought some of his Filipino cohorts with him. In Saigon, Lansdale carried out similar tactics, in this case to help construct a new country, "South Vietnam," and make Diem its head of state. Lansdale bribed military officers, made heavy use of black (crudely deceptive) propaganda, and funneled millions of dollars to support Diem's regime once elected. The U.S.-organized election in 1955 violated the terms of the Geneva peace agreement the previous year, which established plans for politically reunifying Vietnam after the defeat of the French colonial forces by Ho Chi Minh's revolutionary independence movement. Attempting to establish his legitimacy, Diem had simply dictated his margin of electoral victory at over 98 percent. Saigon alone awarded him 130 percent of the city's vote tally. He was soon invited to the United States for a state visit, and the *New York Times* saluted him as a democrat with a "firm concept of human rights" (Fitzgerald 1972, 116–17). Land-reform and nation-building specialists from the United States, plus vast financial and materiel commitments to his military and government, could not save Diem from his dictatorial and nepotistic practices and the unpopularity of the regime. The United States ultimately collaborated with Vietnamese military forces in a 1963 coup d'état that ended Diem's presidency and his life.

Europe was another "theater" of covert CIA election activity. In the late 1940s, the U.S. began to secretly funnel money through the CIA's Office of Policy Coordination to the conservative Italian and French Christian Democratic parties and Germany's Social Democrats as a way of offsetting the political influence of the socialist and communist parties in those countries. U.S. Attorney General Tom Clark determined that those Italians not sharing what he called "the ideology of the United States" would not be allowed to immigrate to his country, nor would the United States countenance a constituent assembly based on the 1948 election results that did not adopt that same ideology (Blum 1995, 27–28). State Department officials were deeply concerned that the Popular Democratic Front of the Italian communist and socialist parties appeared poised to capture the government that year through election. The presumption was that with such an outcome the Soviet Union would eventually extend its influence in the region.

The State Department, National Security Council, CIA, Voice of America, and private groups were mobilized to prevent this outcome. Tactics included organizing a massive letter-writing campaign, some 10 million mail items, from Americans of Italian extraction and Italian war brides to their relatives in Italy, mostly mass-produced form letters needing only signatures and addresses. The U.S. government also arranged for the sending of radio recordings by Frank Sinatra, Bing Crosby, Gary Cooper, and other celebrities to

warn Italians of the dangers of a "communist dictatorship" and rule by (pro-
Soviet) "fifth columnists." Members of the American press served as bagmen
for CIA messages and money to the Christian Democrats. The State Department issued threats about the loss of foreign aid. With "assets" throughout
Italy, the CIA also financed the placement of stories and black propaganda in
the Italian press. Rome's English language *Daily American* was secretly
owned in part by the agency and ran cover for its spies (Bernstein 1977; Blum
1995).

Italian archbishops were mobilized to threaten parishioners that those voting for Communists would not receive absolution or confession, Cardinal Tis-
serant even threatened denial of a Christian burial. A popular anti-Soviet 1939
Hollywood feature film, *Ninotchka* (starring Greta Garbo), was exhibited
widely in Italy, which all of the Italian left acknowledged to be particularly
effective. Adding additional pressure, the State Department declared that any
Italian who voted for the Communist Party would be barred entry to the
United States. Food shipments to the war-ravaged country were leveraged for
political persuasion and control. The mobilization against socialism worked,
as the Christian Democrats easily defeated the left coalition 48 percent to 31
percent. Covert funding for Italian candidates and parties, especially Christian Democrats, continued into the 1970s until halted by the Carter administration. In reality, the USSR had little influence over the election, was more
concerned about a U.S. backlash, and gave only token support to the Italian
Communist Party (PCI) (Blum 1995, 29–32; Gerth 1984, 12).

It was reported that the CIA alone spent $20–30 million annually in the
1950s and $10 million annually in the 1960s to run various programs in Italy.
Private corporations, such as Exxon and Mobil, spent millions more in support of the Christian Democrats. In 1972, Italian political candidates received
$10 million in CIA funds, and in 1976, another $6 million (Blum 1995, 120;
Solomon 1999, 75). In the 1976 election, a CIA-affiliated newspaper, *Il Gior-
nale Nuovo*, ran daily editorial commentaries on Monte Carlo TV, while another CIA outlet, Swiss TV, also carried agency-placed news stories. Both stations' signals were received in Italy (Blum 1995, 120).

Another example of rogue state behavior in southern Europe occurred in
Greece. Following World War II, Greece was embroiled in a civil war in
which the United States aided the country's right-wing military forces
against an independent communist-led insurgency. Committed to blocking
communists from gaining power in that country, the Truman administration
sent $500 million and over 350 American military officers between 1947
and 1949 to assist the Greek army. The communists received no aid from
the Soviet Union, and Yugoslavia closed its borders to Greek leftists seeking sanctuary.

Thereafter, the United States retained its Cold War interest in Greece. In 2002, the U.S. State Department released a top-secret document pertaining to the U.S. involvement in Greece between 1964 and 1968. According to the official report, the CIA station in Athens was involved in a secret operation to fund right-wing parties in the Greek elections in an effort to block the reelection of the liberal Georgios Papandreou government, whose left-leaning son and cabinet member, Andreas, was seen as a particular threat to U.S. state interests. In 1967, it appeared that Papandreou would be elected. Two days before the scheduled election, the Greek military, backed by the United States, staged a coup that brought a right-wing government to power under Georgios Papadopoulos (FBIS 2002, A6–A7).

One of the better-documented cases of CIA intervention in foreign elections is Chile during the 1960s and 1970s. In that country, the CIA, together with a private U.S.-based transnational corporation, International Telephone and Telegraph, channeled money to favored candidates during elections in the 1960s and 1970s to block the first democratically elected Socialist head of state in the western hemisphere. The CIA covered half the campaign costs of the Christian Democrats to keep Salvador Allende, an avowed Marxist, and various leftist parties from coming to power in 1964. Extensive uses were made of the mass media, pamphlets, posters, leaflets, direct mailings, paper streamers, and wall posters, employing disinformation, black propaganda, and scare tactics. Again in 1970, almost $1 billion came from the United States to back CIA-sponsored candidates and thwart Allende's economic nationalization initiatives (Damrosch 1989, 30, n. 128).

Carl Bernstein, the former *Washington Post* Watergate exposé reporter, wrote that "In the Sixties, reporters were used extensively in the CIA offensive against [presidential candidate] Salvador Allende in Chile" (Bernstein 1977, 57). Some 700 articles, broadcasts, editorials, and other features were organized with agency involvement for the Latin American and European media in addition to stories planted in the *New York Times* and *Washington Post*. The leading conservative newspaper in Chile, *El Mercurio*, was CIA financed. Henry Kissinger, Nixon's national security advisor and later secretary of state, said, "I don't see why we need to stand by and watch a country go communist because of the irresponsibility of its own people," and Nixon instructed his subordinates to "make the [Chilean] economy scream!" (Blum 1995, 208–10; Kissinger 1979, 673; McCormick 1989, 185). In 1973, the United States supported a military coup that overthrew Allende's presidency, took his life, and ushered in a long and brutal right-wing dictatorship under General Augusto Pinochet.[4]

The most comprehensive published work on the covert activities of the CIA and its interference in foreign elections is the work of William Blum. The following is but a partial list of other cases involving CIA election interference that he cites:

- Indonesia, 1955: The CIA gave $1 million to an Indonesian Muslim political coalition, Masjumi, to try to block the parliamentary election of President Sukarno's Nationalist Party (PNI) and that of the Communist Party (PKI).
- Vietnam, 1955–1971: During the 1971 election, the CIA secretly assisted Nguyen Van Thieu even as the United States proclaimed its neutrality in the outcome (also see Gerth 1984, 12).
- Japan, 1950s–1970s: The CIA used millions of dollars of U.S. tax money to secretly support individual parliamentary candidates in the conservative Liberal Democratic Party.
- Nepal, 1959: The CIA admitted to carrying out covert attempts on behalf of B. P. Koirala's Nepali Congress Party.
- Brazil, 1962: The CIA and USAID poured millions into federal and state elections and used dirty tricks in helping to defeat President João Goulart.
- Bolivia, 1966: The CIA contributed $600,000 (and additional money to right-wing parties), and Gulf Oil added another $200,000 to the election campaign of René Barrientos.
- Australia, 1972–1975: The CIA financed the opposition to try to block the election of the Labour Party. The U.S. and British governments in 1975 persuaded Australia's governor-general to dismiss Prime Minister Gough Whitlam.
- Jamaica, 1976: Michael Manley overcame CIA efforts to block his reelection via the agency's use of disinformation, arms shipments, incitement of labor unrest, financial aid to the opposition, and assassination attempts.
- Albania, 1991–1992: After the Communist Party won the 1991 elections, the National Endowment for Democracy (NED) went to work on behalf of the opposition Albanian Democratic Party, funding the labor movement and providing party training and civic education programs. The U.S. ambassador threatened that foreign aid would end if the Communist Party was reelected.
- Mongolia, 1996: NED spent close to $1 million in support of the opposition to the Mongolian People's Revolutionary Party (Blum 2000, 145, 157, 168–78).

"DEMOCRACY ASSISTANCE" AND NED

The National Endowment for Democracy (NED) is a quasi-private, congressionally funded instrument, created by the Reagan administration in 1983, for channeling money, equipment, and political consultants and other expertise to certain countries in order "to strengthen democratic electoral processes . . . through timely measures in cooperation with indigenous democratic forces" (Damrosch 1989, 19). That is, NED's goal is to encourage elections in countries undergoing a transition to electoral democracy and support those where elections were already instituted. A number of critics in and out of government see NED as an interventionist, anticommunist Cold War relic falsely claiming to represent itself as serving nonpartisan interests. Allen Weinstein, who helped established NED, admitted that "A lot of what we [NED] do today was done covertly 25 years ago by the CIA" (cited in Blum 2000, 180). There have been several initiatives in Congress to disband the organization.

Resistance to the U.S. war in Vietnam and other foreign policy initiatives brought turmoil within the CIA. Its own agents helped to destabilize the agency. In the 1970s, a Senate select committee to study intelligence activities headed by Senator Frank Church had found widespread abuses committed by the CIA both domestically and abroad, including involvement in assassination plots and secret involvement in American political organizations, which damaged the agency's reputation and led to certain restrictions imposed on it during the Carter administration. NED was to provide an alternative means of encouraging democratic institutions in formerly repressive states. While most people in these postauthoritarian countries no doubt welcomed the possibilities of transparent, multiparty politics, there has remained a widespread suspicion and sensitivity to foreign sponsorship of domestic political institutions. Even when NED's funding of Chile's 1988 election helped push a declining General Pinochet out of power, the opposition parties that benefited nonetheless expressed resentment against U.S. intervention (Conry 1993).

Most of the current NED funding in the form of federal grants goes to four groups: the National Republican Institute for International Affairs (NRIIA or IRI for short), the National Democratic Institute for International Affairs (NDIIA or NDI for short), the Chamber of Commerce's Center for Private Enterprise (CIPE), and the AFL-CIO American Center for International Labor Solidarity. One of the congressional leaders behind the creation of NED, Dante Fascell (D-FL), formerly chair of the House Foreign Affairs Committee, said that this institutional design was intended to give each group "a piece of the pie. They got paid off. Democrats and Republicans, the Chamber of Commerce, along with labor" (Samuels 1995).

Although publicly funded, the activities of these institutes are not reported to Congress. Existing law prohibits money going *directly* to candidates for office. The problem, according to an authoritative study, however, is that NED employs "a complex system of intermediaries in which operative aspects, control relationships, and funding trails are nearly impossible to follow and final recipients are difficult to identify" (Robinson 1992, 18). IRI, for example, receives both NED and U.S. Agency for International Development funding, as well as financial contributions from individuals, foundations, and corporations.

In its mission statement, IRI claims that its programs are "non-partisan and clearly adhere to fundamental American principles such as individual freedom, equal opportunity, and the entrepreneurial spirit that fosters economic development" (Shelley 2000). It does not hide the fact that it has a strong antileftist orientation.[5] Freedom in the IRI weltanschauung generally equates with "free enterprise," and those who resist open-door economic policies are deemed ipso facto to be undemocratic. In the name of nonpartisanship, IRI, significantly more so than NDI, has supported only political parties and institutions in which it sees a shared ideological orientation (Carothers 1996, 137).

Despite its claims of neutrality, there is much evidence that NED in practice is far from being a politically independent and impartial organization.[6] It consistently constructs the meaning of local democracy in terms of corporate market access, unimpeded foreign investment, and rejection of socialism in any form. William Blum writes, "In a multitude of ways, NED meddles in the internal affairs of foreign countries by supplying funds, technical know-how, training, educational materials, computers, faxes, copiers, automobiles, and so on, to selected political groups, civic organizations, labor unions, dissident movements, student groups, book publishers, newspapers, other media, etc." (Blum 2000, 180). Camouflaging its imperial purposes while maintaining a seemingly transparent image, according to one estimate, makes NED a far more effective instrument of state policy than the CIA ever was (Robinson 1996, 110–11).

NED's extensive operations abroad also create opportunities for political consultants, who, unlike CIA operatives, need not assume underground lives or identities. The Republican and Democratic Party institutes under NED turn to people not with experience in development work "but in the war rooms of presidential campaigns, in congressional and lobbying efforts, and through family relationships to top party officials" (Samuels 1995). The extent to which current American political consultants may still rely on covert forms of assistance when working overseas is not certain. A former leading Republican consultant, Douglas Bailey, speculated about this question: "It wouldn't surprise me, by the way," he commented, "if at least some of the consultant money earned overseas comes in the some way from the USIA [United States Information Agency] or CIA. . . . If the U.S. propaganda and intelligence community wanted to make inroads into the fledgling democracies of Eastern Europe, for example, why not invade them with an army of made-in-America political consultants?" (Bailey 1998).

NED's funding activities are chiefly focused on rightist and centrist political organizations but almost never on behalf of left-wing movements or leaders. The organization invests no effort in challenging authoritarian rule in such U.S. client states as Pakistan or in oil-rich Saudi Arabia, Equatorial Guinea, and Kazakhstan. In some cases, NED has been instrumental in helping ease the transfer of power from military to civilian rule, but it has not consistently resisted military rule. In 1984, it funded the military-backed presidential candidate in Panama, Nicolás Ardito Barletta Vallarina, a University of Chicago economics graduate who previously held no political office and who was widely regarded as a puppet of Panamanian strongman General Manuel Noriega (Conry 1993), himself considered a U.S. ally at the time.

Even without direct political experience, Barletta had other U.S.-approved credentials and sources of support. Before returning to Panama that year, he had been a vice president of the World Bank for six years. To help him in his electoral ambitions, the U.S. firm D. H. Sawyer and Associates supplied the word power (the theme of "new leadership") and other campaign expertise—what one writer called another example of "the age-old dream of exporting American democracy to the world" (Stark 1985, 24). Sawyer's contact with Barletta had been arranged by Jimmy Carter's chief of staff, Hamilton Jordan.

Richard Dresner, who in the 1990s worked to get Boris Yeltsin elected in Russia (see chapter 5), did Barletta's polling, even though he admitted knowing next to nothing about Panama. Census data on household television ownership and the addresses of voters were all that interested him. Dresner focused on TV ads and a direct-mail campaign. A former Israeli intelligence officer ran focus groups. The whole affair cost well beyond a million dollars, and Barletta won a narrow victory, but not without extensive vote count fraud organized by Noriega. Barletta was invited to the Reagan White House (Stark 1985, 24–29).

Why did the United States support a military-backed politician with so little political experience? In part, it was that Noriega, at the time a longtime CIA "asset," permitted Panama to be used as a training area for the Contras, the counterrevolutionary Nicaraguan exile group of the deposed Somoza dictatorship that the United States was supporting. Panama also was training Salvadoran army officers to fight against the left-wing FMLN rebellion in that country. NED money was channeled in part to pro-Barletta unions through the AFL-CIO's Free Trade Union Institute (Agee 1992). NED's tactics succeeded—briefly. In less than a year, Noriega forced Barletta out of office.

During the Reagan administration years, the State Department's Office of Public Diplomacy (OPD) under Otto Reich (who later got a temporary "recess appointment" under George W. Bush as Assistant Secretary of State for Western Hemisphere Affairs) ran a propaganda operation to persuade Americans of the evils of Nicaragua's Sandinista government. The Sandinistas had come to power in a 1979 revolution that overthrew the Somoza dictatorship and subsequently were elected to office in an internationally observed national poll in 1984. The Reagan administration organized, financed (in part through illegal arms sales to Iran), and trained (bypassing congressional restrictions on the use of force) the Contras to overthrow the Sandinistas. Part of the intervention strategy involved psychological warfare operations. One example, a "white propaganda operation" memo, was written on March 13, 1985, and sent by the OPD's Johnathan Miller to Reagan's White House communications director, Pat Buchanan, informing him about anti-Sandinista stories prepared by the office that were planted in the *Wall Street Journal*, *NBC News*, the *Washington Post*, and the *New York Times* (Cohen 2001).

"Democracy building" is never without partisan intent. In Nicaragua, NED and other U.S. agencies lined up solidly behind the political opposition coalition, UNO, in an effort to defeat the Sandinistas at the polls (Robinson 1992). Additional support came from the elder Bush administration's covert CIA operation, the Nicaragua Exile Relocation Program, which was largely hidden from Congress. This plan funneled at least $600,000 to 100 Miami-based Contra political organizers to return them to Nicaragua, for eight of them to run for office, and to channel some of the funds on behalf of the anti-Sandinista candidacy of Violetta Chamorro (Post 1991).

With a well-coordinated State Department effort, including significant though indirect NED funding, the United States managed to manipulate the outcome of the 1990 Nicaraguan election. Though NED had been frustrated in an effort to directly funnel $3 million into Chamorro's election campaign, its larger objective was accomplished. "The incident illustrated that NED had no qualms about interfering in elections in general and stopped short in the Nicaragua case only because of its blatantly illegal nature" (Conry 1993). This didn't stop other private American organizations from getting into the act. The U.S. National Association of Broadcasters, with NED's assistance, provided UNO with a production facility. Altogether, some $26 million was estimated to have been given to opposition candidates between 1984 (when the White House refused to accept the certification of many international observers that the Sandinistas had won the national elections freely and fairly) and 1989 in a country with just 3.5 million people (Solomon 1999, 76). Congress officially had approved $9 million in public funds to be spent specifically for the 1990 Nicaraguan election, and even if that conservative estimate is accurate, it is considerably more per capita than the amount the United States allocates in funding its own federal elections.

Expensive elections, whether in the United States or elsewhere, cause significant collateral damage to the democratic process and the allocation of public resources. External funding has forced Nicaraguan parties, the Sandinistas and other parties, to focus high levels of spending on elections. By 1996, for example, campaigning cost Nicaragua more than 73 percent of the national educational budget. That year, IRI claims to have helped register 300,000 Nicaraguans and assisted in the victory of the right-wing Liberal Alliance (Virtual Truth Commission 1998). The very nature of these "democracy assistance programs," in which "American consultants [have] trained tens of thousands of activists in founding elections throughout the world," forces "the proliferation of money- and media-driven campaigning" (Plasser and Plasser 2002, 22, 53). It is a game stacked in favor of elite players.

The deceptive U.S. position offered in 1989 to then-Nicaraguan (Sandinista Party) president Daniel Ortega by ex-President Jimmy Carter, acting as a diplomatic courier, was that NED funding was strictly to ensure a democratic process, regardless of whether the Nicaraguan government shared that perception.[7] Notwithstanding the fact that it is illegal for foreign governments to fund American elections, during the past sixty years, the United States, usually through the CIA, "has installed, subverted and toppled foreign governments; secretly subsidized political parties and fomented coups; bribed politicians, and spent billions influencing public opinion. It has even plotted, sometimes successfully, to murder foreign officials, such as Fidel Castro and Patrice Lumumba of the Congo" (Steel 1997, 27).

NED was actively involved in the politics of other Latin American countries as well. In Venezuela, it was a player in the events leading to the April 2002 coup d'état attempt against the country's president, Hugo Chávez. In the year preceding the failed coup, NED had escalated its funding to opposition groups, including the right-wing Confederation of Venezuelan Workers, which organized work stoppages in protest against Chávez. Parallel to the Reagan administration's involvement with the Contras in Nicaragua, the U.S. government, NED, and their Venezuelan allies were clearly interested in bringing about a political result in Venezuela through force that could not be achieved at the ballot box. For the Bush administration, Chávez's mortal sins included selling oil to Cuba and maintaining state control of the industry at home, criticizing the U.S. bombing policy in Afghanistan after the 9/11 events, visiting with Saddam Hussein and Moammar Gaddafy, and promoting a free-trade and oil-producing bloc in Latin America to make the region more independent of the U.S. economy (Blum 2002).

The *Washington Post* reported that just prior to the coup attempt, "Members of . . . [Venezuela's] diverse opposition had been visiting the U.S. Embassy here in recent weeks, hoping to enlist U.S. help in toppling Chávez. The visitors included active and retired members of the military, media leaders and opposition politicians" (cited in Blum 2002), and the Bush administration openly admitted hosting the opposition at the White House and State Department (McGrory 2002). Meanwhile, NED quadrupled its budget for its Venezuela work to more than $877,000.[8] When it appeared that the Venezuelan coup might succeed, IRI president George Folsom described the military initiative as an effort "to defend democracy in that country" (Corn 2002, 26), even though the coup itself was unconstitutional. One of the first initiatives of the coup leaders was to suspend the national assembly. Yet, despite its undemocratic character, the Bush administration was very quick to endorse the attempted overthrow. The State Department chose to classify it simply as a "change of government." Lorne Craner, the Bush administration's assistant secretary of state for democracy, human rights, and labor, is the former president of NED.

Prior to the coup attempt, one of its funded institutes, the IRI, sponsored the visit of opposition legislators from Venezuela to the United States, a move that usually signals the planning of a covert operation. IRI, with an office in Venezuela, received a $340,000 grant from NED for "political party building" in that oil-rich country. Meanwhile, NED supported a labor demonstration against Chávez that was one of the key events leading to his brief deposal (McGrory 2002). And when this failed, NED contributed $53,400 for "electoral education" in 2003–2004, which, according to that organization, was to "train citizens throughout Venezuela in the electoral process and to promote participation in a recall referendum" through a local organization called Súmate (Lorimer 2004). One political commentator puckishly asked what the public reaction in the United States might be if the British government had chosen to fund the Democratic Party's get-out-the-vote drive in Florida during the U.S. 2000 election (Corn 2002, 24). In 2004, a recall ballot in Venezuela failed by a large margin. (The same year, because of the disputed outcome of the 2000 presidential ballot, several nations announced plans to send poll watchers to observe the U.S. 2004 election.)

This attempt to remove Chávez, even if by more legal means than in the past, raised serious questions about U.S. interference in Venezuelan sovereignty. Ignored by the Bush administration (and the Democratic Party leadership) as well as most of the U.S. press is that Chávez was a democratically elected and popular, though controversial, leader (Marquis 2002a, A8; Marquis 2002b). But the Bush administration was not about to be deterred from pursuing a policy consistent with its oil politics agenda in other countries (cf. the Middle East and the southeastern European–central Asian pipeline), and Venezuela is the fourth-largest supplier of oil to the United States. The problem for the Bush administration and its friends in the oil industry is that the Venezuelan constitution forbids privatization of the country's oil resources.

The conflict with Chávez resurfaced the bitter history of U.S. intervention in Latin America, even if slightly less clandestine than during the heyday of the CIA. The episode also raises serious questions about whether such forms of intervention are consistent with NED's public declarations about its democratic intentions. If NED's transparent use of political consultants in foreign countries represents a departure from the Soviet era, the Venezuelan episode is a throwback to the depths of the Cold War, or perhaps even the gunboat diplomacy of the Theodore Roosevelt presidency. Chávez's education and health programs are similar in goals to those of Castro's Cuba, and his resistance to a muscular U.S. foreign policy directed against his country is suggestive of the showdown that occurred in Chile in the early 1970s. Depending on whether the United States pursues an action similar to that of Nixon and Kissinger, the Venezuelan leader could suffer a fate similar to that of Chile's Allende.

In the Caribbean region, NED has been particularly active in the politics of Haiti. IRI used NED and USAID money to fund and work closely with an alliance of mostly right-wing groups called the Democratic Convergence, which opposed the Fanmi Lavalas (Lavalas Family Party) of Haitian president Jean-Bertrand Aristide. The Bush administration and the State Department's Otto Reich are known to have actively encouraged the destabilization of the popularly elected Aristide government, in part by immediately cutting off all state-to-state assistance. Some $500 million in humanitarian aid from the United States, World Bank, International Monetary Fund, and the Inter-American Development Bank was frozen (Sachs 2004).

Senator Jesse Helms and his former staffer, Roger Noriega, who was U.S. ambassador to the Organization of American States before taking over Otto Reich's position in the Bush administration in 2003, insisted on blocking loans and grants from the OAS to that impoverished nation. The U.S. government has been antagonistic to Haiti since its slave revolt in the early 1800s led to the formation in 1804 of the first black republic in the Americas. In those 200 years, the United States has invaded Haiti more than any other country in the world (Drohan 2002). In February 2004, under threat of an armed uprising and no support forthcoming from the United States for his constitutional mandate as president, Aristide was forced out of power and escorted by U.S. marines into exile.

Another NED target of opportunity is Eastern Europe. In that region, the ineffective statist economic policies and static Communist Party rule that led to its demise made those countries ripe for neoliberal intervention undertaken in the name of democratization. Procedural democracy (open elections) provided the legitimating rationale for establishing a market economy that American neoliberals expected to integrate into the world production and trading system. In most of the former Soviet republics, both democratic institutions and economic development remain weak. As pointed out in a study for the libertarian Cato Institute by Barbara Conry, NED's democratic institution-building program in this region, as elsewhere, has not lived up to its billing. Conry questions whether a private organization with little federal oversight should be empowered to independently carry out U.S. foreign policy in the name of "promoting democracy" (Conry 1993). She also insists that the right of such a private agency to influence the political outcomes of elections is an unwarranted interference in independent countries' political autonomy.

American professional consultants, who are usually given generous service fees for assisting politicians in various parts of the world, often contribute their time to support U.S. "democracy assistance" and benefit from the federal funds allocated for these programs. By 1990, American political consultants were already training future campaign counterparts in Hungary, Poland, and Czechoslovakia. In Czechoslovakia (now two separate Czech and Slovak republics) that year, local party leaders accused NED of funding two favored political parties associated with Vaclav Havel, while ignoring twenty-one others that also were competing for public office. And although NED denied its political interference, a U.S. government budget document made it clear that the organization's funds given to one of the two Czechoslovakian groups, Civic Forum, were intended "to prepare for the June 8 election and consolidate their position as Czechoslovakia's premier democratic movement." German, British, and Canadian political organizations were among several foreign groups that were assisting the country's Christian Democratic Party (Engelberg 1990, 8; Conry 1993; Friedenberg 1997, 203). In Hungary, the Socialists, led by Peter Medgyessy, brought in two Washington, D.C., lobbying firms to help him with public opinion research in his 2004 reelection bid. According to one business publication account, the East European revolutionaries of 1989 "have been shunted aside by pushy, smooth-talking pollsters and consultants" (*Economist* 2004).

By 2002, American political consultants had advised parliamentary and presidential candidates in most of the former Soviet allied countries, including Russia itself, and the newly independent, former Soviet, transition republics. Poland, with close ties to a large Polish immigrant population in the United States (like Italy in the 1940s), was a particularly important opportunity for U.S. state intervention. In the 1980s, even before the collapse of Polish Communist control, NED had already provided Lech Walesa's Solidarity union movement with $5 million (Abrams 1993), even as the Reagan government was aggressively moving to weaken labor organizations in the United States. In Russia, close advisors to President Putin of Russia have been receiving "first-hand insights into strategies and techniques of American campaign practice" (Plasser and Plasser 2002, 22), a form of tutoring that they presumably expect to assist their leader's political ambitions.

In the Romanian election of 1992, IRI provided support for the main opposition (i.e., anticommunist) parties and cosponsored with NDI an observer team; at least one member of each was a political consultant working with an opposition candidate. IRI's goal was to block the reelection of the former Communist Ion Iliescu.[9] A memo it crafted for the political opposition was leaked to the Romanian national press, making it appear that the American organization was little more than an instrument of George Bush and the Republican Party (Carothers 1999, 132–33, 145). As for its claims to be a domestic nonpartisan institution, it is not hidden that IRI is indeed linked very closely with conservative leaders of the Republican Party. Senator John McCain (R-AZ) chaired its board of directors as of 2004.

NED is closely aligned with U.S. government and transnational corporate foreign policy priorities and focuses on countries of interest to those communities. It used its finances, funded by an annual congressional allocation of $30 million, to support the campaigns of forty-one Duma members in the Russian Parliament (Solomon 1999, 75).[10] The IRI member organization concentrates heavily on the post–Communist Party states of Russia and East Europe, with its biggest efforts spent in funding anticommunist party opposition groups in Russia, Ukraine, Mongolia, Bulgaria, Albania, and Romania (Carothers 1999, 144). An NDI assessment of the transformation of Russian elections was that the country's parties, responding to U.S. influence, were

> targeting their communication to voters based on demographic and geographic information . . . conducting research on voter attitudes through focus groups and polling . . . small meetings, coalitions with civic groups, door knocking, phone banks, and public leafleting; organizing more sophisticated press operations *that attempt to create news and respond to events.* . . . Much of this change can be attributed to NDI training. (cited in Carothers 1999, 152; italics added)

In Bulgaria, with the collapse of the Soviet Union, the Bulgarian Communist Party reformulated itself as the Bulgarian Socialist Party (BSP) and won the national elections in June 1990, capturing the offices of president and prime minister, and taking control of the parliament. The BSP was subsequently overthrown in a coup d'état that, according to a widely cited study, was "engineered and financed by the U.S. National Endowment for Democracy." In December 1994, the BSP was reelected to power, and a former Communist Party leader became prime minister. In Albania, NED also financed destabilization, which led to the collapse of the government headed by former communists. The country's Democratic Party remained in power through what even President Clinton recognized as "irregularities of the elections"

(Blum 1997). Although the methods of U.S. intervention in other countries' electoral processes have somewhat changed since the Cold War, its strategic hegemonic goals apparently have not.

GLOBAL ELECTIONEERING MANAGEMENT

Defenders of U.S. electoral intervention usually claim that NED and USAID are merely fostering democratic processes. The problem with supposedly technique-based and process- and efficiency-driven (i.e., professionalized) practices in general is that they tend to be less open to public scrutiny and accountability or to such concerns as political sovereignty and political inclusion. As argued throughout this study, political consulting and the construct of "professionalization" not only facilitate the use and influence of professionals but more importantly the unmediated flow of corporate capital into the campaigns of U.S. and foreign elections. The actors and institutions that help establish modern beachheads of external intervention include not just consultants but also corporate investors, the U.S. Agency for International Development, the U.S. Information Agency (and the Voice of America and other government television and radio transmissions), the Central Intelligence Agency and other government intelligence branches, the mass media, vendors of ICT, market-oriented campaign training seminars, literature and trade journals, and "democracy-assistance" programs (e.g., National Endowment for Democracy, Soros Foundation, IRI, NDI, and others).[11] They also include academic programs (e.g., George Washington University's Graduate School of Political Management, with counterpart training institutions in Hungary and Latin America), American University's Campaign Management Institute, the Bliss Institute, Robertson School of Government, government-assisted foreign visitors' programs, and various professional organizations and academic exchanges. These programs have been established, according to one detailed study, so that hundreds of "party operatives and candidates from emerging democracies in Eastern Europe, Asia, and Africa can observe the U.S. style of campaigning" (Plasser 2000, 36–37).

The USIA, for example, "has been selecting 'established or potential Australian leaders in government, politics, media, education, science, labor relations, and other key fields' for at least 35 years, and sending them on study tours to the United States" (Thompson 1998, 119). Its cherry-picked list of participants has included prime ministers and other cabinet and parliamentary leaders. Beyond this top-tier list, the USIA has sponsored visits to the United States for many other countries' senior, junior, and upcoming leaders. It is impossible to calculate the influence of these propaganda initiatives or the dividends in terms of serving long-term advantages to and legitimation of U.S.

foreign policy and global economic objectives. It is also hard to calculate the costs and subsidies paid by less developed countries (LDCs) to the more powerful ones, as the higher salaries paid by Western-sponsored organizations to Third World participants induces their cooptation and identification with external interests and a brain-drain of the weaker countries' human resource pool. As globalization absorbs the best talents of the LDCs, it also deprives the latter of talented individuals who might otherwise serve as communicators, change agents, and contributors to a more developed and denser local civil society (Ottaway and Chung 1999, 109).

If the quasi-public nature of NED blurs the distinction between official and unofficial conduct of foreign policy, the political intervention of individual American citizens does so even more. When President Eduard Shevardnadze (formerly foreign minister of the Soviet Union under Gorbachev) was forced to resign as head of state in Georgia after a rigged election and a national uprising that followed in late 2003, the billionaire financier and political activist George Soros was seen as having a substantial hand in the events. Soros had been funding the opposition television station Rustavi 2, the newspaper *24 Hours*, and the youth movement *Kmara!* in Georgia, just as he had supported another student movement, Otpor, in Serbia three years earlier. Otpor was centrally involved in the overthrow of Slobodan Milosevic.

Georgian student leaders acknowledged that they had imitated the Serbian revolt step-by-step. "Otpor activists ran three-day classes teaching more than 1,000 Georgian students how to stage a bloodless revolution. Both trips were funded by Soros' Open Society Institute" (Van der Schriek 2003). Soros may be the more visible foreign hand in Shevardnadze's defeat, but USAID, NDI, and IRI also were involved in various ways in the country's electoral activities. Ukraine president Leonid Kuchma described Shevardnadze's defeat as a "western engineered coup" (Warner 2004a, 4).

As the United States has central interests in the Georgia's Baku Ceyhan pipeline, and the Bush administration worried about Shevardnadze's ongoing oil deals with the Russians, the opposition may also have been lent a covert hand of the CIA (Margolis 2003). The Bush administration's first choice to replace him was Mikhail Saakashvili, a George Washington University and Columbia University law school graduate, and the United States supplied his candidacy with pollsters, strategists, and consultants (Traynore 2003). Following Shevardnadze's departure, the United States raised $14 million to help pay Georgian government salaries, and Saakashvili was swept into office in January 2004. To help ensure his victory, his supporters in parliament required Georgians to reregister, a move that reduced registration lists by one-third, thereby guaranteeing the official 50 percent turnout requirement and enabling the election to stand (Warner 2004b, 3).

The Middle East represents another untapped resource for "nation building." In 1990, with the imminent collapse of the Soviet Union, the Yemen Arab Republic, the only Marxist state in the Middle East, merged with the pro-Western Republic of Yemen. This provided another U.S. opening to "democracy building" in that oil-rich region. American political consultant Stephenie Foster was among those who went to Yemen to train local candidates and campaign managers (Lampman 2003). Remarkably, ignorance of the history or way of life of the target country poses no barrier for the democracy builders, because their view is that American political values and techniques represent universal standards that separate the "developed" from the "underdeveloped" worlds and worthy from unworthy states and leaders. And in so many countries, despite "considerable language barriers, sociocultural misunderstandings, an infrastructure of campaign headquarters that is often disastrous, and a diffuse and unpredictable electorate, prominent American consultants have managed to establish themselves as key advisors offering their strategic and technical expertise" (Plasser and Plasser 2002, 25).

Complementing American economic consultants and a range of other business and professional service consultants, election campaign specialists are working toward a generally shared purpose. That purpose is to set up a policy and administrative environment conducive to future opportunities for contact and profitable exchange. The consultants operate under broadly conceived universalist principles and claims that processes of modernization and nation-state building are more important than culturally or politically specific or organic conceptions of change and development. David Harvey sees this universalist approach as often employed in the interest of "maintaining an open field for capital investment, accumulation, and labor and resource exploitation across the surface of the earth" (Harvey 2000, 85). Not all emerging market states so readily absorb the advice of the political and economic consultants. The Poles, for example—who in general seem more skeptical about the role of foreign political consultants than their Russian counterparts, perhaps because they have had more occasion to become suspicious of interventionist motives—often call them, derisively, the "Marriott brigades," referring to the hotel where they usually take up quarters (Wedel 2001, 45).

Though usually couched in politically liberal rhetoric, the U.S. consultants' efforts are not particularly concerned with transferring democratic processes to the rest of the world. In countries such as Iraq, Haiti, Russia, Georgia, and Venezuela, there are more expedient considerations that have more to do with market opportunities. Indeed, according to one study, democratization has been most effective in those countries and situations where the United States has had the *least* influence, which is why efforts to end militarism and authoritarianism have been weakest in Central America and the Caribbean, where U.S. influence has been the strongest (Schmitter 1996, 33). U.S. assistance to human rights and legal aid in Latin America overall was drastically cut back during the Reagan administration, a period when militarism appeared to be entrenched in the region. Since then, U.S. leverage has steadily declined, while democratic institutions have taken firmer root (Carothers 1996, 130, 142–43).

Why then has the United States invested so much effort in staging elections in existing or former dictatorships? According to a study of the Carnegie Endowment for International Peace, "demonstration elections"[12] held under repressive regimes have been "part of a U.S. policy that pursued the contradictory goals of promoting credible electoral processes while also influencing the outcome of the elections through political influence or covert aid, to ensure results useful to the United States" (Carothers 1999, 128). They sometimes succeeded as public relations efforts to impress the mass media, win over a hesitant Congress, and isolate governments such as the Sandinistas in Nicaragua and the communists in Cuba. Some defend this form of intervention as democratic nation-state building. Seen in such structural-functional terms, the holding of American-style elections is regarded as a "stage" of long-term political development (U.S. Agency for International Development, cited in Carothers 2002, 7).

Support for dictatorships and military coups has been on the U.S. foreign policy agenda for many years. Referring to the dictatorship of U.S. marines-trained Rafael Trujillo in the Dominican Republic in the 1930s, Franklin Roosevelt famously uttered, "He may be an S.O.B., but he is our S.O.B." (Smith 1960, 184). From the overthrow of Iran's parliamentary democracy under Mossadegh in 1953 to the ouster of Haiti's elected president Aristide in 2004, the United States continued to lay righteous claim to indirect governance of other countries, even if its embrace of authoritarian regimes contradicts its democratic rhetoric and is neither defensible nor sustainable. The United States did not press for free and fair elections in such client states as the Philippines and Indonesia under the Marcos (1972–1986) and Suharto (1965–1998) dictatorships, respectively (except when faced with their imminent collapse), or for those regimes that ruled South Korea, Taiwan, South Africa, Pakistan, Haiti, and other countries during the 1980s and 1990s.

In other countries where election waivers were not deemed necessary, multiparty electoral contests afforded opportunities for U.S. interests to influence political outcomes and long-term economic policies. But even when competitive electoral processes are introduced to replace juntas and single-party states, the United States often ignores postelection political, social, and economic conditions, regardless of the quality of civil society and the distribution of income that are so important in establishing the underpinnings of viable democracies.

In the long term, the United States is unwilling to maintain the level of economic aid that could sustain American-style democratic institutions. For this reason, say two critical observers, democracy-assistance programs are bound to fail (Ottaway and Chung 1999, 99).

U.S. political and economic support or nonsupport for less developed countries has less to do with their measure of political freedom and more to do with the ease of market entry by U.S. investors and trade companies or where the United States otherwise has strategic interests (e.g., oil in the Middle East, the Panama Canal). The United States has been relatively tolerant of limits on political freedom in China, for example, because of the allure of profit-seeking there by American businesses. The same could be said about U.S. relations with the single party that has continuously ruled Singapore. Cordial relations between the United States and the Egyptian, Saudi, and Pakistani governments hides the fact that these countries are listed as among the world's most politically repressive and worst human rights violators. U.S. sanctions against Israel for its violent policies toward Palestinians and colonial settlement policy in the West Bank and Gaza are unimaginable.

The imperial state is thereby an active agent in setting the borders of power, investing in those areas where returns to the interests of that state are palpable, ignoring for the most part the others. International political consultants provide an important service in helping arrange this political geography, but their legitimating function is limited to places where multiparty contested elections occur. When they do occur, the American consultants often work for different sides, ranging within the spectrum of liberal to conservative politics. But they do not work for politicians advocating protection of the national market from foreign capital or nationalizing core industries—people such as Salvador Allende, Daniel Ortega, Hugo Chávez, or Maurice Bishop. In the neoliberal culture of the political consultant, nationalist, socialist, or radical green political choices do not exist.

An odd, seemingly postmodern, image is that of American political consultants plying their trade in countries once hostile to the United States, particularly those of the former Soviet Union and its Eastern bloc allies. The collapse of the leading socialist state, the USSR, together with the growing hegemony of the transnational corporate economy and the rapid diffusion of communications technologies, have changed the contours of the world's political economic interchange. It is certainly not, however, that ideology no longer matters; it is more a matter of *convergence* between state and capital, between public and private, and, if the professional consultants had their way, between citizen and consumer. But the dialectics of power never end, and certain hegemonic tendencies can change in the most unexpected ways once citizens grasp their (anti)social implications.

Although the presence of American advisors in the inner chambers of politicians around the world is becoming more common, it still remains a controversial issue that challenges the fundamental notion of sovereignty and continues to spark resistance. When Joseph Napolitan was brought in to help manage the French presidential campaign of Valéry Giscard d'Estaing in 1974, it was kept secret from the French press and people. David Garth, another American consultant, was secretly hired to manage Menachem Begin's election effort in 1981 for prime minister of Israel. But in Sweden in the 1990s Prime Minister Karl Bildt openly challenged the opposition campaign of Ingvar Carlsson for employing American political consultant Phil Noble (Halimi 1999). And political consultant Joe Trippi (presidential campaign manager for Howard Dean in 2003–2004) was forced to leave Greece years earlier when his identity as a hired political consultant in that country's election became known to the Greek press.

Critics argue that many of those engaged in "democracy-building" programs are not interested in forms of foreign aid directed toward alleviating poverty but are instead excited about establishing political beachheads for foreign investment and commerce. But democracy does not conflate with neoliberalism. So-called democracy assistance that leads to demonstration elections (such as those in El Salvador, Guatemala, and the Philippines) provides authoritarian regimes with a veneer of legitimacy. Elections often help to centralize power by paying no more than lip service to participatory democracy. In authoritarian societies, elections are thereby used by ruling elites to "reap the fruits of electoral legitimacy without running the risks of democratic uncertainty" (Schedler 2002, 36–37).

The international work of U.S. election consultants, good intentions by many notwithstanding, supports some of the most imperialist and worst neoliberal ambitions in the name of democracy assistance. In such cases, they act as "Trojan horses." The next chapter discusses the global dimensions of American-style electioneering and the worldwide clientele for the professional and technological management services that political consultants and their storehouse of communications technologies bring to bear.

NOTES

1. In 1928, during the rise of fascism, Bernays wrote: "If we understand the mechanism and motives of the group mind, it is now possible to control and regiment the masses according to our will without their knowing it. . . . [T]heory and practice have combined with sufficient success to permit us to know that in certain cases we can effect some change in public opinion . . . by operating a certain mechanism" (cited in Ewen 1976, 83–84).

2. The most blatant example was its sponsorship of the daughter of the Kuwaiti ambassador to the United States, who, without revealing her identity, falsely testified before a congressional hearing on human rights that she personally witnessed invading Iraqi soldiers disposing of Kuwaiti babies from hospital incubators. CNN International, other news media, and Amnesty International carried the story in their respective media outlets. Hill and Knowlton also doctored videos made in Kuwait and coached witnesses to revise their accounts about the Iraqi soldiers in an effort to convince the United Nations to join forces with the United States. Many of these news items were transmitted over the U.S. news media without mentioning their authorship, leaving the impression (and creating belief in their factuality) with viewers that the networks themselves had produced them. The head of the public relations firm's Washington, D.C., office at the time was Craig Fuller, who had been George Bush's chief of staff during Bush's vice presidency. Fuller next went on to become the chief public relations executive at Philip Morris (Sussman 1997, 157).

3. His brother, Stewart, also a well-known newspaper columnist, lent his assistance to the CIA as well (Bernstein 1977, 57).

4. U.S. government documents declassified in 2003 revealed that Kissinger also encouraged a military coup in Argentina that brought 30,000 deaths and disappearances from 1975 to 1983 (Grech 2003, A18).

5. IRI is often joined in its anticommunist crusades by the AFL-CIO's Free Trade Union Institute, which receives a large share of NED funds. In the 1980s, the conservative FTUI supported a $1.5 million grant to block what they saw as dangerous communist influences in François Mitterand's socialist government and to defend democracy in France (!). At the same time, NED channeled money to the right-wing extremist group, the National Inter-University Union. In Romania, the FTUI played favorites by funding one labor federation, FRATIA, and subverting all the other independent unions that didn't affiliate with it (Conry 1993).

6. The political economic interests of the state and the personal interests of individual agents of "democratization" may often coincide for reasons other than principle or philosophy. David Corn described NED as a "pork barrel" for party activists, conservative trade unionists, and those simply promoting free-market ideas for private gain (cited in Conry 1993).

7. Carter assured Ortega in writing that there would be "no covert funding from our government for opposition political parties" and that U.S. financing "will probably not go to any particular party, but will be channeled through the National Endowment for Democracy (NED) to support the democratic process" (from copy of original September 22, 1989, document in Robinson 1992, 265–67). Carter was either naive or disingenuous in offering these assurances.

8. The labor group has close ties to Pedro Carmona Estranga, the pro-U.S. leader of the country's main national business organization, Fedecamaras, who assumed control of government with the backing of breakaway military elements and immediately dissolved the national assembly and assumed dictatorial powers.

9. IRI claimed that Iliescu had sixteen political consultants from the United States working for him (Carothers 1999, 149).

10. Russian law permits financial support in elections from foreign corporations in the country that are not more than 30 percent foreign-owned (Pinto-Duschinsky 2001, 18).

11. Thomas Carothers notes that "The International Republican Institute (IRI), for example, has inserted itself directly into some electoral campaigns abroad, such as Romania and Bulgaria, in the first half of the 1990s, where IRI representatives designed campaign strategies, attempted to broker oppositional coalitions, and generally served as campaign consultants to selected parties" (cited in Plasser 2000, 26). Beyond these forms of direct political influence, U.S. consultants are collaborating with European counterparts, setting up consulting firms in London, Paris, and Stockholm, with the Americans clearly dominating the field (Plasser and Plasser 2002, 26).

12. Demonstration elections (Herman and Chomsky 2002; McCormick 1989) are used to justify U.S. administrative support to otherwise repressive regimes. What journalists and other foreign election observers usually miss are the actions of the government taken prior to the election. These often include "harassing opposition parties, restricting the opposition's media access, commandeering state funds, vehicles, and other resources for their campaign" (Carothers 1999, 132).

5

Globalizing the Political Standard

The key-note of a democracy as a way of life may be expressed, it seems to me, as the necessity for the participation of every mature human being in formation of the values that regulate the living of men [*sic*] together; which is necessary from the standpoint of both the general social welfare and the full development of human beings as individuals.

—John Dewey (cited in Cunningham 1976, 274)

One of the core themes in this study is that the transformation of elections can be understood within the overarching context of the given political economy. The borderless neoliberal economic structure, spurred by the development and diffusion of new production and process technologies, has penetrated areas previously beyond its capacity or socially and politically sanctioned reach. It is not only in the physical spaces of business enterprise that commodification occurs. It is also in the airwaves, in cyberspace, in the interstices between business sites and households, and within the household itself. Telematics, the functional convergence of electronic data processing technologies with telecommunications, and information have become so central to the system of production that worksites are no longer confined to identifiable locations. Accessing workers by cell phone on the road or aboard planes, collecting household consumer information via telephone marketing or surveys, and spamming Internet users with advertising are among the many new media of place-insensitive commodification.

Even the idea of "workers" can no longer be confined to those on business payrolls. Women throughout the world, who have long been uncompensated household workers, are now joined by other earthly dwellers in a seamless global labor force, many unpaid, engaged in the provision of precious data of values, preferences, tastes, habits, and other personal vita with which enterprises produce profitable things, icons, and ideas. That is, households and even vacation spots have become important sites of production. As one cell phone advertisement counsels, "Blur the line between 'the office' and 'the beach.'"

Political spaces too have been commodified by commerce. Electoral processes are now mediated by the same information and communication technologies employed in other areas of the commodity production circuit. Indeed, elections can be thought of as commodities, packaged with all the promotional razzmatazz used in tne selling of brand-name clothing or fast food. Soliciting paid media airtime (advertising), largely on terms set by the media industries, is standard practice in political campaigns. No federal or statewide political campaign can dispense with the use of the election professionals, especially given the enormous funding requirements that go with such a method of getting into office. This is well understood not only in the United States, where high-tech campaigns have become the norm, but increasingly among politicians in other countries.

As discussed in previous chapters, the high-finance, high-tech, professionalized election as a fundament of contemporary American politics has its corollary in the economic sphere. Neoliberalism requires market, not government, regulation and industrialization of electoral processes that make political actors beholden to the patronage and largesse of transnational corporate (TNC) campaign contributors. For their part, organized large-scale economic interests cannot leave political outcomes and the economic legislative agenda to chance. Corporate elites do not necessarily share a common agenda but they do require that administrative and legislative decision making be put in the hands of reliable officeholders. This is nothing new. Since the time of the constitutional framers, control over the electoral process has always been the domain of the propertied classes. The difference now is that the stakes have become global.

TRANSNATIONALIZATION OF POLITICAL RITUALS

Professionalization of elections is usually conceived in terms of modernization. At the end of World War II, the United States began exporting its institutional framework to many of the newly independent Third World countries. In more recent years, the transfer of constitutional, economic, industrial, finance, mass media, and other institutions followed the collapse of the communist party system in Eastern Europe and the former Soviet Union, and the transition to liberal democracies in other parts of the world. In the 1990s, an accelerated transfer of American-style electioneering techniques was added to

U.S. developmentalist and "democracy assistance" programs. Established democracies, too, were turning more to foreign expertise in managing their election processes.[1]

Israel is neither a former Soviet bloc member nor a burgeoning democracy, but it is a client state of the United States and one of the better-documented cases of the professionalization and "Americanization" of election systems. Working behind the curtains in that country's May 1999 election were some of the top-gun political consultants of U.S. national electoral campaigns. James Carville, who managed Clinton's 1992 election, together with veterans Robert Shrum, a speechwriter and TV advertising specialist,[2] and Stanley Greenberg, a pollster[3] for the Democratic Party, were there to make a prime minister of their client, Ehud Barak of the Labour Party. Arthur J. Finkelstein, parachuted in from the Republican Party side, was master electioneering guru for Benjamin Netanyahu, heading the Likud ticket. Carville, Finkelstein, and associates may have been operating outside their turf but not outside their league. This was a heady opportunity to score the national election of the state of Israel.[4]

Carville and Finkelstein, among the leading international consultants in the field in recent years, are famous for having perfected the art of the attack ad.[5] It helped that their Israeli clients came with their own preparation for American-style politics. Barak is a Stanford-trained engineer, and Benjamin Netanyahu is a former student at MIT and Harvard in management and political science. Making the point, Adam Nagourney noted in a *New York Times Magazine* piece that "in assailing Netanyahu, Barak has invoked the line 'too many lies for too long'—the very same slogan that Democrats in the United States used so successfully last fall against another Finkelstein client, Alfonso M. D'Amato." With U.S. professional mentoring and the introduction of the thirty-second personal attack ad, slogans overwhelmed the issues and introduced a level of political aggressiveness that had not been seen in previous Israeli elections (Nagourney 1999, 44).[6]

In Latin America, a region of concentration for American political consultants, there is a noticeable "decreasing importance of traditional campaign practices, [along with] the shifting of campaign activities to television and the influence of party-extern consultants and prominent U.S. overseas consultants." Mass rallies, parades, and appearances of politicians in public plazas have been replaced by scripted televised interviews, events, and debates. These are seen as indicators of the Americanization of politics in that region (Plasser and Plasser 2002, 74, 271), although the financial aspects of electioneering are more central to the changes than the fact that consultants happen to be from the United States. The integration of foreign (as well as domestic) political consultants in Latin America (such as American consultants

Joseph Napolitan on behalf of Oscar Arias's presidential campaign in Costa Rica in 1986 and Mark Mellman for presidential candidate César Gaviria of Colombia in 1990) is directly linked to the system of election financing.

In Latin America, campaigns are largely funded from private sources. In Brazil, for example, business and industry provided 60 percent of Cardoso's successful reelection to the presidency in 1998, outspending the pro-union opposition candidate, Lula, fifteenfold, although Lula ultimately defeated him in 2002. Despite a ban on paid political advertising on television, Brazil has an extremely high level of campaign spending, especially directed toward the use of focus groups, audience studies, media advertising, and polling. Brazil, and countries as far apart as Australia and Russia, now conduct their national politics to the rhythm of the sound bite (Plasser and Plasser 2002, 22–25, 162, 272).

One of the lessons the Latin American political consultants have learned from their northern tutors is the all-important force of money in modern electoral exercises in capitalist societies. Money binds the consultants and the candidates to financial patrons and ultimately makes all elections instruments of conservative interests. One of the leading Latin American political consultants credits his American counterparts for his education on this point: "Americans are world leaders in the field of political consulting. Their vast experience with modern communication technologies and their understanding of the role of money in campaigns make them a very valuable asset" (*Campaigns & Elections* 2004, 17).

Poor countries can ill afford to run the kind of sophisticated, technology-driven, hugely expensive campaigns and elections that foreign governments and consultants urge them to adopt, however. The local availability of import-grade technologies and expertise is scarce, which means that bringing in foreign consultants will lead to a continuing depletion of the country's dollar reserves. Yet this kind of big-money politics and dependence on inappropriate technologies and techniques is spreading rapidly in the Third World. Once one country employs electioneering of this type, there tends to be a contagion effect in neighboring countries. Meanwhile, the costs of running campaigns is driving more politicians to engage in corrupt election practices, for which there is little policing and rare penalties. In the absence of public financing, organized wealthy interests are going to prevail. The average parliamentary seat in Uganda costs the politician, as of the late 1990s, $40,000 to $60,000 — in a country where the annual per capita income is $240 and the salary of a sitting MP is $2,000 per month (Ottaway and Chung 1999, 105).

The presence of American political consultants is becoming common in most parts of the world; some countries rely more on domestic campaign specialists who have been trained in the United States or employ a combination of the two. Major consulting companies in the United States advertise their client victories, domestic and foreign, like trophy resumes. Some big name firms in the United States include Morris and Carrick for media, Garin Hart Yang for polling, and Crounse and Malchow for direct mail. Phil Noble and Associates boasts a client list that includes the British New Labour Party, the Social Democratic Party of Sweden, and the African National Congress—as well as El Salvador's right-wing Arena Party. In Britain, Saatchi and Saatchi, one of the largest commercial advertising firms in the world (with billings in the United States alone reaching $274 million in 1996) and previously on hire for the Tories (and the National Party in South Africa), is said to have "effectively transformed the role of marketing specialists in British politics from technicians to strategists" (Johnson 2000, 43; Scammell 1999, 733).

In some countries, parties prefer not to reveal or play down the fact that foreign consultants, especially those from the United States, are involved in their elections. Under the still emerging culture of neoliberalism, however, this outlook has been on the wane. In Mexico, there remains a constitutional ban, Article 33, against foreign political interference, and it was enforced in the expulsion of foreign human rights workers in Chiapas. But with foreign political strategists, there is an open arms policy, even if there remains an embarrassed attitude about their presence. Phil Noble, a consultant, spoke about this ambivalence: "They love you and they want you around and they want all your love and attention. But they don't want anybody to know about it" (Schrader 1999, A17).

One newspaper reporter observed in 1999 that Mexico's elections were being transformed into a U.S.-style spectacle, "complete with soundbites, rapid responses, nightly polling and searing attack ads" (Schrader 1999, A1). Carville and Greenberg, together with the daughter of Al Gore's campaign manager, Tony Coelho, were on contract to Mexico's PRI ruling party presidential candidate, Francisco Labastida, that year.[7] Another former Clinton political advisor, Dick Morris, a consultant comfortable crossing political party lines and pairing off against other American consultants abroad,[8] was working the other side of the fence for PAN candidate Vicente Fox Quesada. As a former executive for Coca-Cola, Fox was perfect material for an advertising-intensive campaign and was reported to have asked his political marketing manager "to 'sell me' like any other product" (Dillon 2000, A6).

Americans Doug Schoen, Tom O'Donnell, and Zev Furst, none of whom speaks Spanish, advised and ran ads for presidential candidate Roberto Madrazo Pintado, governor of the oil-rich, and by many accounts very corrupt, state of Tabasco.[9] Schoen had been a pollster and consultant for Bill Clinton and New York Mayors Ed Koch and David Dinkins, and, crossing over to the Republican side, Michael Bloomberg. O'Donnell was chief of staff for House Minority Leader Richard Gephardt, and Furst had worked on the elections of Los Angeles Mayor Tom Bradley and Israeli Prime Minister Ehud Barak. Madrazo lost out in the PRI nominating primary, but his Mexican campaign team acknowledged learning from their American advisors the art of "pivoting," which means turning around charges of illegal or questionable behavior with a positive spin (Schrader 1999, A16; Stevenson 2000a, 2000b).

In the desperate but ultimately failed effort to get his PRI candidate elected, Carville provided a slogan that appeared on Mexican billboards and bumper stickers, "It's the right kind of change, stupid." He also inserted a Clintonesque touch by getting Labastida to refer to himself as leader of the "new PRI" but, unlike Americans, Mexicans had difficulty with being called "stupid" by a politician. It would be the first time since 1929 that the PRI lost control of the government, and the high-profile Carville reportedly was asked to leave the campaign (Maggs 2000). Perhaps intending a double entendre, one Mexican writer, Carlos Monsivais, commented on the 2000 election: "It is the Coca-Cola-fication of Mexican politics. . . . The fact that [U.S. consultants] are working in Mexico has enormous consequences. It is the end of the old tradition of anti-*Yanquismo*" (Schrader 1999, A1).[10]

Canadian politics, too, is gradually adopting the habits of its southern neighbor, including the recent trend of politicians using the media to launch character attacks on their rivals. For the 2000 election, the Canadian Election Act lifted certain restrictions on independent issue advocacy groups to purchase advertising on television stations and networks, thereby inducing greater campaign spending. For political parties, television political advertising is unrestricted, and similar to the United States, this medium absorbs about two-thirds of campaign advertising expenditures. Existing limits on polling and political advertising have been challenged in the courts, favoring what looks like a new tendency toward that of the superpower.

There are some important differences between the two systems, however. Canada's parliamentary system does not invest the prime minister, the leader of the dominant political party and the government, with the same degree of power or status that is conferred on the U.S. president. Another difference is that the Canadian House of Commons currently has five established political parties, albeit with unequal national standing, compared to two (some would argue one) in the United States. The political campaign is also a more constrained affair, with only eight days permitted to conduct paid media campaigns (DeMont 1997, 27) and with about two months of intense reporting. Radio and television stations are obligated to provide free airtime to political parties.

As early as the 1960s, pollster George Gallup was hired by Canadian Prime Minister Lester Pearson to take the pulse of Canadian voters (Rath 2000, 27).

James Carville featured as a consultant to the reelection campaign of Liberal Prime Minister Jean Chrétien in the 1997 national poll. The Progressive Conservative Party also went looking for American professionals, hiring Capitol Beltway consultants from the Tarrance Group of Alexandria, Virginia, which had had accounts in the Philippines, France, and Romania. The presence of American consultants has been a touchy issue for Canadians, and the more nationalistic elements in government avoid being associated with U.S. politics and culture. It is the Conservative consultants who have been most aggressive in taking up campaign techniques learned from their mentors to the south. One Canadian consultant, Matthew Johnston, boasts how he and his business partner

> have imported American political strategies and technologies and adapted them to Canada. We already have the largest data base of conservative financial donors in the country, and the most sophisticated electronic direct communications system. We can make literally thousands of pre-recorded telephone calls within one hour, and 1,000 live one-on-one, person-to-person calls in the same period. (Jackson 2002)

It was somewhat of an embarrassment to the federal government when the Ottawa press revealed that "the Canadian Information Office, its so-called unity agency, brought Bill Clinton's famous attack-dog strategist, James Carville, to Montreal in 1997 for a two-day retreat" (Phillips 1999, 38). Ontario's Liberal Party leader, Dalton McGuinty, more recently met with David Axelrod, an American senior consultant to the Democratic National Committee and well-known spin doctor. On retainer for the Liberals, Axelrod gave McGuinty advice on how to run attack ads against Ontario's Conservative premier Mike Harris, who also has the services of John McCain's political consultant, Mike Murphy. The Liberals called Murphy "the merchant of mud" (Blizzard 2001).

In the 1990s, Russia was the plum of American consulting contracts. First, in the production of 1993 TV spots and then in the 1996 Russian presidential election, the country's first American consultants were invited in to spin the world for capitalism and Boris Yeltsin against Communist Party (KPRF) challenger Gannady Zyuganov. The U.S. government and its allies did not rely on the consultants alone, of course, in this epic political battle. Just before the 1996 election, the United States helped bankroll Yeltsin with $14 billion in loans. German Chancellor Helmut Kohl committed an additional $2.7 billion, most of which was fully unconditional (thereby permitting massive vote-buying by the Yeltsin forces).[11] French Prime Minister Alain Juppé added $392 million to the kitty, "paid entirely into Russian state coffers." And the head of the International Monetary Fund, Michel Camdessus, committed his organization, as a "moral obligation," to supporting Yeltsin's privatization plans, with most of the IMF funds going to the state treasury for discretionary spending, but warned that financial assistance would be suspended in the event of a Communist Party victory in the election (Weir 1996, 38–41). "In the end, though, the KPRF's door-to-door campaign was obliterated by the heavily researched, well-financed, media saturating, modern campaign waged by the Yeltsin team" (Mendelson 2001).

Operating under cloak in the Yeltsin campaign were consultants who had worked for California Republican Governor Pete Wilson: his longtime top strategist George Gorton, his deputy chief of staff Joe Shumate, and a political advisor in several campaigns, Richard Dresner. They were joined by Steven Moore, an American public relations specialist, and a Russian TV advertising production company, Video International. Dresner was a former business partner of Dick Morris and former gubernatorial campaign consultant to Bill Clinton. Morris, in turn, was Clinton's main political advisor, and acted as a liaison between the U.S. president and his friends working for Yeltsin, although the White House denied any interference in the Russian election (Deutsche Presse-Agentur 1996b).

Video International (VI) staff were trained for the election by the American advertising firm Ogilvy and Mather, which is part of the worldwide WPP advertising group. The campaign strategy, including archival footage of Stalin's brutality, was to attack the KPRF and Zyuganov with an assortment of anti-communist tactics. Within just a few years of the fall of the Soviet Union, this was an extraordinary turnaround in Russian (former Soviet) politics. As one scholar found in her interviews with VI, the company's producers mocked Zyuganov for failing to grasp the importance of political marketing (Mendelson 2001, n. 76), which indicated another remarkable adaptation in Russian thinking. VI was run by former KGB member Mikhail Margolev, who had previously spent five years with American advertising agencies. Margolev next joined the Putin public relations team for the 2000 election campaign. Since then he has became a "senator" in the Federation Council, Russia's legislative upper chamber. Another VI company executive, Mikhail Lesin, became Putin's press minister. Lesin is known in Russia for harassing media outlets that are critical of the Putin government (Kramer 1996; Mendelson 2001, n. 73), anticipating the growing authoritarian style of that leadership.

The American campaign consultants also worked closely with Yeltsin's daughter and campaign operations manager, Tatyana Dyachenko, passing on to their Russian counterparts the American political art of spin-doctoring (Deutsche Presse-Agentur 1996a; Kramer 1996). According to a published news report, "they advised the campaign on organization, strategic and tactical use of polls and focus groups" with a "central campaign message of anti-communism," a role they shared with Burson-Marsteller and other American public relations firms (Deutsche Presse-Agentur 1996a; Wedel 2001, 143). They also advised Yeltsin to think in terms of how to make the state-run television stations "bend to your will."[12] Boasting that they had saved Yeltsin from certain defeat and Russia from a return to the Cold War, the Republican consultants admitted to employing a host of manipulative tactics in their advertising strategy to sow fear among Russians (Kramer 1996).[13] Gorton defended these tactics with the overblown comment that "Russia needs democracy. . . . I would be remiss in my duty to mankind if I didn't use every political consulting trick I could think of to keep what I felt was a great evil from returning to mankind" (Maxfield and Schlesinger 1996, 15). A *Time* magazine report on the work of the American consultants in Russia came with the brazen cover lead, "Yanks to the Rescue"—later inspiring a Showtime (cable TV) film undertaking, *Spinning Boris*, about how American heroics "saved Russia from communism" (Zolotov 2002). Gorton, Shumate, and Dresner went on to work for Arnold Schwarzenegger's 2003 gubernatorial campaign.

The consultants' political ads, mostly aired over state-run television and radio stations, which Yeltsin fully controlled,[14] had warned that a Zyuganov victory would bring back a command economy and a climate of terror (Hellinger 1996, 10–11). For "personality" styling designed to capture younger voters, the Americans had Yeltsin appear at rock concerts and "dance" onstage at one of them. Some of Yeltsin's Russian advisors did not approve of the stunt (Stevenson 2000b). Ignored in the campaign were the out-of-control economy, Yeltsin's poor health, his alcoholic addiction, and his broad use of repressive tactics while serving as an unelected head of state. Despite his autocratic tendencies as head of state, disregard for constitutionally guaranteed freedoms, frequent money-laundering scandals, and brutal war in Chechnya, Yeltsin received the unreserved endorsement of the leaders of the main market economies, as if open markets were the only real measure of a democracy (Mendelson 2001). A *Time* correspondent rationalized the American intervention in pure Machiavellian logic: "Democracy triumphed—and along with it came the tools of modern campaigns, including the trickery and slickery Americans know so well. If these tools are not always admirable, the result they helped achieve in Russia surely is" (Kramer 1996).

It is, of course, not only the United States that has mastered the art of political propaganda. Russia now has a political consulting industry. This should not be entirely surprising given that much of the rationale for the development of advanced communications technologies and technology-aided propaganda is rooted in the reflexive ideological assumptions and policies of the Cold War. In their post–Cold War political culture, partly inspired by their

American counterparts, Russia now has a Center of Political Technologies, which sells its expertise in joining centers of power to the latest methods of political campaigning (Plasser and Plasser 2002, 35). The Russian business groups have learned to give their money directly to the consultants rather than to the candidates, which more tightly couples policymaking to patronage (Corwin 2002), a tactic that corresponds to soft-money financing in the United States.

Russia also has a Center of Political Consulting, more popularly known as "Niccolo M"—referring to the famed master theorist of political manipulation and spin-doctoring, Machiavelli. By 2002, the Niccolo M public relations organization, which was trained in NED-funded IRI and NDI seminars (see chapter 4), was joined in Russia's new electioneering business by several other new political consulting groups, which not only help design campaign strategies but also arrange contacts between businesses and Kremlin officials. Niccolo M staff used all the methods learned from their mentors, including candidate marketing, polling, focus groups, direct mail, phone banks, heavy use of the mass media, and attack ads. Following the 1996 campaign, the KPRF began studying Western campaign manuals and adopting the same tactics (Corwin 2002; Mendelson 2001).

While Yeltsin's daughter acted as his de facto campaign manager, the person officially in charge was Anatoly Chubais, a person who links the dominant political and economic forces in Russia. He led Russia's privatization plan and related legal "reforms" (seen widely in Russia as mainly reckless schemes to benefit his cronies) and was put in charge of Russian relations with the major international lending institutions as well as other foreign economic consultants. Chubais also served for a time as Yeltsin's first deputy prime minister, minister of finance, and chief of staff. Later he became the CEO of the state's electricity monopoly and went on to help organize the presidential campaign of Yeltsin's successor, Vladimir Putin. His principal American consultant contacts on the privatization plans were from Harvard University's Institute for International Development (HIID), which "served as the gatekeeper for hundreds of millions of dollars in U.S. Agency for International Development (USAID) and G-7 taxpayer aid, subsidized loans, and other Western funds and was known simply as the Harvard Project" (Wedel 2001, 125, 241).

HIID's influence extended to the coordination of $300 million in USAID grants that went to the global public relations firm Burson-Marsteller and the "big six" international accounting firms operating in Russia.[15] The key Harvard-connected economists who were part of the privatization scheme were "shock therapy" specialist Jeffrey Sachs; Russian-born Andrei Shleifer; David Lipton, an associate of Sachs before becoming the Treasury Department's assistant secretary for international affairs; and Lawrence Summers, chief economist at the World Bank (1991–1993) and later Clinton's treasury secretary. USAID eventually cancelled support for the Harvard group because of alleged misuse of its funds for personal aggrandizement by the project's economists. This led to investigations of HIID by the assistance agency, the Department of Justice, and the U.S. General Accounting Office (Wedel 2001, 125–32, 239–41).

American political consulting in Russia has been part of a larger program to transform that country into a market economy and place it under the control of stable and reliable procapitalist, pro-U.S. elected officials, regardless of their less-than-democratic inclinations. Janine Wedel argues that beyond the technical advice of American consultants, "U.S. support also helped to propel [Chubais] Clan members into top positions in the Russian government and to make them formidable players in local politics and economics." This led to the conversion of major state enterprises to private ownership. The Harvard group actually "drafted many of the Kremlin decrees" to this effect (Wedel 2001, 125, 142).

American political consultants also came to the rescue in another former socialist state targeted for U.S. foreign policy intervention: the overthrow of official enemy Slobodan Milosevic in 1999. The U.S. Congress initially appropriated millions of dollars on behalf of political parties, media, and unions opposed to Milosevic. Normally isolationist, Senator Jesse Helms introduced a bill to spend as much as $100 million to overthrow the regime (Myers 1999). In pursuit of regime change, the Clinton administration contracted polling firm Penn, Schoen, and Berland to work the numbers on behalf of the U.S.-backed candidate, Vojislav Kostunica. It is reported that the U.S. government spent $41 million, in which "U.S.-funded consultants played a crucial role behind the scenes in virtually every facet of the anti-Milosevic drive, running tracking polls, training thousands of activists and helping to organize a vitally important parallel vote count" (Dobbs 2000).

Costs included compensating monitors to watch the polls, funds for spray-painting political graffiti, and 2.5 million stickers with anti-Milosevic slogans, paid by USAID and assisted by a private Washington, D.C.-based consulting firm, Ronco Consulting Corp. (Dobbs 2000). Nominally a government institution involved exclusively in economic assistance work, USAID funneled money to other private contractors and nonprofits, including the National Democratic Institute and the International Republican Institute. (See chapter 4.) The IRI was mainly engaged with a Serbian organization, Otpor, in ideological and organizational efforts. USAID previously had had such a nefarious history associated with political and human rights abuses that Congress in 1973 had to formally ban its involvement in foreign police training programs.

This did not end USAID's interference in foreign political affairs, and its police assistance has since been resumed, particularly targeted to Latin America, with little congressional or public oversight.

In Iraq, before the Bush administration got bogged down in attempting to eliminate the growing resistance to the 2003 invasion, the Clinton White House was already seeking ways to build a political opposition in that country and spent $8 million in 1999 toward that end. The public relations company Burson-Marsteller, together with Quality Support, Inc., were paid to bring together some 300 Iraqi opposition leaders at a New York–based convention. Portions of a military appropriations bill designed to topple Saddam Hussein were disbursed by the Clinton administration on office and communications equipment with the intention of launching an Iraqi propaganda war against the Saddam regime. Republicans in Congress mocked the political effort and urged a more direct, military form of intervention (Myers 1999).

Political consultants are part of a larger stream of operatives who work toward objectives that do not venture beyond the Democrat to Republican policy and ideological spectrum. During the height of the Cold War, CIA "advisors" such as Edward Lansdale (see chapter 4) represented the clandestine imagination of U.S. foreign policy. By the 1990s, without the countervailing presence of the USSR, the United States saw less necessity to carry out interventionist policies in such a subterranean way. Although foreign electoral interference remains a delicate matter for many countries, the presence of American consultants operating on their shores as political fixers has become a more open affair than in the past. With U.S.-based TNCs running or subcontracting work throughout the world and increasingly dependent on remote resources, especially in oil and other extractive industries, the stability of the U.S. political economy relies more than ever on governing structures in other countries that are willing to cooperate with the its agenda of open trade and investment, privatization, and minimal state allocations to social welfare. Political consultants are among the vanguard in bringing about such hegemonic dreams.

GLOBETROTTING POLITICAL OPERATIVES

Although it is not certain that political consultants directly or covertly have acted as operatives of the government similar to what many overseas American journalists did from the 1940s to 1970s (see chapter 4), it can be assumed that some receive at least official encouragement to help seat and unseat pro- and anti-U.S. politicians. Invited to El Salvador, Philip Noble, an American political consultant who worked for Bill Clinton, signed up as a strategist to make the strongly pro-U.S. candidate Francisco Flores the country's president. Flores had studied at Amherst College, and his running mate, Carlos Quintanilla, went to American University in Washington, D.C. Noble, on the other hand, spoke no Spanish and knew little about El Salvador.

For Noble, such cultural limitations were inconsequential. It's technology, he argued, that makes the difference in the election process and, he added, "the basic social and policy issues that we're dealing with are largely the same around the world" (Harwood 1999, A1, A18). Apparently, ideological consistency was also of little importance to Noble. Flores ran under the right-wing Arena Party, which a decade earlier had been connected to massive death squad violence under a U.S.-supported regime that had little taste for open electoral contests.

When Noble first went to work for Flores and the rightist Arena Party in 1998, it was Argentinian political consultant, pollster, Latin American secretary for the International Association of Political Consultants, and founding president of the Latin American Association of Political Consultants Felipe Noguera who hired him. Noguera is described as "an Oxford-educated computer whiz who once worked for Andersen Consulting" (a division of the infamous Arthur Andersen, renamed Accenture in 2001). He has been a consultant to right-wing candidates throughout Central and South America. Noguera's goal is to "develop an alternative to the left-leaning neo-populism that is spreading in Latin America" (*Campaigns & Elections* 2004, 17).

On the other side of El Salvador's political spectrum, the left-wing FMLN candidate, Facundo Guardado, hired his own American consultant, Peter Schechter, as part of his own image-modification campaign. Borrowing a page out of the Dukakis campaign, the Guardado message in one TV ad was that it was not about left or right politics, but rather that "It's about solutions" (Harwood 1999, A18). Guardado's new image strategy turned out to be as successful as Dukakis's. Flores won and took office in 1999.

In fall 2001, American consultants gathered in Australia in anticipation of a called election to be contested mainly between the conservative Liberal Party, led by John Howard, and the Labour Party, led by Kim Beazley. In the previous election, Beazley accused Howard of attempting to "Americanise" Australia's political system (Thompson 1998, 119). "Whether it's direct mail or savvy, quick-hit political sound bites on television and radio, many Australian campaigns—already known for a rough-and-tumble style—are increasingly taking on an American flavor" (Mark 2001, 8) and unmistakenly are influenced by past and present American TV political ads and messages (Beresford 1998). Despite these influences, Australians remain sensitive about foreign involvement in their political affairs, and even though American consultants have been working in the country since the late 1960s, they often have had to maintain a low profile. Since their first intensive contacts with American consultants in Australia's elections in the late 1960s, Australian campaign professionals have regularly been trained in the United States in the latest election management skills and techniques, including polling, political marketing, and "American-style techniques of trivialisation." An Australian political scientist, Elaine Thompson, described such techniques as "the deliberate creation of 'pseudo events' . . . to attract television attention," and the regular use of "Richard Nixon–style 'Dirty Tricks'" (Thompson 1998, 116–18). Indeed, Nixon's Committee to Reelect the President (CREEP) permanently altered the ethical grounds of electioneering, and their progeny were still at work at the start of the next century.

Thompson expressed concern that the importation of U.S. ways of employing television advertising, polling, and image making has seriously altered Australian election campaigns and politics, even if some of the language and style of campaigning remains Australian in character. Under such influence, Australian elections have tended to accentuate the importance of fund-raising in politics and political leadership. They also to a greater extent have reduced campaigning to image making rather than issues, and transformed electoral contests "into capital-intensive rather than labour-intensive activities"—putting "further distance between the political parties and the voters, [thus] making the parties seem less relevant as vehicles for mass political representation" (Thompson 1998, 120). Others in Australia are disturbed by the rise of commercial styles, marketing, and voter surveillance, stratification and targeting, along with an "arms race" in the employment of new campaign techniques and technologies in that country's elections, trends that are attributed largely to U.S. influence (Beresford 1998).

American-style electioneering has definitely grabbed hold in Australia (Plasser and Plasser 2002, 28), replacing what's left of an already diminished influence of the British "Westminster model." Australia now extensively uses direct mail and polling, which, as seen by one local consultant, have made elections "very sterile" affairs (Mark 2001, 8). Political parties, meanwhile, have acquired a particularly strong penchant for American-style, hard-hitting, "negative" television political ads, of which there are no legal limits on political parties. This is said to have had a corrosive effect on political practices in Australian campaigning (Beresford 1998, 26, 30). Unlike the United States, however, Australian elections are not funded heavily by soft money or individual donations, and airtime is provided free to political parties—although paid political advertising, since 1992, has existed as well. With compulsory voting in place, parties do not need to strategize around probable voters as in the United States.

To reiterate a core argument, it is not that Australia, or any other country, is in immediate danger of losing its political or cultural identity as a result of the migration of American-style elections. It is rather that a standardization of electoral and other institutional practices are being put in place that are likely to normalize the political authority of technique and finance and reduce ordinary citizens' capacity to determine the rules, vernacular, and players in politics. It is widely observed that television news and entertainment formats in different parts of the world are becoming homogenized, even introducing political talk shows and twenty-four-hour news stations. If some or most of these formats originate in places other than the United States, there is nonetheless a common thread that runs through all the hybrids. That common element is the underlying economic and commercial logic that merges private television channels and other culture industries with advertisers, corporate brand names, and a vast array of profit-seeking commercial interests. Similarly, with the standardization of electoral practices led by institutions concentrated mainly in the United States and a few other leading industrial Western states, it should not be surprising to see reproductions of the election spectacle in various political settings—low voter turnouts (except in compulsory voting countries), growing influence of corporate money, increasing reliance on professional campaign managers and specialists, reduced media coverage or trivialization of issues with more emphasis on candidate personality and appearance, celebrities running for office, media-driven political sex "scandals," and the like.

THE ELECTION STANDARD

Political consulting is now entrenched as part of the global digital-industrial order and the promotional professions. It also can be viewed as a flexible and footloose component of the production system, one that is not tied to place, party, or point of view. With electoral outcomes as the product, political consulting uses the same highly adaptive technologies that are engaged in the restructuring of the world economy. Flexible production of elections is capital and information intensive and, as in other sections of the economy, requires relatively few campaign workers (the remaining labor-intensive campaigns in the world being left to the "amateurs"). It employs digital technologies that can be located almost anywhere, is easily adapted for multiple and recombinant applications, and can be deployed in diverse political settings. A flexible electoral process hires specialists who cross over from other industries and even from other countries. Globetrotting political consultants help establish beachheads for collaboration between different national elites and bring about a fuller integration of politics and market economics, further privileging an elite set of actors and agendas.

The technical sophistication of managing elections has so impressed the power elites in so many countries that American consultants are often regarded as essential in helping national candidates capture state power. The International Association of Political Consultants (IAPC), the who's who of the global consulting industry, was organized in Paris in 1968 by veteran U.S. consultant Joseph Napolitan (commonly cited in the trade literature as the first general political consultant),[16] together with a French colleague, Michel Bongrand. Working with former Democratic Party chairman Lawrence O'Brien, Napolitan had his first foreign election experience in the 1969 presidential campaign of Ferdinand Marcos, the Philippine dictator who, supported by five U.S. presidents, held power for twenty years.[17] Napolitan also served as advisor to Venezuelan president Carlos Andrés Pérez (Bonner 1987, 76; Bowler and Farrell 2000, 162; Napolitan 1999, 24–25).[18] Both heads of state were forced out of office following massive corruption charges, which raises questions about Napolitan's and other consultants' respect for ethical codes in their undertaking of overseas work.

The "international" association Napolitan cofounded is, in fact, overwhelmingly dominated by U.S. consultants. Of the ninety-one registered members in 1997, forty-five were American. Of the thirty-three members who claimed to have worked overseas, 58 percent were U.S.-based (Farrell 1998, 172). Such numbers actually underestimate the influence of U.S. consultants, as many of the non-U.S. members were directly or indirectly tutored under U.S. election consultants, techniques, and campaign processes.

With the aid of networked electronic communications, political consultants are better situated in managing elections than ever before. Their strongest hand is in image management, damage control, and the political makeovers of candidates, their weakest where serious local and domestic issues are up for discussion. On foreign assignment, their political and technological skills seem to work best when not forced to take account of historical and cultural specificities, but rather confined to universalized themes. Latin America—where military rule or strong, caudillo-style presidential leadership has been traditional, though adjusted to more recent demands for symbolically democratic forms—is ripe for U.S.-style electioneering and, in fact, is the region most intensively worked by U.S. overseas political consultants. American consultants have been involved in Venezuelan elections, for example, since 1973 (Peterson 1985). Meanwhile, Latin America's own political consulting industry has been growing rapidly. Campaign training is offered at a number of Latin American universities and institutions, such as the Asociación Latinoamericana de Consultores Políticos, the Instituto Tecnológico Autónomo de México, and the Universidad Iberoamericana.

Argentinian campaign consultant Felipe Noguera comments that U.S. consultants have pressed Latin America to adopt sophisticated technological tools in running elections, which their counterparts in the south have resisted. He also notes, however, that among the changes in Latin American elections, "Television and radio have replaced massive rallies, opinion polls are now to be believed rather than belittled, phone-banks and direct mail work . . . and in short, most politicians have accepted the importance of communications." Politicians, he claims, have had their "first epiphany" that image is reality, although there is less acceptance of a "second epiphany," which is "the rule of money in politics"—lessons he attributes to their American tutors. The latter, Noguera confidently predicts, will change in the next twenty years, "opening the way for greater use of professional fund-raising, and more openness about money and politics in general." At the same time, he admits that Latin American citizens are critically aware of what these changes mean now that they "have been exposed to what has become a permanent campaign," and, as a result, "have become more skeptical, and outwardly reject the political process" (*Campaigns & Elections* 2004; Noguera 2000, 26).

After Latin America, Europe has the highest concentration of American consultants, and this has much to do with the region's growing political economic convergence with the United States in world trade and investment. The neoliberal agenda of the leading industrial countries has weakened the position of the public sector and put corporate objectives and private sector collaboration with the state ahead of national and social welfare demands. As global neoliberal economics is the party platform of both Republicans and Democrats in the United States, it is not surprising that self-proclaimed "liberals" such Carville and Greenberg moonlight for TNCs even as they declare support for the welfare state. Such contradictions are not borne by the Democrats alone. Blair's Labour government in Britain played tail to the George W. Bush's kite in the Iraq and Afghanistan invasions and in the rightward drift of his economic policies. The French Socialist Party government enacted industrial and governmental privatization legislation to a much greater extent than its right-wing predecessor. The enthusiasm of the new social democrats for neoliberalism in which capital, information, and jobs move from place to place with fewer barriers and less controversy than in the past has opened a wide berth to political globalization.

Neoliberalism, the philosophical rationale for economic globalization, is associated with expanded transnational corporate ventures, financial speculation, global communications networking, and the authority of market ideology. The weakening of state enterprise is paralleled in the political sphere, where electoral practices are converging with the needs of commerce and industry. While parliamentary democracy is different from the U.S. system in some important ways, a shift is evident in Europe in the declining importance and distinctiveness of political parties, the growing emphasis on individual candidates, and the efforts to devote more resources to getting individuals elected. One big difference is that parties and the state provide most of the funding for elections in Europe and have the major voice in how campaign funding is allocated, whereas in the United States, there is a far higher proportion of financing from private corporations and wealthy individuals. Also unlike Europe, American political advisors are typically outside the formal party apparatus.

However, with the trend toward privatization of industries in Europe, the corporate sector has found new investment opportunities, which requires stronger linkages with parliamentary and cabinet policymakers. Under Thatcher, Britain denationalized a number of industries, including telecommunications; electrical, gas, and water services, and parts of the national health service system, and introduced private cable companies. With these industries entrenched in the private sector, many members of Parliament became avid enlistees in the neoliberal political-industrial complex. One observer found that

> MPs have increasingly voted and lobbied for bills which have enhanced their business interests. Indeed, privatisation and deregulation have been the main factors behind MPs rushing headlong into the world of commerce. The contracts, franchises, clients and commissions arising from dismantling public corporations have proved an irresistible temptation for MPs keen on providing little pots of gold for themselves . . . [which] has resulted in a boom in consultancies and created a "lobbyists' paradise." (Hollingsworth 1991, 69)

Nowhere in Europe is neoliberalism more enthusiastically embraced as government strategy than in Britain, both in the economic and political spheres.

POLITICAL COMMUNICATIONS IN BRITAIN

Britain has had a long affinity toward U.S. politics. Its ties to American political consultants go back at least as far as the 1960s. The Conservatives developed particularly strong bonds with American consultants in the 1980s. In the 1990s, Britain's Labour Prime Minister Tony Blair, together with his close advisors, Peter Mandelson and Philip Gould, employed a political style and message clearly emulated from Bill Clinton. On the road to the prime ministership, Blair, together with another Labour leader Gordon Brown (later

Chancellor of the Exchequer), visited with Clinton and the new president's advisors in January 1993. Blair's adoption of the term *New Labour*, according to his strategist Philip Gould, was the logical nexus in the modernization of the party. The victory of Clinton's "*New* Democrats" suggested to his British counterpart a logo with which he eagerly attached himself (Gould 1998). It was a "third way" love match of the New Democrats and New Labour (which the ideologically flexible Blair was able to extend in foreign affairs to George W. Bush).[19]

It comes as little surprise, therefore, that Clinton's ex-campaign managers, Greenberg and Carville, teamed up to help Blair win the 1997 British election for the New Labour Party. Greenberg had been a business partner of Gould (Campbell 1999), who, in turn, consulted for the Danish and Swedish Social Democrats and even for Bill Clinton (Farrell 1996, 178). Gould, Greenberg, and Carville collaborated in 1997 on a London-based opinion polling group and high-powered transnational consulting organization, GGC-NOP, owned by United News and Media (Plasser 2000, 45). Greenberg continues to do polling for the Labour Party and consulting for corporations based in the United Kingdom.

A number of critics see nefarious influences of the United States on the electoral behavior of Britain and other countries. Martin Rosenbaum, who has written a book on postwar British campaigning, comments that of late "An Americanization [of British politics] is clearly occurring. You might also call it the trivialization, with politicians speaking in shorter and shorter sound bites" (cited in Grose 1997). Whether or not it's proper to call it "Americanization," the influence on British politics accelerated in the 1990s. One on-the-scene observer in the early 1990s found elections already were "more leader-centred, increasingly stage-managed for the media, particularly television, . . . [with] a greater role . . . played by public relations advisors, advertisers, and opinion pollsters" (Kavanagh 1992, 84). Emphasizing the point symbolically, the Labour Party's 100th anniversary celebration in 2001, attended by Prime Minister Tony Blair, was sponsored by the American fast-food chain McDonald's, giving rise to what one British press pundit referred to as "the McLabour conference." Rather sardonically, he commented that like the fast-food chain, Labour's "packaging is rather more wholesome than the contents" (Monbiot 2001).

In the early postwar years, Britain's dominant two-party structure was not as open to U.S. consultants, which American political consultant Joseph Napolitan criticized as a "chauvinistic shell." The Thatcher government (1979–1990), with its strong probusiness, pro-U.S., anti-union orientation, overcame such inhibitions. "[T]he 1979 campaign of the Conservative Party made extensive use of techniques and personnel from the U.S., prompting

[Larry] Sabato to remark that the 'aloof and skeptical British politicians (were) coming around'" (Farrell 1998, 173). By coming around, he meant that Thatcher was willing to jettison the usual protocols of conducting British elections in favor of a new set of standards borrowed from consumer marketing and outside information management specialists. Thatcher approved the hiring of Saatchi and Saatchi for the creation of television advertisements and the staging of media events—activities orchestrated to attract the attention of eyes and cameras, timed to appear on nightly news broadcasts, and designed to shape the emotional response of voters. Harold Wilson, noting John F. Kennedy's tactic of adopting phrases in his speeches for the benefit of the evening news, did the same in his 1964 campaign for the Labour prime ministership (Mughan 2000, 30; Rosenbaum 1997, 93). This commercial approach also appealed to broadcasters, because it gave them what they were looking for—the exhibition of personality and style as a kind of media commodity. Edelman calls this form of public communication "political spectacle" (Edelman 1988).

Although Britain more carefully regulates the exposure and campaign financing of candidates than the United States, there is nonetheless a growing tendency of politicians, journalists, broadcast media, and campaign advisors in that country to be complicit in the use of sound bites, daily focus groups, news management, rapid-response propaganda tactics, and spin-doctoring. There is also a broadly expressed "disdainful attitude toward . . . party-organized electioneering" (Blumler, Kavanagh, and Nossiter 1996, 68). The most unbending of the national politicians in Britain to resist this trend was Labour leader James Callaghan, who bluntly asserted in the 1979 campaign, "I don't intend to end this campaign packaged like cornflakes. I shall continue to be myself" (cited in Mughan 2000, 31). Despite its defeat that year, Labour's subsequent titular head, Michael Foot, also refused to turn over electioneering to the media and the professionals. Foot's successor, however, Neil Kinnock, put aside tradition and hired a director of communications, Peter Mandelson, who brought Labour into the sludge of "mediacracy" (Mughan 2000, 30–31). "During the 1992 election, party leaders could expect TV soundbites of around 22 seconds on the *Nine O'Clock News* and 16 seconds on *News at Ten*" (Rosenbaum 1997, 94).

One political scientist found that like the United States, "British parties have also been transformed by the gradual evolution of the permanent campaign in which the techniques of spin-doctors, opinion polls, and professional media management are increasingly applied to routine everyday politics," although she considers British politics to be far more "retail" (direct citizen-politician contact) than its American variant (Norris 2000, 174–75). Still, there are important differences between British and American elections. For example, paid political advertising of the American sort is banned on British television and radio but can be bought in newspapers, billboards,[20] and cinemas. Overall spending on national elections, while growing, is only a small fraction of American federal campaign expenditures (Barbash 1997).

In a system of "rationed access" (Blumler and Gurevitch 2001, 391), unlike the United States, British parties are allocated free airtime (both on the public BBC and the commercial networks) for "party political broadcasts" and "party election broadcasts." Free broadcast time for parties is based on their share of the vote in the previous election, while paid advertising is banned. The allotment for Labour and the Conservatives is five five-minute segments during a five-week campaign period, with four segments for the Liberals (Taylor 2002, 20). U.K. television stations are required to provide balanced treatment of the political parties and cannot transmit editorials on behalf of parties and candidates. As for campaign spending, the amount that parliamentary candidates can spend is determined by the number of voters in their constituencies, but the highest, as of the 1997 election, was about $13,000 (Grose 1997). There are no limits on party spending or fund-raising.

By comparison, the average House race in the United States a year earlier was almost $1.1 million. The cost of all U.S. national elections in 2000 rose by some estimates to $4 billion—compared to $60 million for the 2001 British parliamentary elections, including that of the prime minister (Taylor 2002, 20). Michael Bloomberg's self-financed New York City mayoral campaign that year cost more ($74 million) than that. Political campaigns are also considerably shorter in Britain, with the 1997 election season lasting forty-five days, which is relatively long by British standards. And there are fewer opportunities for individual British politicians to seek outside professional assistance, inasmuch as the selection of the party candidates is an internal affair. Compared to the United States, this gives parties more political leverage over their candidates (Bartle and Griffiths 2001, 13). British voters as well as MPs are considerably more likely to vote strictly along party lines than their American counterparts.

However, British parties are increasingly looking to professional image makers to do their political advertisements and marketing. Saatchi and Saatchi went to work for Margaret Thatcher in 1978 to prepare for the national election the following year, which resulted in bringing the Conservatives to power. The agency also did advertising for the party in the subsequent three consecutive Tory victories up to 1992. Thatcher also relied on the advice of Gordon Reece, who tutored her on the importance of her physical appearance. In a 1981 TV interview that brought up her meticulous attention to clothes, hairstyle, and makeup, Thatcher confided, "You have to think— what's it going to look like in black and white on the front page of the *Sun*?

or what's it going to look like on the news on television?" (cited in Rosenbaum 1997, 185).

U.S. influence on British elections has been conspicuous in recent years. William Hague, the defeated Tory leader in the 2001 British election, paid close heed to the message he received from American conservatives, while Blair relied considerably on Democratic Party speechwriter and strategist Robert Shrum. Other Labour parliamentary candidates used the services of American polling consultant Mark Mellman. In 1999, one of Hague's conferees on political strategy was George W. Bush, then governor of Texas (Harwood 1999, A18). The Tories' and Hague's overwhelming defeat in 2001 led to the election of Iain Duncan Smith as the party's new leader. The Conservative Central Office promptly brought in as a key advisor American pollster and political consultant John McLaughlin, the man who is said to have organized the younger Bush's political image from a right-wing, hanging governor to a "compassionate conservative." McLaughlin pushed the British Conservatives to stay the course but give more symbolic attention to the "most vulnerable in society." In the meantime, the party sent "a stream of Tory aides" to visit the United States to study how the Republicans organized their Philadelphia convention in 2000. The Tory conference in October 2002, with blacks, women, and young people seated up front, was designed as a "made-for-TV" event, a "British version of the Philadelphia Story," very American but with "no cheerleaders, no balloons, and no star spangled banner" (Baldwin 2002; Platell 2002).

Tony Blair's move toward the political center is characteristic of Otto Kirchheimer's observation in the 1960s of the tendency of Western political parties and interest groups to formally separate their identities. Conservative parties (e.g., Republicans, Tories) publicly downplayed their associations with big business, and liberals (e.g., Democrats, Labour) with unions, which guided party and interest group leaders to pursue their objectives through catchall rhetorical strategies. "The interest group," Kirchheimer urged, "must never put all its eggs in one basket" (Kirchheimer 1966, 193). This approach has worked well for corporate stakeholders in the United States, which are freed up to patronize both catchall parties and thus block the formation of independent political parties, though not so well for labor unions—as striking pro-Reagan air traffic controllers bitterly learned in 1981. The centrist tendencies of catchall British and American elections deflect attention from serious issues and elevate the importance of personality, "character," style, and the "who's ahead?" elements in the campaign, while increasing reliance on professional expertise, software, and corporate patronage.

Two British political observers find that "British political communications have always appeared to be heavily influenced by American experiences"

(Bartle and Griffiths 2001, 12). Apart from its easy identification with American popular culture, sport, fashion, design, and entertainment, they note, British outlooks also have been affected by the work of an American, George Gallup, who first brought opinion polling methods to the country in the 1930s. In the 1950s, British politicians began to travel to the United States to study political campaign techniques. Conservative leader Edward Heath was impressed by Nixon's 1968 election experience, and Margaret Thatcher much fancied the political style of Ronald Reagan. Tory Prime Minister John Major engaged in White House–style press conferences and agreed to hold a U.S. presidential-style TV debate, both firsts in Britain, in preparation for the 1997 election (Barbash 1997). Labour leaders Tony Blair and Gordon Brown, in turn, took many of their cues from Bill Clinton in the reconceptualization of their party. Techniques adopted from the United States in the 1990s by both Labour and the Conservatives included the use of opposition research and rapid rebuttal. The parties also developed a heavier reliance on computer-generated data in order to maintain an edge in the art of spin and in the mastery of image and propaganda. Blair viewed the package of polling, focus groups, and the marketing of candidates as "part of the democratization of modern elections" (quoted in Frank 2000, 49).

Blair strategist Philip Gould related the powerful lessons he absorbed as an up-close observer of the first Clinton election, his professional relationship with Stanley Greenberg and other Clinton consultants, and the ideological "road map" and war-room tactics that the New Democrats bequeathed to Labour:

> I was not a lone voice for Clinton within Labour. Margaret McDonagh, Hohn Braggins and Alan Barnard, who were to hold senior positions in the 1997 election campaign, were all working in one capacity or another for Clinton. Jonathan Powell, then working for the British Embassy in Washington, now Tony Blair's chief of staff, was observing the Clinton campaign at first hand and building links that were later to prove priceless. Out of all this was born Millbank Tower [Labour Party headquarters] and the "war room" it housed; rapid rebuttal and the Excalibur computer [used to monitor opposition communications]; an obsession with message; and a tough unremitting focus on hard-working people and their concerns. . . . At the time the message of Little Rock was not heard, but it could not be silenced. The Clinton experience was seminal for the Labour Party. Within five years almost everything that was written in my document had been implemented. Modernisation of Labour did not depend on Clinton, it would have happened anyway, but his election did give modernisation a road map. (Gould 1998, 176–77)

The Conservatives also accepted campaign lessons from their transatlantic partners. Emulating American-style elections, Saatchi and Saatchi undertook a more "scientific" and psychographic approach to winning, studying what one of its executives called "the emotional attitudes which emerge when ordinary people discuss politics." He noted that in the 1983 election the agency engaged in "hours of discussion about finding the right tone, which had to be 'warm, confident, non-divisive, and exciting'" and focused on "directional research, target areas, how to attract women voters, skilled workers and much else" (quoted in McNair 1999, 110). Saatchi and Saatchi also put clever political advertising slogans in posters and print media for the Thatcher campaign in 1978–1979, such as "Labour isn't working" (with a photo of a group of disheveled "unemployed" individuals standing in queue), "Educashun isn't working," and "Cheer up! Labour can't hang on for ever" (Rosenbaum 1997, 14–15).

Following the 1987 election, the Conservatives, still in power but suffering some setbacks, brought in Republican consultant Richard Wirthlin, who extensively used computers to organize psychographic classifications in gauging public values, attitudes, and lifestyles and also introduced the Tories to the practice of "power phrases" (Rosenbaum 1997, 171–74). The Conservatives sent a delegation to the United States in 1991 to speak with Republican leaders in preparation for the 1992 British election, and in February 1999 their leader, William Hague, visited with both the Republicans and the Canadian conservative leadership. Labour too did not shrink from the opportunity to garner foreign advice and use foreign consultants, hiring the U.S. Democratic Party firm of Mellman and Lazarus to teach them the art of "people metering" (also known as "perception analyzers")—the use of electronic handsets to test focus group members' visceral reactions to phrases, slogans, advertisements, styles, and other political symbols and behavior. The Conservatives also took the lead in the use of computers in the election of 1992, although Labour bypassed them in the use of this technological application in the 1997 campaign. Computers were particularly important in the expanded use of direct mail.[21]

As in the United States but on a slight time-delay basis, communications technology has become increasingly central to British electioneering. In the early 1970s, well below half of British households had telephones, but by 1994, the penetration rate had reached 91 percent. This made it feasible to employ telephone marketing as an important technique in election contests, and it also made possible the extension of the traditional period of campaigning by months or even years. As in the United States, professionals have a free hand in collecting citizens' past voting records, along with other personal information about their habits and lifestyles, which helps candidates profile their political values and chart and thereby influence their political behavior. Consistent with the principles and logic of the industrialization of politics is the tendency for professionals to invest their energies and resources in capturing the marginal (or swing) voters, those whose voting habits are not very predictable (Denver and Hands 2001, 80–82).

Compared to the United States, however, the British press plays a more active role in articulating the range of the nation's political opinions, while British television, on the other hand, is not as dominant an influence in news coverage. However, with the televising of the proceedings in the House of Commons, starting in 1989, television has become more influential, and members of Parliament have learned to play to the camera as a way of soliciting public attention and support (Rosenbaum 1997, 85–87). The major British newspapers and magazines are considerably more vibrant, sometimes outrageously so, than their American counterparts, and their management is more willing to work with political parties and openly express partisan viewpoints. Rupert Murdoch, Australian turned American in the 1990s, owns a number of media enterprises in the United Kingdom, including the *Times*, *Sunday Times*, *Financial Times*, *Sun*, *News of the World*, and the all-European satellite Sky Channel. An archconservative, Murdoch nonetheless supported Blair as prime minister in the last two elections, although he has not had much use for the Labour Party. As a major player in the United States and Asia, Murdoch represents the global commercial interests and outlooks of the media industry on both sides of the Atlantic and the Pacific. One should not necessarily consider these influences on media and politics as American per se but rather as transnational, commercial, and hyperindustrial.

PROFESSIONALIZATION, AMERICANIZATION, OR HYPERINDUSTRIALIZATION?

As discussed in chapter 1, the understanding of political change based on Weberian notions of "professionalization" and institutional "modernization" does not adequately address questions of entrenched systemic power, particularly in corporate market economies. The Weberian approach suggests that the preemption of the electoral process is a reflection of the growing complexity and maturation of industrial society. Hence, professionalization of elections occurs as a result of the rationalization and technological transformation of society as a whole, which, in the postindustrial state, increasingly relies upon expertise in the new "knowledge economy." As a functionalist concept, professionalization holds that as elections are conducted on a more technical and information-intensive basis, such as with the use of voter databases, telemarketing, focus groups, and so forth, there arises a greater need for new forms of expertise that become central to campaign management. It is a reading that largely ignores and precludes a political economic interpretation, which generally associates the control of politics with the defense of organized political and economic power and privilege. Professionalization is also an argument that provides an easy segue to the conclusion that U.S. political campaign practices are logically transferable as countries begin to "modernize" to levels approaching those of the West and may even speed up the process.

Taking the functionalist approach, Mancini and Swanson see elections as the most important measure of democratic societies. For them, it is the process, not the larger configuration of power in society, that seems to matter most:

> The manner in which democracies conduct their election campaigns is in some ways as important as the results of the voting. The concept of democracy rests, after all, on a view of appropriate procedures for selecting representatives and making political decisions. Governments are regarded as democratic not because their rhetoric describes them as such, but because their manner of choosing decision makers is consistent with a recognizable conception of democracy. The way in which a democracy conducts its election campaigns can empower or silence particular segments of the electorate, achieve or disrupt a balance of power among institutions of government, support or undercut the strength of political parties, and foster public support or alienation from government. (Mancini and Swanson 1996, 1–2)

They and others argue that methods for choosing leaders in modern polities have given rise to a realignment of political actors. They find that political parties are less important in the political process, and it's mass media executives, political consultants, and other election management specialists who are now the key players in developing the political candidate. What has emerged is "a 'marketing' approach to campaigning," they say, "relying on experts in public relations, opinion polling, and communications for advice about how to craft an appealing message tailored to the voters' opinions and concerns." This gives rise to an emphasis "on the personalities of party leaders, for appealing personalities are currency of high denomination in media logic" (Swanson and Mancini 1996, 251). Perceptive as this is, financial and business interests do not feature as consequential in their writing.

Professionalization is premised on the apolitical assumption that the "modernization" of politics, including elections, is essentially a management process, and that it represents an advancement over the traditional reliance on citizen participants ("amateurs") and local party activists. Challengers to political incumbents are advised that they will succeed only when they recognize "the positive influence of professionalization" and learn how to "move from amateur to highly professionalized campaigns." Professionalization is concerned more about strategies of "winning" elections and less about the extent and quality of citizen engagement (Medvic 2000, 102–3). For the electioneering professionals (as with NFL football coaches), "winning isn't everything, it's the *only* thing." Issues of sovereignty, political inclusiveness, and social justice get lost in campaign literature that is steeped in promotionalism and the stock-in-trade of the professionals—the speeches, polling, media advertising, telemarketing, and so forth—with nary a word of objection to the system of corporate financing and agenda setting.

It's no wonder that even mainstream "liberal" presidential candidates like Carter, Clinton, and Kerry fail to challenge corporate domination of politics, and why the Nader campaign, even while marginalized and eschewing professionalization, is such a compelling form of protest. Nader's lack of high-priced professional electioneering tactics is one reason the mass media fail to give his campaign serious consideration. Professionalization excludes challenges from critics of the system, especially from the left. Scammell (1998), on the other hand, uncritically conceives professionalization to be the "hallmark of modern campaigning" (269).

The central question that the professionalization thesis ignores is, Where does *power* actually reside, and how is it wielded in the electoral process? Elections are decidedly not about how campaign specialists orchestrate events, even if Jimmy Carter's celebrated pollster Patrick Caddell prefers to believe, "We are the pre-selectors. We determine who shall run for office" (Clark 1996, 869). The professionalization argument fails to consider the legal and material regime of wealth creation that operates in the United States and elsewhere, the political options that elite interests are able to and must exercise to defend and perpetuate their privileged and hegemonic agenda in society. Is it even conceivable that organized corporate interests, such as the pharmaceutical, airline, electronics, automobile, and energy industries, could ignore or play a passive role in the electoral process? Yet the technocentric arguments that the professionalization "school" puts forward about the established and authoritative technique of politics do not lend themselves, precisely because of their technical rationale, to open public engagement and debate, nor are they treated by their proponents as being in any serious way controversial. Such an approach normalizes citizen indifference or a spectator relationship to politics.

This approach also assumes an axiomatic principle within elite circles that ordinary people cannot be entrusted to set the social and political agenda. That responsibility properly belongs to the educated, management-oriented, and professionally assisted political strata. Edward Bernays (1947), the early master of public relations, called the elite system of social control "the engineering of consent." And famed journalist Walter Lippmann referred to the same idea as the "manufacture of consent" (Herman and Chomsky 2002, 332, n. 5). Earnest Elmo Calkins argued in his widely read *Business the Civilizer* (1928) that advertising is necessary to "civilize" people to wants they didn't know they had (Mayhew 1997, 191).

Although nominally independent, the administrative classes ultimately derive their authority from what C. Wright Mills identified as the "power elite" and their ruling institutions. This self-selected group acts as the "critics of morality and technicians of power, as spokesmen of God and creators of mass sensibility." Mills allowed that the "power elite are not solitary rulers" but rely on "[a]dvisers and consultants, spokesmen and opinion-makers [who] are often the captains of their higher thought and decision" (Mills 1956, 4). Referencing only that small elite fraction of political organization, the professionalization thesis evades intrinsic controversies concerning the locus and uses of political power.

Professionalization assigns little value to analyzing the larger political economic context in which politics is situated or the factors that historically joined modern technological development as we know it, its underlying processes, and administrative policies to corporate interests and necessities. (See Sussman [1997], especially chapters 3 and 4, for a discussion of the embedded politics in technology.) Ignoring this historical power context, professionalization assumes intrinsically natural, inevitable, logical, and progressive characteristics in the submission of elections to "expert"-mediated management. Formal politics is not simply about planning and administration by technique, technicians, and technology; such an argument masks what elections, in fact, have become: more industrialized, commercialized, and merchandised. The "pay-to-play" precondition for candidacy and office prefigures political control by highly financed, organized interests. This makes natural allies of the consultants, public opinion specialists, media advisors, mass media, the transnational corporate sector, and other friendly governments, ideologues, and politicos in pursuit of common neoliberal objectives—in short, the political-industrial complex (PIC).[22] Within the ranks of the PIC, this system of selecting leaders is seen as a normal aspect of a highly stratified democracy, but one in which a narrow stratum is presumed to be fit to rule.

Mancini sees the key political fallout from professionalization as the demise of the political party. He doesn't consider, however, how parties have been internally restructured to the needs of the new political economy. In the professionalization argument, there is no animate force, only a passive narrative, in the changes Mancini describes in "the becoming" and "the undergoing"—leaving a deep sense of mystery about what is actually driving "professionalization." He writes,

The "digital citizen" prefigures the possibility of direct interactions among citizens, leaders, and officials, which, bypassing the mediation of the political parties in favor of technical skills already developed in the fields of research and business, further undermine the parties' role and importance. In short, the process of professionalization has accelerated, producing effects not only in party structures but also, as shown later, in the very functioning of democracy. Not only *the party is becoming more professionalized*, but also *the whole field of politics is undergoing the same process*. (Mancini 1999, 236; italics added)

In modern elections, unelected political consultants indeed have superseded to a great extent the function of political parties, and party issues and ideological coherence have been replaced by a new form of propaganda—candidate image construction. Particularly in the United States, where the primary system is used to build name recognition and voter familiarity, political consultants are a crucial resource to the candidates in capturing the attention of a largely disinterested electorate (Blumler, Kavanagh, and Nossiter 1996, 57). It is a much easier campaign for those candidates, such as Jesse Ventura, Ronald Reagan, Arnold Schwarzenegger, or a son of a president, already with name recognition. Former senator and presidential candidate Robert Dole complained that the new political faces are often those of celebrities, not those of people, like himself, who have worked their way through the political party system (Witcover 1999, 34).

At the end of the nineteenth century, participation among eligible voters was above 80 percent in presidential elections, almost 90 percent outside the south, and close to 70 percent in midterm congressional elections. Since the 1960s, presidential election turnouts have been declining, reaching 49.1 percent in 1996. Even a tightly contested race in 2000 interested only 51.3 percent of the electorate. Midterm congressional polls typically have brought out just over a third of the electorate (Ginsberg and Shefter 1999, 18, 20). Had the United States adopted a law like those used in Serbia or Georgia, that turnouts of less than 50 percent invalidate the election, the 1996 contest would not have counted, and well over 90 percent of (nonpresidential year) congressional, state, and local electoral outcomes would have to be thrown out as well.

Despite the fact that the majority repeatedly choose not to vote in local, state, and national elections, the elite strata, including the mass media, still hold up the ritual as the crucial test of a government's legitimacy. In the 1988 presidential election, the turnout was 50.1 percent, and half of those who voted, according to an *ABC News* exit poll, did so primarily to block either the Democratic or Republican candidate (Denton and Woodward 1990, 99). Congress apparently does not regard low turnouts and voter disinterest as a serious problem, else it would act to raise the level of participation, such as by changing the voting day, or determining and acting on the social causes of public disaffection. Is voting a meaningful exercise in representative democracy or merely a defense of the status quo, engaging the public in a spectacular but largely meaningless citizen activity in which the "process is pitched almost entirely toward winning . . . not toward governing afterward" (Bennett 1996, 161)?

Performing key informational, commercial, ideological, and legitimating functions in industrialized society, media corporations are central to the PIC and very much at home with the professionalization trope and the practical business of organizing political contests. At the heart of this trope is an ideological premise that disembodied technique, rather than organized groups, is the agency of political change. Professionalization thus assures that a predictable revenue stream will flow to "the messenger." Each election cycle (federal, state, and local elections) confers a multibillon-dollar windfall upon the mass media (especially television), which draws half or more of all campaign expenditures.

The media maximize income from the electoral process by spinning its "dramatic" elements: personal conflict, superficial controversies, character issues, campaign activities and tactics, and the "horse race." Television and newspaper companies are fond of reporting, conducting themselves, or commissioning, sometimes jointly, polls on political trends. Polling appears to put them in touch with the public mood. Often, the poll itself is the news, which news organizations and their favored media pundits can then use to help frame a political discourse—one that is contained within elite agenda-setting possibilities (Lewis 2002, 79). Nothing requires the media or politicians to take up serious social issues that do not interest them, regardless of how widespread certain critical opinions may be. Polling is particularly fruitful for the media when it helps them report on which candidate or party happens to be ahead at the time (or on which issue, as the media frame the issues, happens to be favored in the public initiative process)--again, the horse race.

Indeed, the tighter the "contest," the higher the level of candidate, party, or interest group expenditures, which means more revenue for the media in the form of political advertising. Of the campaign stories covered by the nightly network news in the 2000 presidential campaign, 71 percent were about the horse race, not about the issues (Taylor 2002, 11). Reporting on political tactics trumps candidates' policy orientations. In the process, substantive controversies such as growing income disparities, high rates of poverty and underemployment, inadequate educational, housing, and health care investment, capital flight, the class composition of combat forces, and a host of other issues pertinent to working- and middle-class voters—and what should be treated as the scandal of extremely low voter turnouts (see table

Table 5.1.   National Legislative and Presidential Election Turnouts[1]

Region and Country	Turnout Percentage[2]	Population (millions)
Asia		
India (1999)	59.7	986.8
Indonesia (1999)	93.3	207.1
Japan (2000)	62.0	126.9
Malaysia (1999)	68.7	22.5
Pakistan (1997)	35.2	137.6
Philippines (1998)	81.3	73.0
Singapore (2001)	94.6	3.0 (1997)
Thailand (2000)	70.0	62.8
Latin America		
Argentina (1999)	78.6	36.5
Brazil (1998)	78.5	161.7
Colombia (1998)	59.0	36.4
Venezuela (2000)	56.5	24.1
Middle East		
Iran (1993)	53.2	58.43
Israel (1999)	78.7	6.0
North America		
Canada (2000)	61.2	31.2
Mexico (2000)	64.0	93.0 (1994)
United States (2000)	48.5	284.9
Western Europe		
Denmark (2001)	87.1	5.2 (1998)
Finland (2003)	69.7	5.1
France (1997)	68.0	58.5
Germany (1998)	82.2	82.1
Italy (2001)	81.4	57.6
Netherlands (1998)	73.2	15.3 (1994)
Norway (2001)	75.0	4.4
Sweden (1998)	81.4	8.7
United Kingdom (2001)	59.4	59.4

1. For Latin America, North America (except Canada), and the Philippines, the presidential election is used
2. Compared to registered voters
3. For Iran, the turnout is based on all eligible voters
Source: www.idea.int/voter_turnout/

5.1 for comparative data)[23] — get lost in mass media coverage and in how the political advertisers package the "issues."

When U.S. consultants take their electioneering package abroad, they help reshape the local style of campaigns, introduce fund-raising into politics, and alter the meaning of leadership. In Australia's experience, American consultants helped trivialize issues and turned campaigning and fund-raising into capital- rather than labor-intensive activities. The result places further distance between the political parties and the voters, making the parties seem less relevant as institutions for mass political representation (Elaine Thompson, cited in Plasser 2000, 44). This pattern of increasing dealignment of voters from parties has occurred in almost all of the leading industrial states during the past thirty years or so (Plasser and Plasser 2002, 304–6), as elections have become more industrialized and professionalized, as parties have adopted a more centrist and probusiness ideology, and as politicians seem to be more remote from ordinary people and discourses severed from the public interest.

Under neoliberal restructuring, the separation of the public and private sector has broken down, and politics is more directly administered by corporate interests. Corporations, including the major ones in the media industries, have become much larger economic and more spatially dispersed entities,[24] and their financial contributions to political parties and candidates in the United States and elsewhere have rapidly accelerated. In the United States, political consultants, politicians, cabinet members, federal regulators, and other government officials glide giddily between public service and private enterprise. The centrist politics of Clinton and Blair, more than the reactionary Reagan and Thatcher governments, represented the full triumph of corporate politics and the end of the social welfare state.

Neoliberalism'a attachment to privatization and commodification of public sphere activity has also stimulated a technology-intensive, businesslike system of producing and marketing political candidates to corporate patrons and the voting public. Jürgen Habermas in 1974 called this the "scientificization" of politics, referring to the broader use of instrumental means to control the harvest of information, voter behavior, and election outcome—and the rationalization of the political and public sphere (Mancini and Swanson 1996). A focus on technique displaces a discourse about values and a "deliberative democracy" of active citizens. For the publisher and editor of the consulting industry's leading trade journal, *Campaigns & Elections*, Ron Faucheux, who himself consults for both Republicans and Democrats, the conduct of campaigns is technologically determined. In his view, "Technology—and not candidates, consultants, or the press—is driving change" (Faucheux 1996, 5). To assign change to technology is to relieve the latter three, not to mention citizens, of political agency and accountability.

A contributor to that journal, American Association of Political Consultants president Ray Strother, who worked with Dick Morris for Bill Clinton in Arkansas, believes it is the consultants who are in charge. Strother exults in the idea that "our [political consulting] profession is teaching corporate America how to influence public opinion and is playing an increasing role at the boardroom table." In praise of the industrialization of politics, he continues, "Our expansion into corporate America broadens our numbers and gives us room to expand our industry. We are good, damned good. And our secret is out. Let's take advantage of it" (Strother 1999/2000, 17). By "taking advantage," he presumably means expanding opportunities for American consultants to market themselves as indispensable to electoral victory either at home or abroad.

A number of observers cite an "Americanization" of elections around the world, a thesis that speaks to American-style professionalization. Mancini and Swanson ascribe Americanization to certain features of modern campaigning in the following way: "Increasingly, we find such common practices as political commercials, candidates selected in part for the appealing image they project on television, technical experts hired to produce compelling campaign materials, mounting campaign expenses, and mass media moving center stage in campaigns" (Mancini and Swanson 1996, 2). Most academics analyzing various countries' adoption of professionalized election processes conceive of the phenomenon as evidence of either Americanization or, more likely, modernization. The first implies the imposition of American practices upon other countries' political cultures; the second speaks more to a functionalist, linear, and universal rationality intrinsic to economic and technological innovation and development, including, per Durkheim, increasing segmentation and specialization of everyday life. Farrell, Swanson, Mancini, Scammell, Negrine, and others discuss the transfer of the professionalized election prototype only between these two narrowly differentiated constructs.

"Americanization" falsely imputes a particular *American* character to the way monied interests dominate the political process, and "modernization" infers an inevitability, a trajectory of progress in the way that the election process is converted from a "pre-modern," public to a "modern," largely privately organized spectacle.[25] The narrow terms of debate about the transformation of politics ignore the intentionality and collaborations behind political change—of state elites who help set the rules for electoral competition and stand to gain when the organization of campaigns is professionalized. Professionalization as a high-powered discourse of and rationale for change also forecloses serious discussion about citizen engagement in the political system and, to cite Robert Putnam's (1995) concern, what is needed to create a more dense civic society. In the end, the professionalization argument defends the legitimacy of a top-down and elitist power structure, even when it allows for modest reform, and shields it from critical scrutiny of a public alienated from a system that purports to represent it.

A more critical interpretation of political change resides in the concept of *hyperindustrialization*. This idea suggests that as elections become more technically managed, they thereby become more industrialized (that is, process centered), corporate in character, socially engineered, and intensely managerial and bureaucratic—and significantly more expensive. With hyperindustrialization, there is a deeper penetration of industrial processes and centralization into decision-making structures of public and private space that previously was constrained by technical capacity or the public's sense of legitimate encroachment. The industrialization and commodification of politics reduces the uncertainty of long-term policy outcomes, particularly with respect to an increasingly authoritarian state and a globally "decentered and segmented corporatism" (Joachim Hirsch, cited in Robins and Webster 1999, 90).

The capturing and integration of politics into the nexus of worldwide production and circulation is irresistible to globally organized corporations driven by what is for them an inexorable historical logic and dream of a market-managed world order. With advanced information and communication technologies now at their disposal, corporate elites and their political and ideological allies see such a project as fully realizable. Mario Tronti, writing in 1962, anticipated the need of capitalism with its expansionist logic to continually colonize and industrialize physical, social, and political space:

> The more capitalist development advances, that is to say the more the production of relative surplus value penetrates everywhere, the more the circuit of production–distribution–exchange–consumption inevitably develops; that is to say that the relationship between capitalist production and bourgeois society, between the factory and society, between society and the state, become more and more organic. At the highest level of capitalist development social relations become moments of the relations of production, and the whole society becomes an articulation of production. In short, all of society lives as a function of the factory and the factory extends its exclusive domination over all of society. (translated by and cited in Cleaver 1992, 137, n. 13)

Technoindustrial convergences enabled by digital electronics and telecommunications have spearheaded the invasion of spaces and places previously beyond the grasp or even imagination of capital, including the intensive surveillance of citizens for political and commercial purposes. Telemarketing, for example, which infiltrates and mines households for valuable profile data, or cell phones that valorize commuting, other nonworkplace spaces, and even vacationing by "virtually" tethering employees to the office, further integrate and industrialize information, time, and space as factors of production. The dial meter or perception analyzer, discussed in chapter 3, is used to harvest values, sensibilities, and cultural data from largely unpaid groups of individuals in order to transfer and transmute such information for business marketing and sales and political campaigns. In effect, people's consciousness, sometimes probed at the subliminal level, has become an unpaid factor of production in this panoptical hyperindustrial era—a kind of "consciousness industry" (Enzensberger 1974) or industrialization of consciousness.

Hyperindustrialization converts, standardizes, and Taylorizes much of modern nonmanufacturing work into scripted, repetitive, and deskilled technology-mediated tasks, extending factory-like work processes to the supermarket, department store, fast-food restaurant, data processing center, and to other service employment. In production and distribution, corporations have adopted "synergizing" strategies to merge, concentrate, and vertically integrate industries and gain greater control over the branding and cross-marketing of products, icons, and lifestyles. A profit-seeking din of commercial transactions with telecommunication portals to households has penetrated other built and cultural environments, including public schools and universities; it is also experienced in the growing commodification of public information, extending all the way to the private patenting and reproduction of life-forms. These transformations are part of a political culture in which business organization is internalized and in which remaining unincorporated public spaces are assumed to be frontiers of future industrialization and commoditization. With the escalation and fuller integration and extension of corporate funding, production technologies, and professional expertise into political space, the electoral campaign process is less recognizable as a public activity as much as a social management custodianship of the political-industrial complex and their retainers.

It is, therefore, not simply a matter of politics being essentially "American" or evolving from premodern to postmodern "stages," as Pippa Norris suggests (Norris 2000, 160). Rather, politics has become commercial, market oriented, commoditized and industrialized, privatized and less public, centralized while more decentered.[26] The professionalization thesis overlooks the neoliberal global context in which electioneering and transnational capitalism are now intertwined in an industrially interlocked world, a political economy that operates within not national but global boundaries. And it is not a "postindustrial" politics, as Mancini (1999) would have it, but rather a hyperindustrial politics that has adopted the principles of industrialism and articulated them more deeply into spaces of civil society, from the domestic public sphere to the borderless geography of TNCs.

The current mode of U.S. electioneering follows core hyperindustrial principles: professional segmentation and specialization; subcontracting; wide use of flexible and convergent forms of media and digital information technologies for the collection, processing, and editing of data and images, and so on; customized mass-produced messages; and the integration of citizens and households as *factors* in electoral production. One author referred to the modern election process as dominated by "the three 'Ts' of electioneering: tech-

nology, technocrats and techniques" (Farrell 1996, 171). He might allitera-
tively have added "treasure." As elections become more commercial and industrialized, they also become much more expensive, a condition that favors
well-funded organized interests, making confederates of the consultants, the
media advisors, the public opinion specialists, the mass media, the corporate
political action committees (PACs), and associated governments and foreign
parties and politicians in pursuit of common neoliberal market objectives—in
short, a transnational political-industrial complex.

Polling results regularly show that Americans hold the political system in
deep suspicion.[27] But despite the tarnished reputation of many political consultants and politicians because of improper ties to big business, the Enron
scandal being only one of the more perfidious examples, the founder of *Campaigns & Elections* bemoans the fact that political campaign teaching programs are not directly located in business schools. Hitting the nail on the
head, he reasons that "in spite of the different ends—the one social and the
other economic—the methods of business to produce a profit are not essentially different management-wise from the methods of political campaigns to
produce votes" (Reed 2000, 28). This is the kind of neoliberal straight talk
that explains precisely where the political system and the remaining public
sector (Social Security, public schools, public broadcasting, government employment, etc.) have been heading. Chapter 6 further explores the monetary
nexus in the management of electoral politics.

NOTES

1. Of all the countries where foreign political consultants work, 66 percent were in
"new democracies," primarily Eastern and Central Europe and Latin America (Farrell, Kolodny, and Medvic 2001, 23).
2. Shrum wrote the "Dream Will Never Die" speech for Ted Kennedy's 1980 presidential campaign and four of Bill Clinton's State of the Union addresses and, with
Stanley Greenberg, penned the "A lot to do, a lot done" for Tony Blair in 2001. In
2002, the victorious Fianna Fail Party of Ireland was helped by Shrum and his consulting partners, Tad Devine and Mike Donilon. Tony Blair, Ehud Barak, and Gerhard
Schröder also retained his company's services. In 2000, Shrum was Al Gore's political strategist, and in the 2002 midterm elections, he went to work for Senator John
Edwards's reelection bid. Shrum is well known for his "brutally effective, and expensive, strategies" (*Business and Finance* 2002). His senatorial clients had beaten
Finkelstein's in three previous elections: New Jersey, Rhode Island, and North Carolina. In 2003, he went to work for Republican Arnold Schwarzenegger's California
gubernatorial campaign and as senior strategist in John Kerry's Democratic presidential race. Shrum is a Harvard Law School graduate.

3. Like Carville, Greenberg has clients in many countries. He has been invited to consult in Germany (spinmeister to the Schröder government), Eastern Europe, the Balkans, and several African countries, including the African National Congress of South Africa, and remains an advisor to Tony Blair, whose New Labour Party he helped in defeating Scottish nationalists in 1997 (McIntyre 1999; Prusher 1999, 1). In 2000, Greenberg was in Italy, together with his colleagues Jeremy Rosner and Tal Silberstein, providing strategic polling and advice to the center-left candidate for premier, Francesco Rutelli.

4. American consultants have advised Israeli politicians since the early 1980s, and Greenberg, Finkelstein, and Shrum all had previous living experience in Israel (Hockstader 1999). David Sawyer, a New York consultant of the Sawyer-Miller Group, had worked with Labor Party leader Shimon Peres in a 1988 political campaign (Spielmann 1988). In 1992, Israel changed its electoral system to introduce direct election of the prime minister, which first came into effect in the 1996 election, and opened the way for more foreign election expertise. That year, Netanyahu hired Finkelstein, who played a major part in the campaign. Aware that the new rules required a new kind of personality politics and a TV persona, Netanyahu instructed his election staff to "Listen to him [Finkelstein] because he's talking for me" (Nagourney 1999, 46).

He was also quoted as saying Finkelstein is "a very professional man, and he will be in charge of it all [the campaign]. What he says goes" (Rodrick 1996). In one of his ads, Netanyahu, seated in his study "dressed in a friendly blue sweater, looking like Jimmy Carter giving a fireside chat," asks the audience, in a line borrowed from the American campaign book, "Do you feel safer today than three years ago?" (Wilkinson 1999, A16). When Finkelstein wasn't casting Netanyahu as a man who could be loved, he was designing TV ads that "showed pictures of bombed-out buses, over the wailing of police sirens, followed by the slogan: 'No security. No peace. No reason to vote Peres'" (Halimi 1999). Following the 2001 election, Israel eliminated the direct-election provision.

5. They are far from being alone in using these tactics. One news report discovered that consultant Phil Noble issued the following guidelines in one of his campaign seminars in 1990: attack ads should be simple enough to explain in less than ten seconds; radio is more effective than television for attack ads; ridicule and humor are effective attack techniques; last-minute attacks may look like acts of desperation; do not indicate the name of the candidate on whose behalf the attack ad is designed (Tu 1993).

6. Previously, Israeli prime ministers were selected by the dominant party. Now they've tasted the American electoral system, "one that rewards simplicity over complexity, shock over substance and Election Day victory over governing and nearly everything else" (Nagourney 1999, 44). Roni Rimon, an Israeli political consultant for the rightist Likud Party, noted that "The best thing about bringing them is not that they know better, but that people listen to them more [than Israeli consultants]" (Prusher 1999, 1). One result is that Israelis got exposure to the "mudslinging and snide jokes [that] are the staple fare in a TV blitz" of campaign advertising. The advertisements "are slick and negative, with concise sound-bite themes" (Wilkinson 1999, A16). Despite their defeat in 1999, Likud and Finkelstein lived to fight another

battle, reuniting to win the prime ministership for Ariel Sharon in 2001, while Shrum and Greenberg this time backed the loser, Barak.

7. The consulting team behind Labastida was accused of using "dirty tricks" in the campaign. Greenberg, hired by Pearson Research, allegedly conducted a poll that gave Labastida "a fictitious 16 point lead" (Ross 2000). Mexican elections also have been tainted by big money. According to one source, presidential candidate Ernesto Zedillo accumulated $25 million in his successful election effort in 1994, drawing the funds from bankers, who were later bailed out by the president (Ross 2000).

8. Morris previously opposed Carville's presidential candidate in an Argentine primary and again during the 1998 Honduran election contest between Carlos Flores and Nora de Melgar.

9. Another Mexican journalist reported that on behalf of Madrazo, Schoen, O'Donnell, and Furst, a local public relations firm also employed tactics never before seen in Mexican politics, namely, attack ads (Aguayo Quezada 1999).

10. Anti-Yanquismo feelings tend to resurface in Mexico. In 2003, there was an outcry in Mexico about revelations that paid political consultants, no names provided, transferred large quantities of Mexican voter data to U.S. agencies, ostensibly to monitor illegal migration (*Wall Street Journal* 2003).

11. Meanwhile, Germany has itself used both American as well as local political consultants, who engage in American-style campaigning and TV debates.

12. His political heir and successor, Vladimir Putin, who won the 2000 election, likewise enjoyed the complete loyalty of state TV and radio stations, which gave no broadcasting access to his opponents (Herman and Chomsky 2002, xxvii).

13. George Gorton presented his moral position as: "I would be remiss in my duty if I didn't use every political consulting trick I could think of to keep what I felt was a great evil from returning to mankind" (Maxfield and Schlesinger 1997, 15). At the same time, the three consultants had found in focus groups that Yeltsin was widely regarded as corrupt, and "more than 65% believed he had wrecked the economy." This did not deter them, and perhaps the $250,000 fee they were paid plus all expenses helped them to think "professionally" about it (Kramer 1996). From the perspective of Russian professionals who had firsthand experience working with foreign political consultants, according to what Plasser and Plasser (2002, 259) found in their interviews, the external campaign assistance was generally regarded as superficial in quality.

14. Ellen Mickiewicz writes that "the Yeltsin campaign, with the advice of new media savvy advisors, actively moved to coordinate and dominate television programming (both state and private), including news coverage and as much as possible the more fragmented newspaper market." Zyuganov, on the other hand, faced a more hostile press and much tougher questioning (Mickiewicz 1998, 45). It did not appear to trouble the "free-speech"—and "free-enterprise"—loving American advisors that their work product was carried over a state-controlled medium.

15. The "big six" are Deloitte and Touche, Coopers and Lybrand, KPMG Peat Marwick, Arthur Andersen, Ernst and Young, and Price Waterhouse.

16. Although Napolitan also formed, with F. Clifton White, the American Association of Political Consultants, of which they were the first president and vice president,

respectively, the claim that he was the first general political consultant is misplaced and somewhat chauvinistic. Political rulers have had advisors or consultants since ancient times. Machiavelli, author of *The Prince* in 1532, can be regarded as one of the modern members of that profession.

In any case, Clem Whitaker and Leone Baxter were hired as consultants in 1933 to help defeat a California initiative directed against the Pacific Gas and Electric Company and were brought back to that state a year later to help defeat Upton Sinclair's Socialist candidacy for governor. Whitaker and Baxter engaged in a deceitful anti-communist attack on Sinclair, including the use of movie theater newsreels that portrayed him as an admirer of the Soviet Union, a smear tactic similarly applied the following decade in the first congressional campaign of Richard Nixon.

17. In the Philippines, where people were used to American razzmatazz, Napolitan sent out fifteen flatbed trucks with a screen and projector and had them tour the country to deliver hours of Marcos political advertisements. In the villages, where movie showings were quite rare, the idea was quite an entertaining novelty (Stark 1985, 24).

18. Altogether, Napolitan claimed to be a "personal consultant to nine heads of state," including former dictator Hugo Banzer (Bolivia) and the caudillo leader Omar Torrijos (Panama). During the U.S. negotiations with Torrijos over the future of the Panama Canal, Napolitan was called in by the U.S. ambassador to that country to share his professional expertise on the proposed treaty (Maggs 2000).

19. The year (1997) that Blair, adopting much of the Clinton "New Democrat" lexicon, captured control of Parliament for the first time in eighteen years, Mary MacAleese also took a page from Clinton's 1996 "building bridges" campaign rhetoric and won the presidency of Ireland (*Business and Finance* 2002).

20. In the 1997 British elections, the share of the advertising budgets spent by the Conservatives and Labour on posters and billboards was 80 percent. And with far less paid broadcast advertising than the United States, Austrian and German parties spend up to 40 percent in these media (Plasser and Plasser 2002, 298).

21. In the 1992 campaign, the Conservatives used personal computers in 79 percent of the contests (but 93 percent in close races), while Labour used them in 77 percent of the contests (97 percent), and the Liberal Democrats uses them in 68 percent (84 percent). By 1997, the respective numbers were 88 percent (96 percent), 90 percent (99 percent), and 77 percent (100 percent) (Denver and Hands 2001, 79). Direct mail is greatly on the upsurge in most of Western Europe.

22. One measure of the political-industrial complex is transnational advertising. A U.S. company, McCann-Erickson, is the world's leading advertising agency. Proctor and Gamble, with $1 to $1.2 billion spent (1996) on television promotions alone ($2.6 billion overall), is the nation's largest product advertiser (Eliot 1997, C1, C8). By the early 1990s, the largest two U.S. ad agencies already earned more than half their income abroad (King 1990, 26).

23. The United States has by far the lowest elections turnouts of any of the leading industrialized countries. Were Third World countries, especially "enemy" states, to have election participation rates of 50 percent or lower, which is typical of the United States, it is likely that the State Department would not recognize their legitimacy. Average turnouts of industrial countries in lower house elections between 1960 and 1995

include: Australia (95 percent), Austria (92 percent), Belgium (91 percent), Italy (90 percent), New Zealand (88 percent), Denmark (87 percent), Germany (86 percent), Sweden (86 percent), Greece (86 percent), Netherlands (83 percent), Norway (81 percent), Israel (80 percent), Portugal (79 percent), Finland (78 percent), Canada (76 percent), France (76 percent), United Kingdom (75 percent), Ireland (74 percent), Spain (73 percent), Japan (71 percent), United States (54 percent) (Franklin 1996, 218). In 1994, the Republican "landslide" congressional victory was achieved with 21 percent of eligible voters. A 2002 first-round election for president in France brought out 72 percent of the electorate, the lowest in the country's postwar history, and the French press treated it as a sign of mass apathy.

24. The concentration of newspapers in the United States does not match that of France, however, where 70 percent of the national newspapers is in the hands of two armament manufacturers, Dassault and Lagardère.

25. It is not Americanization or professionalization that led to the impeachment of Lithuanian president Rolandas Paksas in April 2004. However, the transformation of Lithuanian elections permitted private campaign contributions, in this case an apparently corrupt arrangement in which a Russian arms dealer, Yuri Borisov, gave Paksas $400,000 for his election in 2003 and in return was given preferential treatment in arms sales as well as restored Lithuanian citizenship. It is reported that Borisov worked through a Russian consulting firm, Almax, which is linked to the Russian foreign intelligence service (Myers 2003). One might call this an industrialization of politics, inasmuch as electoral activity was used as a conduit to effect economic exchange relationships.

26. The decentering of politics enables campaign headquarters to centrally control the management of the election, while encouraging local, customized advertising messages to be used in places where they are most effective.

27. For example, a *Business Week* poll in 2000 found that 74 percent of Americans believed that corporations have "too much influence" over politicians, policies, and policymakers in Washington, D.C. A 2002 *CBS News* poll revealed that 72 percent of Americans think that many public officials alter policy decisions in response to major campaign contributions (M. Green 2002b, 243–44).

6

Elections and the Corporate Agenda

I hope we shall take warning from the example and crush in its birth the aristocracy of our monied corporations, which dare already to challenge our government to a trial of strength and bid defiance to the laws of our country.

—Thomas Jefferson, 1816

Congress is the best money can buy.

—Will Rogers

PLUTOCRACY

The focus of this chapter is an elaboration of the nexus between corporate power and the political and electoral process. To the corporate business community, their interest *is* the public interest. There are many entry points through which large-scale corporations can pursue and protect their stakeholdings and set the economic agenda in the political and policy arenas, but none is as important as the capture of the means by which political "leadership" is enthroned and socially legitimated. No establishment of power is as enduring as one in which public consent is enjoined in the system of social control (Gramsci's idea of hegemony), and no governing idea has been more accepted as legitimate in the world than democracy. But a formal democratic system whose political life and institutions of public information and persuasion are dominated by corporate elites presents a formidable challenge to those who would change this mode of governance. Jefferson and Lincoln were among those who recognized the fragility of American democracy and visualized its decline under the control of a wealthy oligarchy.

The way in which U.S. elections are conducted and financed is central to the maintenance of elite power, but the capturing of state power does not begin and end with elections. As Thomas Ferguson (1995) forcefully argues, the penetration of money into the political process permeates a large number of institutions that one does not always associate with organized political interests. These include charities, churches, lawyer organizations, universities, the mass media, and a range of other institutions. In politics, money, the lingua franca of the polity, is exchanged through a complex system of reciprocal relations and alliances, which are formed well before election time. Such institutionalized relationships create static codependencies and lead to horse-trading in which advantageous legislative treatment and subsidies are negotiated or bartered. This money-for-favors approach fosters a conservative political culture.

Politics has become almost synonymous with business, and corporate financing of elections is regarded as simply a cost of doing business. In the 1970s, following the war in Vietnam and a decade of public criticism directed at government and big business, corporations began to aggressively reassert their political clout. After *Buckley v. Valeo,* most of their political largesse was vested in Republicans—particularly as a reaction to the Carter administration and the liberal influence in Congress in that period—which led to a surge in the number of corporate political action committees (PACs). A large proportion of corporate PAC money went to Republican challengers in the 1980 poll and helped bring about a conservative sweep (a party turnover in the Senate and a thirty-four-seat net gain in the House by Republicans) and the election of Ronald Reagan. The new president's political advisor, Lee Atwater, bragged that his party's "congressional campaign committee and the Republican National Committee are having meetings with every PAC in town" (Eismeier and Pollock 1988, 84–86). Both parties have since become increasingly solicitous of and aligned with corporate backing, while the welfare politics of Franklin Roosevelt's New Deal and Lyndon Johnson's Great Society has been permanently put on the defensive.

Elections present opportunities to make procedural democracy work on behalf of a narrow range of economic and financial interests that are present in every important corridor of state representation and decision making.[1] It is not, of course, only in elections where corporate power is politically exercised. Public-private investment networks (the "growth machine") continually reinforce and reassure large private economic and financial interests of their privileged standing in the polity. Moralistic, "freedom-loving," "national interest," and other diversionary public rhetoric provides a shield to disguise the actual workings of the political economy.

With the shift to global neoliberalism, former government officials can more easily trade on their public status to form lucrative associations with the international business community. Henry Kissinger, for one, has made very profitable use of his years in government (former national security advisor and secretary of state to Nixon and Ford) and his Harvard pedigree to become a consultant to major blue chip companies while frequently moonlighting for the U.S. government. His business consulting ties include American Express, IBM, and the American International Group, and, with Bill Clinton's chief of staff and senior advisor, Thomas McLarty, Exxon, Mobil, United Parcel Service, and Delta Airlines. Former deputy director of the CIA Frank Carlucci and Ronald Reagan's chief of staff, James Baker, formed a consulting group, the Carlyle Group (which included the family of Osama bin Laden as multi-million-dollar investors), a key player in the Middle East political economy. A protégé and former consulting partner of Kissinger's, Alan Stoga, and Lawrence Eagleburger, respectively, were hired, along with Bill Clinton's former deputy treasury secretary, by the Duhalde government in Argentina. At the same time, Kissinger is said to be "of interest to Argentine prosecutors for his alleged role in egregious human-rights violations committed in South America during the 1970s." An estimated 20,000 Argentinian civilians were kidnapped and murdered by a military junta that was supported by then-Secretary of State Kissinger. Many of the Argentinian junta came from Duhalde's Péronista Party (Andersen 2002).

Many other government officials have moved on to the private sector as corporate consultants and lobbyists. These include William Cohen, Clinton's defense secretary; Samuel Berger, Clinton's national security advisor; Richard Holbrooke, former ambassador to the United Nations; William Kennard, former FCC commissioner; and George H. W. Bush, former U.S. president. Still others have become executives or board members of major corporations. Cohen, for example, is on the board of Nasdaq, Global Crossing, Cendent, and Head Sports (Wayne 2001). Since 2000, at least two Democrats and fifteen Republicans have left Congress to work for lobbying firms in D.C.

On the intersection of American business and politics, Serge Halimi (1999) wrote:

> Today US politics is dominated by business methods, as political parties have virtually ceased to exist, campaigns have become personalised and, because of the cost of advertising, money plays an ever greater role. Once the distinction between voter and consumer—and between democracy and the market—has been obliterated (which is an explicit part of the doctrine of some theoreticians of pluralism), a good election strategy is to try and split a fragile opposing coali-

tion. The stress must be on topics that can serve to detach a sufficient number of supporters (or customers). The less politicised the electorate, the less emphasis should be placed on genuine political differences.

Leading actors and institutions in the modern capitalist system become established on the basis of symbiotic and mutually reinforcing relationships among politicians, political consultants, corporate executives, media pundits, and an inner circle of other managers, wealthy individuals, ideologues, and professionals. Political campaigning solidifies these bonds through the solicitation and securing of funding, political favors, policies, privileges, and public relations between each election. The ability of consultants to acquire major corporate clients works to the interest of their political candidates and ultimately benefits all three parties. Without secure relationships with legislators, consultants will have difficulty landing corporate accounts. The working relationships among corporations, consultants, and candidates eradicates effective boundaries between the public and private spheres. "It's all one big party right now. . . . I mean party as in whoopee," says one consultant, "because these guys [the consultants] just make a fortune, and they're totally manipulating the system. And the system is entirely prone to manipulation" (Galizio 2002).

The professionalization of elections facilitates manipulation by encouraging big business to channel vast amounts of money and influence directly into the political process with little interference or public notice. This contravenes the basic tenets of democratic government being of, by, and for the people. Former Texas Agricultural Commissioner Jim Hightower, among others, sees political consultants as deliberately pushing expensive media-based campaigning as a way of obstructing grassroots initiatives in public decision making. Democratic Party candidates, he points out, who would disproportionately benefit from directly enlisting higher voter turnouts from poor and lower-middle-class constituents, are persuaded instead to put their money into TV ads. What consultants are saying is, "Hey, I own the computerized, annotated, and cross-indexed list of current November voters, which I get to resell to you dimwitted candidates every four years for about a quarter-million bucks a pop. I do not, however, have a list of these on-and-off voters" (Hightower 1998, 266).

Michael Bloomberg, the media tycoon who switched to the Republican Party in order to win the New York City mayoral election, brought in some of the top hired guns to manage his campaign. Some of his normally Democratic consultants saw no problem in working the other side of the fence against the liberal Democratic Party candidate, Mark Green. Bloomberg's media firm, Squier Knapp Dunn Communications, ran $23.5 million in TV, radio, and print ads from May to November 2001, of which $2.3 million went as earnings to the company. A year earlier, Bill Knapp had consulted for Al Gore's 2000 presidential campaign. Anita Dunn had worked on behalf of Senate Majority Leader and Democrat Tom Daschle. David Garth, who had previously worked on New York's Giuliani, Koch, and Lindsay mayoral campaigns, was paid $720,000 from February 2001 to election day in November, about three times what candidate Mark Green had offered to pay him over that period. Bloomberg's spokesperson William Cunningham was paid $239,000 over nine months, and Penn, Schoen, and Berland Associates, the polling group that had worked for both Bill and Hillary Clinton, took in $4.5 million. Bloomberg spent another $156,000 to get advice from Frank Luntz's Republican consulting company. Even a liberal academic from New York University, Mitchell Moss, cashed in on the bonanza with a $7,500 paycheck for offering advice to Bloomberg to run as a centrist "good government/good management" candidate (Robbins 2001).

The mass media are also integral to the plutocratic system of electioneering. Money that pours into television political advertising encourages the medium's management to limit news coverage of candidates. In a neoliberal market economy, formal politics is given no special public status. This works to the detriment of the public at large, which depends on major news outlets to be "the people's intelligence service" (Kelley 1956, 204). TV coverage of candidates, campaigns, and party conventions have all heavily declined since the 1950s and even significantly since the 1980s.[2] A study by two leading university political research centers found that more than half (53.4 percent) of the 2,454 news programs surveyed across the country between September 18 and October 4, 2002, carried no campaign coverage at all, even at the height of a tight battle for control of both the Senate and House in the November 5 elections (McClintock 2002). The simple logic of it is that the less that stations provide (free) coverage, the more candidates are forced to get their messages across through expensive broadcast advertising in which both the media and the consultants, with their hefty commissions, directly benefit.

Into the twenty-first century, the United States remained one of the very few countries (along with Ecuador, Honduras, Malaysia, Taiwan, Tanzania, Trinidad, and Tobago) that did not provide free broadcast airtime for political parties and candidates. Almost all other countries do, including most of Central and South America, virtually all of Europe, Australia, Britain, Canada, Israel, Japan, Mexico, New Zealand, and Russia. Even several poor African and Asian countries, such as Ghana, India, Senegal, South Africa, Turkey, and Zimbabwe, give free airtime to candidates. It is truly remarkable that the United States does not recognize that state support for voter education strengthens civic capacity by adding opportunities for hearing and debating diverse political points of view.

Senators McCain and Feingold introduced a Senate bill in 2002 to require private commercial TV stations to provide free airtime to parties or candidates. Without free airtime, politicians and parties, especially third parties, have limited means of transmitting their messages over the broadcast media. The commercial, sensation-hungry style of news coverage, with twenty-four-hour surveillance of any controversial utterance of a candidate (often taken out of context), constantly repeated across the broadcast spectrum, often trivializes and corrupts political speech. Candidates in the pretelevision era may have been more explicit (though not necessarily more sincere) in their spoken views before targeted audiences or interest groups (e.g., organized labor, ethnic minorities, professional and business organizations); today, they would not be advised to do so in front of national television cameras given the commercial media's salacious tendencies toward personal exposé and public humiliation of well-known individuals.

In the last weeks of the 2000 election, the national networks and local stations devoted an average of one minute per night to candidate discourse (Alliance for Better Campaigns 2001). TV stations, which are given free licenses from the federal government to use the public airwaves, provide few if any set-asides for the public interest, and they profit immensely by rationing political information. (See table 6.1.) NBC, which provided the least amount of the 2000 campaign coverage among the three largest networks, took in the most political advertising revenue (Alliance for Better Campaigns 2000; Taylor 2002, appendix 3) and, along with Fox, refused to televise the presidential debates. During the final three months of a tightly contested California gubernatorial race in 1998, the seven largest cities in the state on average focused one-half of 1 percent of their news coverage on the campaign (Taylor 2002, 10).

Despite the fact that television stations are required under a 1971 congressional act to offer politicians the "lowest unit charge" during election season, they in fact frequently spike advertising rates during the heat of the campaign. One way is by offering those who can afford it guaranteed "non-preemptible" rates, which means that their ad slots cannot be bumped by commercial advertisers. In actuality, most political candidates, unable to pay inflated rates, have to take their chances and go head-to-head with the likes of General Motors for limited airtime. During the fall (and the beginning of new program season), rates are four times those of the early part of the year when political contests have not yet picked up full steam (Alvarez 2002a).

With bigger war chests, incumbents tend to benefit the most from these pricing arrangements. Congress, which itself is overwhelmingly dominated

Table 6.1.   Top Media Recipients of Political Advertising, 2000

Corporation	Ad Revenue
1. NBC	$83,031,180
2. ABC	$82,429,321
3. Paramount/CBS	$68,133,713
4. Gannett	$49,605,994
5. Fox Television	$46,905,461
6. Hearst-Argyle	$42,020,558
7. A. H. Belo Corp.	$37,578,442
8. Cox Broadcasting	$28,028,160
9. Scripps	$24,528,035
10. Post-Newsweek	$24,182,071

Source: Taylor, 2002, appendix 3
Note: This accounts for only the top 75 markets

by repeat incumbents, has done virtually nothing to prevent these pricing practices. It's a system that mutually reinforces the power of corporate, media, professional consulting, and political interests and confers most of its rewards on those who engage politics from perches of great financial advantage. Over 40 percent of the money that goes into TV political ads comes not from the candidates themselves but from PACs and the parties (Taylor 2002, 7). Starting in the 2004 election cycle, a growing share started coming from independent political groups.

It has been argued (Phelps 2001) that the problem with American elections is not the amount of money spent on them per se but rather the main sources of those funds. In 1996, for example, 96 percent of Americans made no direct campaign contributions at all, and less than 0.25 percent gave more than $200, while each of the top Fortune 500 corporations gave no less than $500,000 to the two dominant parties during the preceding decade (Hartmann 2002, 222). The biggest fund-raiser of all time is George W. Bush, for whom 200 backers alone, called "pioneers," raised most of the $70 million in bundled contributions in the 2000 primary campaign (Powell and Cowart 2003, 230). But far more money than that might be well spent if it were dedicated to the political education of voters and not used to manipulate public opinion and policy. "It *is* a little pathetic that we spend less as a society on political debate than we do on yogurt or toothpaste" (Phelps 2001, 50; italics in original).

Similarly, it is argued that seeking to influence politicians is not necessarily corrupt. The problem is that only a narrow stratum of individuals and organized interests, backed by what is essentially bribe money, has access to political leaders and the process for putting them into power.[3] Financial persuasion overwhelms reasoned public discourse, debate, and collective interests in order to protect corporate privilege (Phelps 2001)—what Ferguson (1995) calls an "investment theory" of politics. To ensure the best return on this investment, the most effective technique is for trade association companies or executives within a firm, together with their relatives, to "bundle" their individual contributions, so as to sidetrack Federal Election Commission (FEC) imposed restrictions on corporate contributions to candidates (Weinberg 2001).

Exposure of the corrupt practices and political influence peddling by the Enron corporation revealed its financial links to over 250 legislators in both major parties over a twelve-year period. The scandal extended to bribery charges against the company in several other countries where it operated with the aid of its high-level political connections in the federal government. As of mid-2004, only the company treasurer had been convicted of corruption, but there was little fallout for the members of Congress and Presidents Clinton and Bush, who took millions in financial contributions from the company before it filed for bankruptcy. Enron was the largest corporate energy contributor in the 2000 election. Apart from possibly influencing what turned out to be largely ineffective campaign finance reform, the exposé failed to generate a national debate about the failings of the neoliberal capitalist political economy and its impact on the governing system.

CORPORATE WELFARE: PACS AND LOBBYISTS IN POLITICS

Since time immemorial, monied interests have slipped financial and other incentives to rulers as a way of maintaining or purchasing favorable positions in society. It may seem rhetorical to ask, but is there any serious reason to think that this system of currying protection and privilege has changed in modern democratic polities? Although explicit interest group bribes to or votes by legislators for laws or administrative acts in which either party has a direct financial stake are generally illegal and are occasionally exposed in anticorruption investigations, there is nothing that otherwise keeps officials from supporting legislation on behalf of favored clients (or their own trust accounts) in public and private life. Powerful stakeholders and interest groups need not use bribes to secure legislative favors, however, because their lobbyists normally work more indirectly through communication with executive branch officials and key congressional committees. They typically seek out those legislators who usually vote along lines that suit their mutual interests and who are not at all hard to identify. Large corporate interests and their lobbyists can wield influence over the political process in a number of ways.

Along with the slick brochures, expert testimony, and technical reports, corporate lobbyists still offer the succulent campaign contributions, the "volunteer" campaign workers, the fat lecture fees, the stock awards and insider stock market tips, the easy-term loans, the high-paying corporate directorship upon retirement from office, the lavish parties and accommodating female escorts, the prepaid vacation jaunts, the luxury hotels and private jets, the free housing and meals, and the many other hustling enticements of money. (Parenti 1995, 207–8)

Mark Hanna once said, "There are two things you need for success in politics. Money . . . and I can't think of the other" (cited in M. Green 2002b, 1). Tip O'Neill, former Speaker of the House, who, as a longtime veteran of political life, was in a position of knowing, commented (echoing others before him) that money is "the mother's milk of politics" (Living on Earth 1997)[4]— but he should have specified lobbyists' money. Money in politics is nothing new, but the scale of financial support from large corporations to grease the political wheels of governance and its penetration into every nook and cranny of public offices is unprecedented. Rational, sustainable, and democratic policymaking cannot occur when special interests are writing the legislation and the legislative agenda. The Enron scandal is emblematic of political corruption, but it is only the tip of the iceberg. George W. Bush's provision of huge tax breaks to the wealthiest 2 percent of the population, who provided millions in return as campaign financial contributions, reveals rather conspicuously how the quid pro quo works in contemporary U.S. politics.

To be sure, patronage and pork barrel have been part of the American (and other countries') political culture even before the formation of formal state systems. The overwhelming share of patronage that goes to private interests and lobbyists is entirely legal, even if it is often indiscreet—from prestigious ambassadorial appointments to the 938 sleepovers at the Clinton-era White House Lincoln bedroom.[5] Table 6.2 indicates that many of the choice ambassadorial postings are little more than rewards for hefty political donations. Of those newly awarded ambassadorial appointments following the 2000 election, almost all their financial contributions had been given to the Bush campaign or to other Republicans. None of the appointed ambassadors had given any significant amount of money to Democrats; most gave nothing to the defeated party. Bush's most successful fund-raisers, including the top three, were all given ambassadorial positions. Tom Ridge, who was made secretary of homeland security, had raised more than $250,000 (Oppel 2003, A17). The system of rewarding donors with ambassadorships and other plums, however, did not originate in the new century. Franklin Roosevelt and presidents since made this a standard political practice.

The usual conception of professional lobbyist does not capture the full extent to which individuals in or with access to high-level policymaking work

Table 6.2.   What Donors Get: Republican Donors as Noncareer Diplomats, Post-2000 Election

Donor	Amount Donated (1999–2000)	Ambassadorial Posting
J. Thomas Schieffer	$2,000	Australia
W. L. Lyons Brown	$37,450	Austria
Richard Blankenship	$32,000	Bahamas
Stephen Brauer	$13,830	Belgium
Russell Freeman	$3,750	Belize
Clark Randt Jr.	$24,000	China
John Danilovich	$21,000	Costa Rica
Craig Stapelton	$61,500	Czech Republic
Stuart Bernstein	$182,600	Denmark
Hans Hertell	$23,000	Dominican Republic
Bonnie McElveen-Hunter	$107,750	Finland
Howard Leach	$399,359	France
Daniel Coats	$3,500	Germany
Nancy Brinker	$125,000	Hungary
Robert Blackwell	$1,000	India
Richard J. Egan	$480,100	Ireland
Mel Sembler	$127,600	Italy
Sue Cobb	$139,250	Jamaica
Howard Baker	$20,250	Japan
Denis Coleman	$105,000	Luxembourg
Anthony Gioia	$36,411	Malta
John Price	$585,181	Mauritius
Margaret Tutwiler	$3,200	Morocco
Clifford Sobel	$299,700	Netherlands
Charles J. Swindells	$42,000	New Zealand
John Ong	$181,735	Norway
John Palmer	$166,850	Portugal
Robert W. Jordan	$2,500	Saudi Arabia
Frank Lavin	$4,500	Singapore
Ronald Weiser	$42,250	Slovak Republic
George Argyros	$134,000	Spain
Charles Heimbold Jr.	$365,200	Sweden
Mercer Reynolds	$456,173	Switzerland
Robert Royall	$30,000	Tanzania
William S. Farish	$142,875	United Kingdom
Martin Silverstein	$37,325	Uruguay

Source: Adapted from Kitfield 2001, 2660–61

on behalf of corporate interests. In recent decades, presidential cabinets, for example, increasingly have been drawn from the Fortune 500 business sector, which has raised innumerable concerns about conflict of interest. The younger Bush cabinet is packed with direct or indirect representatives of the telecommunications, electronics, high-tech, airline, aerospace, pharmaceutical, food, chemicals, automobile, finance, tobacco, oil, energy, and other major industries. This begs the question about how policymakers with close ties to particular industries (or corporations in general) can be expected to be neutral in regulating them.

First and foremost among the corporate interests represented in the G. W. Bush executive branch is the oil industry. Bush himself was an oilman, though not a successful one, whose company was eventually bought out by Harken Energy (on which he had a board membership). His vice president, Dick Cheney, after leaving the position of defense secretary under the elder Bush, was CEO of Halliburton, the world's biggest oil field services corporation. Halliburton, through its European subsidiaries, sold spare parts to Iraq's oil industry, despite UN sanctions during the 1990s (Center for Responsive Politics 2001). Cheney cashed out of Halliburton in 2000 with $36 million in salary, bonuses, and benefits to join the Bush administration. The following year Halliburton got a $140 million contract from Saudi Arabia to develop an oil field, and one of its subsidiaries shared a $40 million Saudi contract to build an ethylene plant. Cheney continued to receive deferred compensation from Halliburton, in 2003 amounting to $178,437, almost as much as his vice president's salary of $198,600 (Mulvihill, Myers, and Wells 2001; White House 2004).

The privatization of government contracting enables corporate friends and major contributors to the White House and other people in high office to get special treatment when lucrative projects are in the offing. As private entities, corporations are not subject to Freedom of Information Act inquiries or many other investigations that public institutions, such as the Army Corps of Engineers, would be required to entertain. With Cheney's support, Halliburton was given the principal contracts for reconstructing the oil industry in Iraq following the U.S. invasion. Other oil interest representatives in the executive branch include commerce secretary Donald Evans, who was chair of a Denver-based oil and gas company, Tom Brown Inc., and sat on the board of TMBR/Sharp Drilling, an oil and gas drilling operation. Gale Norton, the interior secretary and a lawyer, had represented Delta Petroleum, and Christine Whitman, EPA secretary, held corporate shares in five oil companies and owned significant oil-producing property in Texas. Condoleezza Rice, national security advisor, sat on the board of Chevron, which (now merged with Texaco) does extensive business in Saudi Arabia (Center for Responsive Politics 2002).

Chemical, pharmaceutical, high-tech, and other industries are also well represented in the Bush cabinet. Ann Veneman, Bush's agriculture secretary, served on the board of directors of Calgene Inc., which produced the first genetically engineered food item, the Flavr Savr tomato, before it was bought out by Monsanto in 1997. Donald Rumsfeld, defense secretary, had been CEO of the pharmaceutical company, G. D. Searle (now Pharmacia) and was also CEO of General Instruments (now Motorola), a telecommunications corporation. Paul O'Neill, treasury secretary (until fired in 2002), was chair and CEO of Alcoa, the world's largest aluminum manufacturer. Mitch Daniels Jr., director of the Office of Management and Budget, was a senior vice president for the drug company Eli Lilly (Center for Responsive Politics 2002).

Oil and defense companies with stakes in the Middle East are tightly interlocked with the Bush administration. Among the top oil industry contributors to Bush and the Republican Party during the 2000 election were Chevron ($769,588), Texaco ($353,118), Unocal ($42,600), Halliburton ($383,947), Marathon Oil ($161,500), and Amerada Hess ($165,400). When Bush was still governor of Texas, a close political associate, Kay Bailey Hutchison (R-TX), sponsored a Senate bill in 1999 that cancelled $66 million in royalty payments owed to the federal government by the oil industry. Four oil companies alone—Exxon, Chevron, Atlantic Richfield, and BP Amoco—had contributed $2.9 million in PAC and soft money during the previous election cycle. In the defense sector, major contributors to the 2000 Bush and Republican campaigns included TRW Inc. ($378,450), SAIC ($313,000), and the Carlyle Group ($108,560) (M. Green 2002b, 225; Mulvihill, Myers, and Wells 2001).

These high-powered corporate linkages to the inner circles of political power represent only a slice of the political-industrial complex (PIC). During the 1995–1996 election cycle, businesses and their executives already accounted for 96 percent of Republican and 87 percent of Democratic soft money ($263.5 million total) contributions (with another 11 percent to Democrats coming from organized labor) (Johnson 2001, 184). One New York City ZIP code alone accounted for more in contributions to congressional candidates that year than any of twenty-four individual states (Donnelly, Fine, and Miller 2001, 7). The epicenter of soft-money contributions has been Washington, D.C., especially K Street, the favorite address for 17,000 lobbyists and the nation's biggest PACs. And within the business world, the sector making the largest campaign contributions and that spends the most on lobbying is finance, insurance, and real estate, which is also the most profitable (Phillips 2002a).

Hardly a day goes by inside the Beltway when a trade association, corporation, political action committee, or other lobbying or interest group is not organizing a fund-raising breakfast or dinner for members of Congress at rates often well beyond $1,000 a plate. It starts almost the day that the new member of the House, Senate, or Oval Office takes her/his seat. The money comes in part from local constituents but in larger amounts from big national or international donors. People running for or wishing to remain in national office spend more time fund-raising than for any other single political activity. One politician says candidates don't "run" but rather "fund-raise for office" (M. Green 2002b, 105). The money chase structures the entire system of governance and legislative behavior.[6] As payback to the corporate PACs that fund U.S. elections, the federal government doles out an estimated $50 billion annually in various private sector subsidies (M. Green 2002b, 162).

That is exactly as it should be, says direct-mail marketing firm executive David Himes. In his view, "The people who vote you into office should be the people who give you most of the money to pay for the campaign. The more true this is, the greater the chances of winning the election" (Himes 1995, 64). That's not an original sentiment. John Jay, one of the country's founders, president of the Continental Congress, and the first chief justice of the U.S. Supreme Court, stated it even more frankly: "The people who own the country ought to govern it." Most Americans are not unaware of the control of the political-industrial complex. The *New York Times* reported in 1997 that 75 percent of Americans believed that "public officials make or change policy decisions as a result of money they receive from major contributors" (cited in Schlesinger, ca. 1997).

American electoral victories are big investments and highly prized commodities. Races for House and Senate seats in 1996 cost $840 million, and spending in all federal, state, and local elections that year was $2.7 billion. The average Senate campaign absorbed $4.5 million ($4.7 million for the winners), which means that each senator had to generate $14,000 in contributions per week over the six-year term. House members, the winners spending an average of $673,000, had to raise an average of over $5,000 per week (*Economist* 1997; Johnson 2001, 170; Schlesinger, ca. 1997) and also have to run for office three times as frequently as their Senate counterparts.

In the 2000 election cycle, 20 percent of congressional campaign financing came from families with $500,000 or more income; 46 percent came from families with $250,000 or more income, and 81 percent came from families with $100,000 or more income. According to one finding, families with less than $50,000, about half of all families in the United States, contributed 5 percent; according to another, 95 percent came from just 1 percent of the population (Phillips 2002b, 328; Weinberg 2001). The 340,000 millionaires in the United States, representing about one-hundredth of 1 percent of the population, is a sufficient donor pool to finance any and all elections. The higher the cost of elections, the greater the influence of the high-roller interests that can purchase access to policymakers. Multibillion-dollar election cycles are designed for a plutocratic system of decision making. No successful challenger for a House seat in 2000 spent less than $850,000 to win. And once in office, those candidates who might want to support issues that concern ordinary voters soon discover, according to former labor secretary Robert Reich, that it "is difficult to represent the little fellow when the big fellow pays the tab" (cited in M. Green 2002a, 18). In Canada, too, money is increasingly becoming an issue in political campaigns. In June 2002, amidst frequent charges of corporate payoffs to his government, Canada's prime minister, Jean Chrétien, was forced to announce changes that would require fuller disclosure of sources and amounts of contributions to his cabinet members.

Money effectively has become the currency of speech. Large corporate-based PACs share with the media a love for the private bankrolling of politics, because it enables concentrated financial power to exercise direct electoral management and elections to have money multiplier effects.[7] In the 1995–1996 election cycle, PACs raised $437.4 million for various office seekers, including $203.9 million to House and Senate candidates (out of $790.5 million raised), plus $10.6 million more in independent expenditures for and against candidates, according to Common Cause and the Federal Election Commission. The total congressional and presidential campaign expenditures for that year was $2,131.2 million,[8] of which the presidential campaign expenditures amounted to $471.6 million. Party hard and soft money amounted to $894.3 million (Common Cause 1999; Federal Election Commission 1997). By the 2000 election, the party hard/soft coffers reached well over $1.2 billion, an increase of over 34 percent in just four years (Opensecrets 2001).[9] Campaign spending in all federal elections in 2004 had already surpassed the previous election cycle before the party national conventions were over and was expected to more than double the 2000 amount. If workers' wages increased at that level, poverty in the United States would be almost nonexistent within a decade.

In the 1996 poll, the top ten donors in soft-money contributions alone contributed more than $14.2 million to congressional campaigns (Center for Responsive Politics 1997).[10] Even in state House and Senate elections, a large campaign war chest is critical for success. In 1998, state House campaigns cost an estimated $1.4 billion. The average state Senate race cost $75,000 ($600,000 in California and $400,000 in Texas). The average state House race cost $30,000, but as much as $200,000 in some cases (Wayne 2000, A1, A21). With unrelenting commodification, neoliberalism leaves no stone unturned.

CAN CAMPAIGN FINANCE BE REFORMED?

A 1979 change in the law opened the way to soft-money contributions, a mechanism created to bypass federal restrictions on campaign financing. This form of financing allowed funding sources to spend unlimited amounts of money on campaigns as long as the money did not go directly to candidates. Soft-money spending rose from $19 million in 1980 to $80 million in 1992. By 2000, it shot up fivefold to $498 million (Rosen 2003). (See table 6.3.)

A ruse for pulling in large bundles of money from wealthy contributors was to channel it to nominally "party-building" efforts, an area exempt from federal spending restrictions. Robert Farmer, fund-raiser for the Michael Dukakis campaign in 1988, made use of this exception in the law, and his Republican rivals backing George Bush soon followed his lead. Dick Morris continued to exploit the soft-money loophole for Bill Clinton by funneling financial contributions into unregulated "issue advocacy" advertising both before and during the formal campaign season (Witcover 1999, 78–79).[11] On the supply side of the money circuit, the Health Insurance Association of America spent millions in issue advocacy ads between 1993 and 1994 to block Clinton's proposal for a national health care program.

Heavy campaign spending lifts all boats of those directly employed by the electoral process—including the biggest ships of state and corporate capital. The money-driven election is an effective means of insulating the two-party system from serious challenges by radical third parties or the collection of less mobilized, less well-financed public and private interests. The large-scale private financing system that protects the political duopoly enables corporations to maintain a disproportionate hold on political discourse and action. Membership in the duopoly requires national politicians to engage in a full-time money chase during their entire legislative tenure, allowing corporate industry lobbyists and wealthy donors proprietary access to politicians and to

Table 6.3.   Federal Campaign Sources, 1996 and 2000 Funding Cycles

	1996	2000
Campaign donations below $200	$734 million	$550 million
Large individual donors	$597 million	$912 million
Soft-money contributions	$262 million	$498 million
PAC funding	$243 million	$267 million
Public funding	$211 million	$238 million
Candidate's personal funds	$161 million	$205 million
Other	$200 million	$57 million
Total	$2.4 billion	$2.7 billion

Source: Phillips 2002b, 324

legislative and administrative policy. Although the interests of ordinary people are not completely ignored, under a conservative agenda that has largely controlled federal politics since the Nixon era, they have become increasingly marginalized. Income for workers in the United States has declined almost steadily since the early 1970s. In terms of income disparities, the United States is the most class stratified among the leading industrial states.

A genuinely democratic transformation of American politics requires major changes in many areas, including the institution of a system favoring multiple political parties; proportional representation in federal and state legislatures; an instant runoff voting procedure (discussed in chapter 3, note 5), as adopted for city elections in San Francisco and Berkeley, California; mandatory full public financing of federal and state elections; and free television airtime for candidate and party addresses and political debates. Many see the Democrats and Republicans as almost undifferentiated in political structure and orientation, particularly with respect to their linkages to and dependence upon private corporations, and a financing system that is extremely biased toward those two parties. This was a consistent theme of Ralph Nader, whose Green Party presidential candidacy in the 2000 election and reappearance as an independent in 2004 attracted a significant protest vote in a "survival of the fittest," winner-take-all election system (Hill 2002, 148). Proportional representation in Congress, on the other hand, the method of vote counting used in a number of democratic countries, would have made the Green Party's 2000 electoral participation meaningful, instead of provoking Democrats' hostility toward Nader for "spoiling" Al Gore's opportunity for victory.

The United States is exceptional among leading industrial states in having only two viable parties that supposedly cover the range of citizens' political orientations. European democracies offer more coherent ideological and political choices to voters, even when there are only two or three major parties. In those democracies, the smaller parties are potential coalition partners, which means that voters identifying with the minor parties will have their voices represented in government instead of being ignored, as they generally are in the United States. Table 6.4 lists alternative, mostly quite obscure, parties in the United States, both those that have put forward or endorsed candidates for political office and those that have not. The vast majority of Americans have not heard of any of these alternative parties, save for one or two that have seriously contested national elections in recent years. What is notable about the list is that it covers a much fuller spectrum of political ideas in the United States—from the far right to social democrats, communists, and anarchists on the left—than do the two dominant parties, which, if anything, have only converged ideologically in the last twenty-five years or so.

Table 6.4.   Third Parties in the United States

Parties with political candidates

America First Party	Natural Law Party
American Heritage Party	New Party
American Independent Party	New Union Party
American Nazi Party	Peace & Freedom Party
American Reform Party	Prohibition Party
Communist Party USA	Reform Party
Constitution Party	The Revolution
Family Values Party	Socialist Party USA
Freedom Socialist Party	Socialist Action
Grassroots Party	Socialist Equality Party
Green Party of the United States (Green Party)	Socialist Labor Party
The Greens/Green Party USA (G/GPUSA)	Socialist Workers Party
Independence Party	Southern Independence Party
Independent American Party	Southern Party
Labor Party	U.S. Pacifist Party
Libertarian Party	We the People Party
Light Party	Workers World Party

Parties that have not yet fielded or endorsed political candidates

American Falangist Party	Pansexual Peace Party
Constitutional Action Party	Pot Party
Constitutionalist Party	Progressive Labor Party
Democratic Socialists of America	Revolutionary Communist Party USA
Knights Party	The Third Party
Libertarian National Socialist Green Party	Workers Party, USA
Multicapitalist Party	World Socialist Party of the USA

Source: "Directory of U.S. Political Parties." Online at www.politics1.com/parties.htm

Little has been done to challenge the lock on the political system by the Democrats and Republicans. Instead, most of the attention about reforming the system has been focused on the issue of campaign spending, a conspicuous spigot of political corruption, and the need for changes in campaign financing. In 1906, President Theodore Roosevelt declared, "I again recommend a law prohibiting all corporations from contributing to the campaign expenses of any party. . . . Let individuals contribute as they desire; but let us prohibit in effective fashion all corporations from making contributions for any political purpose, directly or indirectly" (cited in Hartmann 2002, 131). The following year, bank and corporate financing of elections was banned under the Tillman Act, and the law still remains on the books. Adequate enforcement mechanisms have never been established, however. In 1947, Congress extended the ban on corporate campaign contributions to labor unions. Both corporations and organized labor have gotten around the ban by directing their contributions to the soft-money category of campaign funding.

Table 6.5. Campaign Contributions ($1,000 or More) by the Wealthiest Political Donors, 1999–2000

Contribution Category	Number	Amount
$1,000–$9,999	325,747	$ 619,040,837
$10,000 plus	14,888	$ 444,617,244
$100,000 plus	719	$ 151,642,813
$1 million plus	6	$ 7,770,700
Total	341,360	$1,223,071,594

Source: Adapted from Phillips 2002b, 328

Prevented from giving directly to candidates, the political action committee was formed as the principal mechanism to channel money indirectly to campaigns. The strength of PACs is not only in their own contributions to candidates and parties, which Republicans were the first to fully exploit, but in their coordinated use in support of politicians, political parties, and government administrative policies. (See tables 6.5, 6.6, and 6.7.) One of the most influential of the corporate PACs over the years has been the Business Industry Political Action Committee (BIPAC), to which a large majority of corporate PACs have had an affiliation (Eismeier and Pollock 1988, 81–82). In its own words, BIPAC "identifies and supports pro-business candidates who have demonstrated the skill and leadership necessary to fuel a pro-business Congress" (BIPAC 2004). Over time, corporate PAC money and the contributions from the wealthy elite have mastered political parties with their influence in the electoral process, starting with the "seed money" that corporations give to office seekers to test their candidate viability.

How important is PAC money? In 1974, there were 608 registered PACs; by the end of 2000, there were 3,907, 76 percent of which were organized, mostly corporate, interest groups. PACs gave $246.7 million to all federal candidates in 2000 and $28.7 million to political parties. Close to 80 percent of financial contributions to congressional candidates come from PACs, from individual contributions of $200 or more, or from the coffers of wealthy candidates themselves (Congressional Research Service Report for Congress, 2001).

Although corporate financing of elections is often bracketed with campaign contributions from unions, the comparison is very misleading. Businesses provided half of all the congressional contributions (eleven times greater than those coming from labor unions). Corporate profits are about 500 times greater than the combined income of all labor unions and are expanding at an accelerating rate (Center for Responsive Politics 2001; Parenti 1995, 216; Weissman 2000). Even after the 2002 campaign finance reform efforts in Congress, one New York politician ruefully commented that "[Corporate]

Table 6.6. $1,000 Donors and Their Political Recipients, 2000 Campaign

Candidate	Individual Contributions	Amount of Money from $1000 Donors	Percentage from $1,000 Donors
Republican			
Bush	$92.3 M.	$59.3 M.	64%
McCain	$28.1 M.	$10.1 M.	36%
Keyes	$8.2 M.	$0.5 M.	6%
Bauer	$7.9 M.	$1.4 M.	18%
Forbes	$5.8 M.	$1.8 M.	31%
Dole, E.	$5.0 M.	$3.0 M.	60%
Quayle	$4.1 M.	$1.5 M.	37%
Alexander	$2.3 M.	$2.0 M.	87%
Hatch	$2.1 M.	$1.1 M.	52%
Smith	$1.5 M.	$0.08 M.	5%
Democratic			
Gore	$33.9 M.	$19.3 M.	57%
Bradley	$29.3 M.	$18.4 M.	63%
Total	$220.6 M*	$118.5 M*	54%*

*Rounded
Source: Corrado 2000b

PACs are more alive than ever" (Live Online 2002). Money, like water, will always find an outlet. (See table 6.8.)

An initiative in the U.S. House and Senate to reform the election campaign finance system, namely the McCain-Feingold bill in the upper chamber and the Shays-Meehan bill in the lower chamber, resulted in a compromised version of the two that passed into law in 2002 (as the "Bipartisan Campaign Reform Act"), following the Enron political influence–peddling scandal.[12] An amendment offered by Senator Paul Wellstone (D-MN), which would have enabled states to have publicly financed campaigns for congressional elections, got only thirty-six votes (Forsberg 2001, 5). The intent of the bill that passed was to curtail the influence of unregulated (and indirect) soft money going to national parties and their committees, while raising limits on individual and corporate (direct) hard money that goes to or advocates for candidates. Critics find it difficult to believe that the political process could be seriously reformed in this way, because to do so would restrict the privileged position of corporate money to control the selection and behavior of the country's political representatives. Opposition to McCain-Feingold came from a disparate group: among them were the National Right to Life Committee, the American Civil Liberties Union, the National Rifle Association, the Republican National Committee, and the AFL-CIO.

Table 6.7. Top Ten Soft-Money Contributors from U.S. Corporate Subsidiaries, 1995–1996 Campaign Cycle

Source of Funds	Main Business	Base	Amount
1. Joseph E. Seagram	Alcoholic Bev. and Media	Canada	$1,938,845
2. News Corp.	Media	Australia	$674,500
3. Brown & Williamson	Tobacco & Tobacco products	United Kingdom	$642,500
4. Glazo Wellcome	Pharmaceutical	United Kingdom	$510,000
5. CS First Boston Corp.	Banking and Finance	Switzerland	$296,000
6. BP America	Petroleum	United Kingdom	$274,579
7. Sony Corp. of America	Electronics and Media	Japan	$207,319
8. Toyota Motor Sales	Automobile	Japan	$ 188,475
9. Citgo Petroleum	Petroleum	Venezuela	$188,450
10. Zeneca, Inc.	Pharmaceutical	United Kingdom	$184,700

Source: Adapted from Schlesinger, ca. 1997

Table 6.8.   Top 20 PAC Contributors, 1999–2000 Election Cycle

Political Action Committee	Amount of Contrib. ($)	Going to Dem. Cand. (%)	Going to Rep. Cand. (%)
National Assoc. of Realtors	3,423,441	41	59
Assoc. of Trial Lawyers of America	2,661,000	86	13*
American Federation of State, County, and Municipal Employees	2,590,074	95	5
Teamsters Union	2,565,495	93	7
National Auto Dealers Assoc.	2,498,700	32	68
International Brotherhood of Electrical Workers	2,470,125	96	4
Laborers Union	2,255,900	90	9*
Machinists/Aerospace Workers Union	2,188,138	99	1
United Auto Workers	2,155,050	99	1
American Medical Assoc.	2,028,354	48	52
Service Employees International Union	1,871,774	89	11
National Beer Wholesalers Assoc.	1,871,500	21	79
Carpenters & Joiners Union	1,869,920	84	15*
National Assoc. of Home Builders	1,824,999	36	64
United Parcel Service	1,755,065	35	65
United Food & Commercial Workers Union	1,743,652	97	2*
National Education Association	1,717,125	95	5
Verizon Communications	1,677,617	33	67
American Bankers Assoc.	1,657,615	35	64*
American Federation of Teachers	1,599,555	98	2

*Percentage rounded
Source: Wayne 2003, 107

Prior to the 2002 reform legislation, one professor of government commented that even if a campaign finance bill were passed, "The money is going to squirt out somewhere" and that "All the reform is doing is rechanneling where the flow is" (cited in Lynch 2002, E1). And as might be expected, the majority (67 percent) of political consultants think campaign finance reform is not a good idea (Pew Research Center 1998). Before the reform act could take effect, the two parties broke records in 2002 for soft-money fundraising, more than doubling the amount of the previous midterm election (1998) and even surpassing the 2000 presidential election by 20 percent. Even preparations for a war in Iraq did not deter the president from raising millions on the campaign circuit for Republican candidates in the congressional election that year (Oppel 2002, A1, A19).

The campaign finance reform bill only impacts the unregulated, so-called soft-money portion; the big money in the 2000 election still came from hard-money contributors (Donnelly and Fine [preface] in Cohen and Rogers 2001, xiii). Just months after the bill's passage, the antireform FEC already had taken initiatives to gut it, interpreting its language narrowly so as to create major loopholes for candidates and parties to continue the money chase with few constraints. By August 2002, soft money was flowing into the coffers of both major parties, especially the Republicans. The Republican National Committee had a 12 percent increase in soft-money contributions over the 1999–2000 election cycle, the National Republican Congressional Committee had a 46 percent increase, and the National Republican Senatorial Committee had a 60 percent increase. The Democratic National Committee and Democratic Congressional Campaign Committee experienced declines, but the Democratic Senatorial Campaign Committee had a 72 percent increase (Common Cause 2002). By May 2003, a federal panel of judges had struck down major portions of the McCain-Feingold bill, which counseled the two major parties to continue raising massive soft-money war chests for upcoming campaigns (Tucker and Eilperin 2003, A1). In December 2003, however, the Supreme Court ruled in a 5-4 decision in favor of key parts of the law.

Even if contributions to the national parties slowed down after the new provisions on soft-money restrictions went into effect (November 6, 2002), state and local parties, which are allowed to raise unlimited soft money for party-focused advertising, stood poised to become a much larger destination of campaign financing.[13] Federal officeholders can engage in state and local soft-money fund-raising, provided they don't *ask* for the money, and a new wave of advocacy and interest groups predictably surfaced to make up for the shortfall in federal soft-money fund-raising. This simply means an altered money-flow pattern from state to national parties instead of, traditionally, the reverse. Moreover, national parties can and did use independent committees for raising unlimited and undisclosed soft money, as long as they were created before November 6, 2002 (Tompkins County Green Party 2003). In one of several challenges to the campaign reform act, the FEC in 2002 opened the door for state parties to use soft money in attacks on or support for federal candidates. The commission also approved conditions under which state and federal parties can spend unlimited soft-money contributions for political activity over the Internet, direct mail, phone banks, and other media (Common Cause 2002; Justice 2003, A25). The precise legal restrictions of paid advertising used in directly advocating or attacking candidates are still open to court determination.

Already, issue advertising on television has begun to shift from networks to local channels. Earlier "reforms" merely changed the strategies for soliciting funding, without changing the highly stratified system of funding itself. This, in fact, has led to dramatic increases in the amount of corporate money invested in electoral outcomes. Federal matching funds for candidates has mirrored this elitist pattern of campaign financing in that those who have the wealthiest backers get the most in government assistance, and those with even greater financial assets can waive federal funds altogether.

Under the 2002 McCain-Feingold legislation, individuals are allowed to contribute $2,000 in hard money to each of two candidates per year (previously, the limit was $1,000 per candidate), $5,000 to a political action committee (as long as the money is not earmarked to the same candidates), and $25,000 (previously $20,000) to a political party per year—or an aggregate of up to $95,000 to federal, state, and local candidates and parties per two-year election cycle and periodically indexed for inflation (*American Prospect* 2002). Some have argued that the principal beneficiaries of restricting soft-money contributions are incumbent politicians. Where most observers agree is that with the presumed elimination of soft money under McCain-Feingold, the most immediate winners are Republicans, whose hard-money contributions were 70 percent higher than the Democrats in the 2000 election, whereas Democrats had previously enjoyed an advantage, though a smaller one, in the soft-money category (Engel 2002, 15). The Bush and Republican 2000 presidential campaign outspent Gore and the Democratic Party, 58.6 percent to 41.4 percent and 56.4 percent to 43.6 percent, respectively (Holman and McLoughlin 2002, 41). The losers, déjà vu, are ordinary citizens, who are largely reduced to spectators of the election process, save the final day. With heavier dependence on hard-money contributions, federal pay-per-view candidates are expected to spend even more time on the fund-raising trail, driving the electoral system as a whole deeper into the captivity of wealthy elites and transnational corporate interests. For those who feel no hesitation gliding between the upper tiers of the government and business worlds, this may present no burden. George W. Bush was off and running under the new rules, raising $259 million at the conclusion of the primaries. And for the first time, the early front-running presidential primary contenders on the Democratic side, Howard Dean and John Kerry, both decided in late 2003 to forego federal matching funds, which would have imposed a $45 million primary spending cap, in an effort to try to close the huge fund-raising gap between themselves and Bush. At the time of the Democratic Party convention, the nominee Kerry had already raised $233.5 million (Getter 2004, A9; Justice 2004).

Differences between the parties tend to divide along the principles of polity versus property. Republicans, who generally oppose restrictions on campaign spending, see campaign financing as a free speech issue. Others, mainly liberal Democrats, contend that financing is less an issue of speech and more an assertion of property rights, the latter of which interferes with the principle of one person one vote. The broadcast industry, including the National Association of Broadcasters, a regular victor in the election spectacle, successfully lobbied to eliminate a key provision of the final finance reform bill that would have required radio and television stations to offer reduced rates for a particular form of public speech, political advertising. In the midterm 2002 election, advertising revenues by mid-October were already $250,000 above the 2000 campaign year, promising a blockbuster year for the television industry and their best political clients. South Dakota, a state of 775,000 people (fifth smallest in the country) but locked in a tight Senate race that could tip the balance to either party nationally, led the nation in the number of political commercials (Alvarez 2002a). Given this windfall, one would expect South Dakota's local television stations to be strong advocates for maintaining the status quo on campaign financing.

The impact of the Supreme Court's decision in *Buckley v. Valeo* (1976), which drew an equation of money with free speech, is that there is little likelihood that in the near future the legal system will permit serious controls on campaign spending, even if particular types of expenditures are constrained. Lower courts have thrown out limits on campaign contributions in several states. By 1982, *Buckley v. Valeo*, even in its limited and inadequate attempt to impose campaign finance reform, ended up inspiring a wave of special interest PACs. That year, 3,149 of them, dominated by the corporate sector, contributed $240 million to various political campaigns (*New Internationalist* 1985). It is an Orwellian twist that the First Amendment, which was written to defend citizens in the new republic against the historic abuses of the British state, would be ultimately employed to protect the interests of the most powerful elements, corporate "persons," in the modern U.S. state. Given the Court's history of interpreting the Bill of Rights and other constitutional amendments largely in favor of private corporations and the wealthy (Hartmann 2002), it would have been truly revolutionary for the supreme judicial body to have subordinated the status of the propertied classes to the governance of the majority interest. The Declaration of Independence declared that governments derive "their just powers from the consent of the governed," not the "monied corporations" of which Thomas Jefferson, *supra*, spoke.

REVOLVING DOORS

Ignoring or downplaying the financial nexus, it is easy to see why Farrell, Mancini, Scammell, and others regard professionalism as the driving force in modern politics. But it is actually the money game of politics, not merely professionalism, that fuels professionalization, industrialization, and corporate domination. More than controlling campaign spending, *Buckley v. Valeo* was a major step toward the commercialization of political speech, and indeed the First Amendment. Even with its restraints on the amount of money that can be given by individual and PAC contributors, there is no lid on the total amount of money that a candidate or the candidate's backers can ultimately spend on a primary or election. In financial contributions, Senate Republicans were clearly favored over Senate Democrats, 61 percent to 31 percent in the 2000 election (Nelson 2002, 32). The sea of dollars during each election cycle opens the gates for the entry of the campaign professionals and managers, but the real owners of the political system, per Chief Justice John Jay's infamous assertion in favor of paramount rights accruing to the rich, are the corporate elite.

At least three-fourths of open-seat contests and two-thirds of incumbents in the House employ professional consultants, while mainly for lack of money, only 16.5 percent of challengers use them (Thurber 1998), a rate almost certainly increased by both groups since the late 1990s. Moreover, for many political consultants, such as President Clinton's pollster, Stanley Greenberg, advertising, marketing, polling, and public relations are seasonal occupations that share revolving doors between political and corporate clients.[14] The accounts of George Bush's pollster, Jan van Lohuizen, include Wal-Mart, Qwest, Anheuser-Busch, and Microsoft. Conducting a poll on behalf of a Microsoft advocacy group in 2001, van Lohuizen found data to support dropping the government's antitrust lawsuit against Microsoft (J. Green 2002). Jimmy Carter's pollster, Patrick Caddell, did public relations for Mobil Oil. Peter Hart, pollster for Walter Mondale's 1984 presidential campaign, also worked for Chrysler, Kodak, American Airlines, and Time Warner. As one regular political commentator notes, "The pollsters, strategists and media experts who shape political campaigns are playing an increasingly prominent role in campaigns for nonpolitical clients, helping corporations, trade associations and advocacy groups sway public opinion and win support on Capitol Hill" (Barnes 1995, 1330). Of the fifteen most expensive U.S. Senate campaigns in 1994, almost three-quarters of the expenses went to political consultants (Heclo 2000, 26), giving some illustration of the harmony of interests between big money and the electioneering industry.

There are great incentives and rewards that go to politicians and other government officials who play to the interests of corporations and their lobbyists and vice versa. In exchange for servicing those interests, politicians can generally rely on significant campaign contributions, which, in turn, buys entry for lobbyists to the offices of those officeholders. Beyond that, lobbyists, of which there are 17,000 in Washington, D.C., alone, provide most of the information that politicians and government technocrats use in policymaking. Indeed, they and their law firms are frequently directly involved in the writ-

ing of legislation, speeches, and press stories on behalf of their political patrons and generally can count on having the ears of politicians at their disposal. Moreover, lobbyists offer public officials alluring possibilities of a lucrative life after government.

Richard Wiley, who ran the FCC during the Ford administration, established a law and lobbying firm in 1983—now the largest communications
practice in the country—with at least six of his partners having previously
worked at the commission (Gallavan, Rebholz, and Sanderson 2000, 35). His
clients have included CBS, Gannett (the largest newspaper chain in the
United States), and A. H. Belo (a Texas-based media company with twenty-
seven TV and cable stations and ten newspapers). Roger Ailes, former strategist for the elder George Bush and also former executive producer for the ul-
traconservative talk show of Rush Limbaugh, was made president of Fox
News. Wearing two hats, Ailes advised the younger Bush administration on
how to handle the post–September 11 political situation, which provoked a
public controversy. The news network acts as a semiofficial voice of establishment conservatives, making it a kind of special interest public relations
group.

Fox News became the news itself after its 2000 election night analyst, John
Ellis, was the first to call the Florida count—and the presidency—for George
W. Bush. He did so without the benefit of data from Voter News Service, the
polling consortium owned by the major news networks, which provided state-
by-state election counts to all the major news outlets until it was dissolved in
2003. The other TV news networks all quickly followed Fox's lead before re-
alizing that the call had been premature. The controversy became greatly
magnified when it came to light that Ellis is the first cousin of Bush and his
brother, Florida governor Jeb Bush, and, further, that he illegally had been
feeding both Bushes exit poll data during the evening of the election (De
Moraes 2000), an action defended by Ailes. This not only exposed Fox as a
highly partisan news network but also drew unfavorable attention to the close
connections that exist on several levels between corporate media and the narrow stratum of organized political power. Despite the controversy, Fox News
apparently did not learn any new lessons about journalistic integrity. In its
2004 coverage of the election, Fox News chief political correspondent Carl
Cameron was captured in the highly critical documentary footage of *Out-
foxed: Rupert Murdoch's War on Journalism* cozying up to George W. Bush
during an interview and revealing that his wife was actively working, along-
side the president's sister, on the Bush reelection campaign.

The Bush family and their foreign policy advisors have even more impressive connections abroad. One newspaper report uncovered (subsequently exposed in the documentary *Fahrenheit 9/11*) that the elder Bush is a senior and

highly paid advisor to a major investment bank, the Carlyle Group, based in Washington, D.C., which is well connected to the Saudi royal family and invested in U.S. defense corporations that have armed and trained the Saudi military.[15] The Carlyle Group sold its interest in BDM, a defense contractor whose subsidiaries have "multimillion-dollar contracts . . . to train and manage the Saudi National Guard and Saudi air force," to TRW. These three companies, the report found, "are all stocked with high-level Republican policy makers." The Saudi royal family contributed $1 million to the elder Bush's presidential library. For his part, George W. Bush was a director of a Carlyle subsidiary until 1994, and some of his gubernatorial appointees in Texas served on a teachers' pension fund board that voted to use $100 million of its money to invest with Carlyle (Mulvihill, Myers, and Wells 2001).

Such casual public official–corporate linkages are pervasive in the United States. Michael Parenti noted that over a six-year period in the early 1990s, congressional members took $36.5 million from banking interests and in return granted $500 billion in deregulation and bail-out benefits to that industry (Parenti 1995, 211, 223). And when politicians' terms of service end, there is a path into the future paved with money for those so inclined. This, of course, is nothing new in American or other countries' politics. Woodrow Wilson, who sometimes spoke very frankly, offered the following: "Suppose you go to Washington and try to get at your Government. You will always find that while you are politely listened to, the men really consulted are the men who have the big stake—the big bankers, the big manufacturers, and the big masters of commerce" (cited in Parenti 1995, 210). Political consultant James Carville said no less, acknowledging in his usual blunt manner that "I'm going to talk to somebody with money way before I talk to somebody with ideas" (quoted in Witcover 1999, 73).

To whom do the political parties talk? Political journalist Kevin Phillips, who identifies himself as a Republican, offered the following in his analysis of the money-for-legislation style of American politics during the 2000 political campaign:

> The Timber Industry spent $8 million in campaign contributions to preserve the logging road subsidy, worth $458 million—the return on their investment was 5,725%. Glazo Wellcome invested $1.2 million in campaign contributions to get a 19-month patent extension on Zantac worth $1 billion—their net return: 83,333%. The Tobacco industry spent $30 million in contributions for a tax break worth $50 billion—the return on their investment: 167,000%. For a paltry $5 million in campaign contributions, the Broadcasting Industry was able to secure free digital TV licenses, a give-away of public property worth $70 billion—that's an incredible 1,400,000% return on their investment. (Phillips 2002b, 326)

The power of corporations to secure favorable political treatment derives not only from their wealth but also from the concentrated form of power characteristic of American capitalism. A U.S. Senate study, *Structure of Corporate Concentration*, last undertaken just before the strongly pro-corporate Reagan administration took office, documented a vast array of interlocking directorates that dominate industry, commerce, and banking. Interlocking directorates in this study referred to individuals serving as directors on two or more of the largest customer, supplier, and financial institutions that nominally are in competition with one another. In the telecommunications industry, for example, directors of AT&T, IBM, Exxon, Xerox, Sperry, and Eastman Kodak at the time were all on the board of Citicorp. Directors of IBM, RCA, Sperry, Eastman Kodak, and Exxon were represented on the board of Metropolitan Life. IBM, AT&T, Xerox, and GTE were on the Bankers Trust board. AT&T, IBM, Eastman Kodak, and Exxon were directors of Continental Illinois. AT&T, IBM, RCA, and Exxon sat together on the board of Chemical New York. AT&T, IBM, and GTE were all directors on Conoco.

The most competitor interlocks at the time were between the two largest computer and telecommunications firms in the country, IBM and AT&T (Sussman 1997, 181; U.S. Senate 1980, 26). The names and specific interlocks have changed somewhat since that study was undertaken, but the degree of financial convergence has only accelerated. Interlocking directorates represent an informal structure of collusion, allowing for market coordination and a restraint on competition, a system that enjoins the political process in its grip on economic resources and the exercise of political power. Ralph Miliband argued that while the capitalist class may not govern, it most certainly rules (Miliband 1969). Were Miliband alive today to witness the number of CEOs and other wealthy elites who have captured political office in the United States, his assessment of the political directorate would probably be that they govern as well as rule.

The corporate empire employs a revolving-door system for both shuttling its executives into government and hiring ex-government officials, sometimes as board directors or executives and often as lobbyists. These practices help insulate the political-industrial complex from what otherwise could be a more transparent, democratic, and accessible political process. With a cabinet already full of revolving-door appointees, George W. Bush hired the chief lobbyist for General Motors, Andrew Card, who earlier had been the secretary of transportation under George Bush Sr., to be White House chief of staff. A Bush nominee to coordinate the government's global HIV-AIDS program, Randall Tobias, was previously the CEO of Eli Lilly, a leading pharmaceutical corporation, which, together with Tobias himself, was a major contributor to the Bush presidential campaign in 2000 (and contributed more than $1.5

million to Republican campaigns in 2002). Critics of the appointment said that Tobias's background would put him at odds with the need of poor Third World countries to buy cheap generic drugs to combat the disease (Beattie 2003, 2).

Some politicians don't wait to leave public service to sideline in private enterprise. Although former Montana governor Marc Racicot left office in 2001 before becoming a Washington lobbyist, almost immediately afterward he assumed the chair of the Republican National Committee The RNC post provided him highly privileged access to party business in Congress. In 2004, he was made chair of the Bush-Cheney campaign. Technically, high-ranking party officials are exempt from conflict of interest rules that apply to legislators, and personal ethics also appeared to impose no restraint on his conduct. Racicot refused party officials' requests to put his lobbying on hold but eventually conceded, while still retaining a $700,000 salary in a major D.C. law firm involved in lobbying for corporate clients (Lewis 2004, 89–96).

Lobbying is also becoming a favorite pastime for retired politicians and White House officials, such as former House Speaker Tom Foley, Congress members Dan Rostenkowski and Pat Schroeder, and Senators Bob Packwood, Dennis DeConcini, Paul Laxalt, and George Mitchell, as a way of parlaying insider status into a service for arranging corporate influence peddling. Mitchell (D-ME) had been Senate majority leader until 1995, when he left government to join the board of directors of the Disney Corporation, becoming its chair in 2004. In 1999, CBS's *60 Minutes* counted 128 former members of Congress serving as registered lobbyists. By 2003, the count was at least 160. Among them, former Republican senator and presidential candidate Bob Dole worked for one of Washington's biggest lobbying firms. And former Congress member Thomas Hale Boggs Jr. is a partner in Patton Boggs, perhaps the king of the (Capitol) Hill in the lobbying industry (CBS 1999; Chaddock 2003).

Howard Baker, former Republican senator from Tennessee (1967–1985), became a registered lobbyist for the pharmaceutical corporation Schering-Plough, a company that has been investigated in recent years by the Federal Drug Administration and fined $500 million for numerous and serious violations of the agency's "current good manufacturing product" regulations. In October 2003, it was reported that Schering-Plough, with $9.4 billion in untaxed overseas profits, was among a group of companies that was offered windfall tax benefits as part of a Senate bill, conditioned upon their returning a portion of their profits to the United States. One of the main lobbyists for a coalition of companies that supported the proposal is Bill Archer, former chair of the House Ways and Means Committee; another is Donald Carlson, his former chief of staff (Andrews 2003, A1). Reagan's aide Lyn Nofziger and media advisor and deputy chief of staff Michael Deaver both went on to become lobbyists of some notoriety. Haley Barbour, former Republican National Committee chair and one of the highest paid lobbyists in Washington, D.C., went the other direction and became governor of Mississippi.

U.S. Rep. William Tauzin (R-LA) was one of the principal authors of a 2003 Medicare prescription drug bill that added hundreds of billions of federal dollars for drug benefits and barred the government from interfering in the price structure. This particular provision was pushed by the pharmaceutical trade association, PhRMA, which stood to become the biggest financial beneficiary of the act. According to the public interest group *Public Citizen*, Tauzin received almost $120,000 from the trade group while he was in the process of drafting the legislation (*Public Citizen* 2004). Soon after the bill's passage, Tauzin announced that he was leaving Congress to become president for the very same drug group, which made him an offer that "would be the biggest deal given to anyone at a trade association." A month earlier, Thomas Scully, an administrator at the Department of Health and Human Services, and another author of the same legislation, accepted a position with a law firm "that represents drugmakers, hospitals and other health-care businesses" (Ahrens 2004; Sevastopulo and Harding 2004).

They are among a long list of former government representatives and agency officials, including many from the Federal Trade Commission and Federal Communications Commission, who have gone on to work for the companies they once regulated. The revolving door raises questions about the depth of public officials' public service commitments at the time that they held high-level positions of public responsibility. One of the most notable examples of a revolving door beneficiary is Dick Cheney, who spent six terms as a member of Congress from Wyoming before becoming George Bush Sr.'s defense secretary. When Cheney was defense secretary, a Halliburton subsidiary, Brown and Root, was given major Pentagon contracts in the Balkans, and later benefited from U.S. "police actions" in Bosnia, Kosovo, Rwanda, Somalia, and Haiti. With no prior business executive experience, Cheney temporarily left government to become CEO of Halliburton, where he is said to have become a multimillionaire, before returning to the public sector as G. W. Bush's vice president. At the end of their 2002 terms, four prominent Republicans—J. C. Watts (OK), Jim Hansen (UT), Phil Gramm (TX), and majority leader Dick Armey (TX)—left the House and used their government connections to seek their greater fortunes with K Street firms.

Gramm was cosponsor of a 1999 Senate bill (Gramm-Leach-Bliley Act) that, according to Jim Hightower, expanded the rights of financial institutions

to collect, create, and store personal financial, consumption, and credit profiles in their computers, and sell the information to affiliates and other corporations under joint marketing agreements and without the individuals' knowledge or consent. Hightower reports that at "the behest of the industry (which,
coincidentally, just happened to be his major campaign funder), Phil
[Gramm] dutifully maneuvered this body-snatching bill into law. Gramm left
the Senate last year and was rewarded with—what else?—a fat cat job with a
giant financial firm that had lobbied for this bill" (Hightower 2003). Gramm
is, of course, not alone among politicians in trading on public official experience for lucrative opportunities in the business world.

Rudolph Giuliani turned his spectacular exit from the mayorship of New
York City, following the 9/11 World Trade Center attack, into a highly visible
and profitable consulting group. In 2002, he agreed to be a consultant to Mexico City, for the fee of $4.3 million a year, paid for by a group of very wealthy
Mexican businessmen, to advise the police force on crime reduction. The
same year, Merrill Lynch also hired the former mayor when the firm came
under an investigation by the New York State Attorney's General's office.
Giuliani additionally served as advisor to WorldCom, at the time the second-
largest long-distance phone provider in the United States, which went bank-
rupt the same year following a multibillion-dollar accounting fraud. For guest
appearances, he reportedly charged $100,000 per speech (Herszenhorn and
Atlas 2002, C2; Weiner 2003, A4).

In Britain, one case of influence peddling involved a Conservative member
of Parliament, John Browne, who began forming a business partnership in the
early 1980s in an integrated communications corporation while speaking up in
Parliament for deregulation of the emerging cable-TV industry. Browne also
approached the media industry group, Thorn EMI, with a proposal to become
the company's consultant, selling his credentials as "someone . . . who is close
to William Whitelaw (Home Secretary), Kenneth Baker (Information Technology Minister), and to the back-bench media committee." But Browne was
not unique in his entrepreneurial political style. "Many of the MPs who backed
cable television [parliamentary acts] later picked up shares and directorships."
Presumably, what occurs in the MP-communications nexus also occurs to an
equal or greater extent in other political-industrial relationships. The first
decade of deregulation in Britain was "as prosperous for lobbyists and MPs as
it has been for merchant bankers and contract-seeking companies. Back-
benchers have run willingly into the arms of the brokers and consultants, despite the conflicts of interest." And for their services, MPs and civil service
workers collect on average thousands of pounds in fees, effectively rendering
them as paid advisors for major business corporations (Hollingsworth 1991,
85–90, 99, 111–12).

$PECIAL INTERESTS AND AMERICAN DEMOCRACY

Fueled by the overall speculative investment frenzy in the United States in the 1990s, congressional and gubernatorial campaign spending has been rising at a phenomenal rate, which parallels the increasing use of consultants, media, and communication technologies. Spending for House and Senate races went from $88.2 million in 1974 to $735.8 million in 1998, more than an eightfold increase, and more than double the consumer price index over this period. (See table 6.9.) Presidential and congressional elections broke spending records, even factoring for inflation, again in the 2000 election. At the state level, both New York's and Pennsylvania's gubernatorial election spending in 2002 increased threefold over the previous election cycle (M. Green 2002a, 16). And in the U.S. House, spending on elections increased at a higher rate than the Senate, the average campaign that year costing over $1 million.

Money is clearly the critical factor in politics. In the 1998 congressional races, it was recorded that 96 percent of House and 91 percent of Senate victors were those candidates who spent the most (Johnson 2001, 175). In the 2000 congressional races, winners outspent losers on average by three to one and enjoyed victory margins of 70 percent to 30 percent, while 98.5 percent of incumbents were reelected (98.2 percent in 2002, raising an average $900,000 for the pleasure of serving). In 2002, more than 90 percent of the

Table 6.9. Congressional Campaign Expenditures, 1972–2000 Adjusted for Inflation in 2000 Dollars

Election Year	Total Expenditures (millions)	House Expenditures (millions)	Senate Expenditures (millions)
1972	318.5	191.6	126.5
1974	308.1	186.9	121.2
1976	349.5	216.4	133,2
1978	514.5	289.5	225.0
1980	499.5	284.4	215.0
1982	611.0	364.0	247.0
1984	620.0	337.4	282.6
1986	708.4	375.9	332.5
1988	666.2	373.3	292.9
1990	588.0	350.3	237.7
1992	832.5	499.1	333.4
1994	841.5	472.0	370.7
1996	839.5	524.4	315.5
1998	782.2	478.1	304.0
2000	1,005.6	572.3	434.7

Source: Nelson 2002, 29

winners outspent the losers, with 299 of the former outspending their opponents by 10 to 1 (*BusinessWeek* 2004, 74; Taylor 2002, 4; Tompkins County Green Party 2003). The fact that money generally flows to safe seats makes most incumbents quite secure about reelection and also tends to make them less responsive to voices for change.

In the Senate, the cost of winning a seat grew from an average of $609,000 in 1976 to $7.2 million in 2000, a year in which 82 percent of incumbents were returned to office (M. Green 2002b, 4). In New York State, incumbent Alfonse D'Amato spent over $27 million in the 1998 Senate race but was still defeated by Charles Schumer, who spent more than $16 million (Corrado 2000a, 78–79). In New York's 2000 U.S. Senate contest, Hillary Clinton and Rick Lazio combined to spend well over $80 million, the most expensive congressional race to that point. And in California, Republican tycoon Michael Huffington emptied $28 million from his personal vault ($30 million overall) in a failed bid to "buy" a U.S. Senate seat in 1994, a flop outdone in 1998 by Al Checchi's $40 million third-place finish ($58.66 per vote) in the state's governorship race (Bennett 1996, 60; Johnson 2000, 42, 174).

On the other hand, billionaire media baron Michael Bloomberg converted almost $69 million (or $92.60 per vote) of his personal fortune to gain a New York City mayoral victory in 2001, an election season marked by the trauma of the September 11 terrorist attacks and the political resurrection of Rudolph Giuliani (Cooper 2001, A1). By comparison, Ken Livingstone spent 80 cents per vote to win the mayoralty of London the same year (M. Green 2002a, 16). Bloomberg's single campaign expenditures matched the $70 million that another media tycoon, Republican Steve Forbes, had personally laid out on two failed presidential candidacies in 1996 and again in 2000 and topped the $63 million that Democrat (ex-Republican) and former Goldman Sachs CEO Jon Corzine spent in capturing a U.S. Senate seat from New Jersey the same year. In his first month in office, Bloomberg was already involved in a $15,000-per-plate reelection campaign fund-raiser, with George W. Bush in attendance, for New York governor, George Pataki, held at his swanky Upper Eastside townhouse (Steinhauer 2002, A27).

In defense of their privileged position in the campaign money circuit, media/communications conglomerates are themselves among the leading PACs and lobbyists working in opposition to campaign finance reform. Earlier initiatives of the FCC to require free campaign airtime were strenuously resisted by such "reformers" as Senate commerce committee chair John McCain, until the commission, threatened with funding cutbacks, was forced to retreat (Lewis 2000b). From 1996 to mid-2000, the fifty largest media companies and four of their trade associations spent $111.3 million to lobby Congress and the executive office, $31.4 million in 1999 alone, in addition to providing legislators with regular "fact-finding mission" junkets, which often happened to be located in beautiful resort locations. A *Newsweek* journalist reported that "300 members of the House are in bed with the National Association of Broadcasters" (Alter 2002). The communications industries have easy access to the FCC. To cite one example, lobbyists from AT&T, SBC, WorldCom, along with industry executives, participated in at least thirty-eight of forty-three ex parte proceedings of the commission, held from June 4 to June 7, 2001 (Barsamian 2001, 6–7).

McCain collected almost $700,000 (1993 to mid-2000) from the broadcast industry, the most of any Congress member. In return, the senator came through for the industry by leading a bill that would raise the ownership cap for any television network from a 35 percent to a 50 percent share of the national audience and supported FCC chair Michael Powell's parallel efforts in 2003.[16] Time Warner, which announced what became a $106 billion media/communications merger with AOL, spent $4.1 million in lobbying expenses in 1999, and Disney was right behind with $3.3 million. The two kicked in almost $9 million in campaign funds since 1993 (Common Cause 2000a).

Another one of the most powerful special interests in Washington through the 1990s was the tobacco industry. In 1997 alone, the big five tobacco companies spent $30 million on lobbying, and tobacco interests overall were the biggest soft-money contributors to the two major national party committees[17] ($1.6 million to the Republicans, $400,000 to the Democrats). That year, not coincidentally, "Trent Lott and Newt Gingrich inserted a single and mostly unnoticed 46-word sentence into that year's massive tax law . . . [that] granted the tobacco industry a $50 million tax break" (Hartmann 2002, 182). In the 1995–1996 election cycle, Philip Morris alone gave over $2.5 million to the Republicans and $500,000 to the Democrats (Center for Responsive Politics 1997; West and Loomis 1999, 49–50).[18]

Tobacco lobby payouts were overtaken, however, by other industry soft-money interests in 1999. The securities and investment firms that year contributed $8.2 million, telecommunications $6.3 million, real estate $5.1 million, transportation $5 million, insurance $4.9 million, and pharmaceuticals and medical supplies $4.3 million (Common Cause 2000a).[19] Overall, however, tobacco interests contributed more than $28 million to national parties and federal candidates between 1987 and March 1998 (Common Cause 2000b). Although both parties are paid off, among all the major industries, only the communications/electronics sector leans toward the Democrats (largely because of contributions from the Hollywood and music industries). The Republicans are the favored, however, in total corporate protection money handouts (Weissman 2000).

Lobbyists have no permanent friends or permanent enemies, only permanent interests. During and between elections, the dominant political and economic special interest groups, primarily large corporate-scale industries, are continually paying for access to Congress and legislators at every other level of government. To cite one industry payoff, of the 213 congressional members who voted to boost spending by $493 million for Northrup-Grumman's B-2 stealth bombers, each received an average $2,100 from the company in campaign contributions. Of the 210 who opposed, each received an average $100 (Donnelly, Fine, and Miller 2001, 8).

More than 85 percent of congressional members involved in the investigation of the Enron corruption scandal had received campaign contributions from the company. The ring of federal political connections did not end there. Enron was the largest source of campaign funding for George W. Bush, going back to his governor races. The energy giant was also closely linked to a string of high-ranking officials: Vice President Dick Cheney (who invited the company to help draw up federal energy policy), Attorney General John Ashcroft ($61,000 in Enron donations in his failed 2000 Senate campaign), Secretary of the Army Thomas White (a ten-year executive of the company involved in market and price manipulations), chief Bush political advisor Karl Rove (a major stockholder in the company), Secretary of Energy Spencer Abraham (recipient of Enron contributions while a senator), U.S. Trade Representative Robert Zoellick (on Enron's advisory council), Don Evans (Bush's chief campaign fund-raiser and secretary of commerce, who had received campaign funds from Enron chair Ken Lay), former Montana governor Marc Racicot (former Enron Washington lobbyist before becoming Republican national chair), and other White House insiders (*Public Citizen* 2003).

This pay-to-play style of policymaking points to an invisible government of unelected elites who have the ears of elected and other government officials, who orchestrate much of the day-to-day policies of government, who write much of the legislation through hired high-powered legal attorneys, and who patronize the electoral process on behalf of themselves and their favored government officials. It's a sweetheart deal writ large. When one speaks in an academic sense of the "state," it is these sets of players who comprise, together with the government and other political influentials, the larger formal and informal governing strata of society. In marxian terminology, it is called "the ruling class."

Much is made of organized labor as a "special interest," but the total spending of labor unions, representing millions of working people—from welders to firefighters to hospital and hotel workers—on lobbying in 1997–1998, $44,379,999, was minuscule compared to spending by corporate lobbyists.

Labor groups provided only 15 percent of the top fifty soft-money contributions in the 2000 election; the rest largely came from corporations and business groups (Holman and McLoughlin 2002, 62). Citizen organizations, too, such as consumer and environmental protection advocates, spend a small fraction of the funds that are used for information and lobbying. In 1996, corporate energy groups contributed $21 million to congressional candidates, whereas environmental interest groups gave $2 million (Donnelly, Fine, and Miller 2001, 14). Overall, the five biggest lobbying interests in the 1997–1998 election period were:

Finance, Insurance, and Real Estate	$378,159,242
Communications/Electronics	$338,453,610
Health Care Industries	$325,415,297
Energy and Natural Resources	$282,602,274
Transportation	$227,324,383

(Adapted from Loomis 2000, 177)

THE ENGINEERING OF CONSENT

This kind of money buys a lot of image making, which becomes important to the political process only at the final act—the election event. A critique of political practices in the United States needs to focus not on the characteristics of individual candidates but with an examination of the organization of power that selects for such candidates. The selection, presided over by organized political (e.g., Christian Coalition, National Rifle Association, AFL-CIO, party organizations) and economic interests (e.g., Fortune 500 companies and industry associations) and gatekeepers (e.g., party power brokers, media influentials), starts long before the formal campaign. While professionalization is involved in further segmentation of functional roles in U.S. politics, professionals themselves are not independent of the larger role that interest elites have always played in the society. The emphasis on professionalism supports a technocratic approach that tends to ignore how organized elites regulate the ideological structures and institutions (media, civic organizations, schools, churches) and helps to inculcate political legitimacy. It is consistent with much of postindustrial and postmodern thinking that technocracy and the crafted image should assume such an elevated status. For postmodernists like Baudrillard, image is reality, and political "reality" is constructed by professional image makers.

It is suggested here that the core principles that govern the changing roles and functions in the political process are part of a rapidly accelerating pace of commodification of public life that has been opened up by elites' (in both major parties) adoption of neoliberalism in the economic sphere and deregulation and market hegemony in civil society and the public sphere. The power players in the electoral process include transnational corporate executives, lobbyists, PACs, the mass media, the advertising and public relations industries, producers of ICT, public officials, *and* the election professionals—certainly not simply the professionals alone. Mancini and Swanson thus reach a narrow understanding of the agencies of power when they argue, "The United States offers a clear example of how advertising tends . . . to influence the entire content of political campaigns and . . . the requirements of effective advertising can become constraints that shape all forms of political discourse" (Mancini and Swanson 1996, 13). Rather, there is an array of elite interests and individuals that coalesce, without necessarily full coherence, around the *process* of electing officials and a narrow spectrum of participatory and policy alternatives that in fundamental ways excludes the interests of the majority.

Adopting the professionalization thesis, Mancini sees only a demise rather than a restructuring of the political party and does not seem to recognize how these changes have been impelled by forces in the new political economy. His explanation of political change leaves a sense of mystery about what drives "professionalization." For example, he writes,

> The "digital citizen" prefigures the possibility of direct interactions among citizens, leaders, and officials, which, bypassing the mediation of the political parties in favor of technical skills already developed in the fields of research and business, further undermine the parties' role and importance. In short, the process of professionalization has accelerated, producing effects not only in party structures but also, as shown later, in the very functioning of democracy. Not only the party is becoming more professionalized, but also the whole field of politics is undergoing the same process. (Mancini 1999, 236)

The linkage of the professionalization of politics and the decline of political parties has long been noted (Nimmo 1970; Sabato 1981; Salmore and Salmore 1989), not only in the United States but also in other Western democracies, including Britain, Germany, France, and Italy. It's been observed that Tony Blair's campaign relied heavily on communications professionals for news management and spin-doctoring. For Mancini, it is the political consultants who oversee not only the technical aspects of elections but even what used to be the exclusive domain of the party—campaign organization and everyday decision-making authority (Mancini 1999, 236–37). It is a bewildering explanation that begs the question of how the consultants could have captured this central domain of political life, and it ignores the role of organized political economic forces in nations and in the world economy.

Within a Weberian, McLuhanesque, and neoliberal framework, professionalization makes much sense—at the local, national, and global levels. However, to discuss the work of professionals and the uses of advanced communications systems as simply a necessary, even if flawed, outgrowth of modernization and progress is to envision such developments as part of a technologically determined worldview (one of process and expertise, not of power and participation). In such a view, professionalization is ultimately more efficient (though the real costs of such "efficiencies" are never fully conceived) than citizen-intensive political and election practices. In effect, it depoliticizes politics, strips it of the conflicts of interests on which it actually rests, and renders citizens as passive observers and consumers of a theater of media-orchestrated spectacles. Political choice operates only after all the props on the lot are constructed and campaign rules have predisposed the outcome to a set of intraelite, corporate governed options. Voting becomes a mere simulation of democracy.

Politics in the United States certainly has shifted in the postwar era—from a system dominated by political parties and party machines to one more directly supervised by organized and global economic interests. Campaign professionals are important as mediating agents in the management and construction of successful candidacies, which to a great extent relieves the latter of party dependency and accountability to a governing program or ideology. Professionalization as discourse and practice facilitates more direct influence of political action committees and direct contributions from corporate and other wealthy interests, eliminates much of the guesswork as well as reciprocity in politics, and rationalizes the best electoral system that money can buy. But it is the material costs of elections and the symbiotic and mutually constituting relationships between the candidates' organizations and their financial and industrial backers that explains the reduced role and relevance of political parties and party activists at the grassroots level. As Shea and Burton (2001, 10) point out, politicians still rely upon parties to a certain extent to organize petitions and volunteers, raise money, make telephone contacts, and canvass at the neighborhood level. However, central campaign strategies and tactics are now largely in the hands of campaign professionals, which is a result of restructured campaign rules, the growth of corporations, and almost unlimited campaign financing. Those without deep pockets, corporate support, and the favorable attention of the mass media are generally excluded as serious political contenders.

Media corporations have a multifunctional interest in elections. They make windfall profits from paid political advertising and interest in their news coverage. How media cover campaigns confers a degree of king-making power on their management. And the limits of that coverage and the ideological characterization it takes (dramatic contests of personal ambition) insulates the hegemonic power of the corporate system in which the mass media are among the most prominent members and in which they have an extremely privileged role. The mass media thus help to shield the political system from public knowledge and scrutiny and public empowerment, which is understandable given the material stakes of the mass media in the making of the news agenda.

The watchdog and social responsibility obligations of the mass media with respect to electoral activities are in practice very limited. Under FCC licensing provisions, broadcasters can only deny political advertisements that fail to meet the time and technical standards of their stations, that do not name sponsors, or that are considered obscene. They have no duty to screen for the truth. The result is that what the public learns about political candidates is often based on false or misleading statements uncorrected by the media, manipulation of data and symbols, and deceptive audio and visual cues. Success in political campaigns, especially at the statewide and national levels, highly correlates with the amount of money spent per voter in procuring advertising, and those parties and candidates not backed by corporate capital are effectively blocked from reaching the ears and eyes of most voters (Jamieson 1992; Bennett 1996).

Elections in the United States have come to resemble the cycle of commodity production, which routinely includes the use of focus groups, advertising strategies, media saturation, and texts that play to consumer (voter) gratifications. Nicholas Garnham observed that

> Politicians appeal to potential voters not as rational beings concerned for the public good, but in the mode of advertising, as creatures of passing and largely irrational appetite, whose self-interest they must purchase. The campaigners thus address citizens within the set of social relations that have been created for other purposes. Thus the citizen is addressed as a private individual rather than a member of the public, within a privatized domestic sphere rather than within public life. (Garnham 1990, 111)

After a lifetime in politics, former U.S. senator Mark Hatfield pessimistically concluded, "When you look at the political-industrial complex, you see a whole new industry . . . reaching such heights that neither the public nor the political institutions are in a position to do much about it. It's a runaway" (Hamilton 2000, A12). The question for the public is how to recover their lost position and their rights as citizens.

Lodged within a political structure governed less by accumulated wealth and monopoly power, communication professionals might just as easily be hired for an election style that catered to the ideal of dense public participation and enlightenment. Their methods under such a mode of governance would have to be less gratuitously dishonest, manipulative, and self-serving. Even Mancini concedes that under different rules of governance, "Bearers of proven specific specialized skills, these [commercial sector communications] professionals would lend their expertise to the service of a civil cause" (Mancini 1999, 242). The focus of the problem of U.S. elections is misplaced, however, when it singles out the professionals and professionalization. The real issue is a political structure that has been and continues to be flexibly adapted to the needs of an expansive corporate class that will leave no stone unturned in its quest to monopolize and seek profit from both the economic and the political sphere—and annihilate what is left of the public interest.

NOTES

1. Even the nonpartisan-sounding Commission on Presidential Debates (CPD), which established in the 2000 campaign the ground rules for participation in the fall debates, was funded by private corporations, including the Anheuser-Busch beer company. Essentially, the CPD served as a front for the two dominant political parties determined to keep third parties out of contention. In 2000, the CPD set a minimum 15 percent vote threshold in five polls taken just before each debate in order to qualify third party candidates, effectively shielding the public from hearing Ralph Nader and other serious candidates challenge the front-runners (Hill 2002, 186–87).

2. The three major networks reduced coverage of the 2000 campaign by 28 percent compared to 1988 and the conventions by two-thirds. The political sound bite of candidates declined from forty-three seconds in 1968 to 7.8 seconds in 2000. Of the twenty-two television debates in the 2000 presidential primary campaigns, only two of them were televised over a broadcast network—and not during prime time. NBC and Fox offered sports and entertainment (counter)programming during some of the presidential debates (Taylor 2002, 11–12).

3. Physicist and global environmental activist Vandana Shiva observes that Indian elections have become corrupted by bribes from the corporate sector. She accuses Enron of having paid part of the campaign costs of certain Indian candidates for parliament ("Rich World, Poor Women" program aired on the PBS *Now* series in 2003).

4. The origins of the aphorism is usually attributed to Jesse Unruh, former California assembly speaker, first uttered in 1968 (Thurber 1995, 6).

5. Clinton was strongly criticized by Republicans for using the White House in this manner. However, the list of sleepovers in the Bush White House between January 2001 and July 2002 is not significantly different. Based on numbers provided by his administration, Bush had 164 sleepover guests, keeping pace with the Clinton White House, 70 of whom were political contributors. The seventy contributors gave over $858,000 to federal candidates and parties since 1999, 80 percent of which went to Republicans (Center for Responsive Politics 2002).

6. When it comes to whom it is that federal candidates most rely upon, "The dependence on Wall Street money really suppresses [the] argument," says Bill Clinton's ex-press secretary, Michael McCurry. "If you . . . schlep up and down Wall Street with your tin cup," he adds, "then you listen to these guys making their arguments about the efficiency of financial deregulation and so forth, you begin to say, yeah, they've got a point" (cited in M. Green 2002b, 145).

7. The ten largest industry soft-money donors from January 1, 1999 to mid-2000 were (figures rounded): securities and investments, $24.2 million; telecommunications, $17.8 million; labor unions, $16.1 million; computers and electronics, $13.1 million; real estate, $12.8 million; lawyers and lobbyists, $12 million; insurance, $10.2 million; pharmaceuticals and medical supplies, $9.2 million; entertainment and media, $8.9 million; and transportation, $8.9 million (Common Cause 2000c).

8. The *New York Times* reported at the end of 1997 that the figure was up to $2.2 billion (Abramson 1997, A18), up from $1.6 billion in 1992, of which three-fourths was spent on television and mail advertising (Strother 1999, 188).

9. In recent national elections, the Democrats have taken in almost as much as Republicans in soft money, but the Republicans draw far more hard-money contributions: $266.3 million to $155.5 million in 1992; $407.5 million to $210 million in 1996; and $465.8 million to $275.2 million in 2000 (Opensecrets 2001).

10. The top ten were (in order): Philip Morris, Joseph E. Seagram and Sons, RJR Nabisco, Walt Disney, Atlantic Richfield, Communications Workers of America, American Federation of State, County and Municipal Employees, AT&T, Federal Express Corp., and MCI Telecommunications. The calculation of hard- and soft-money contributions, monitored by groups such as Common Cause, does not include spending by "Stealth PACs," which are organizations that use a loophole in the 1996 federal tax code to hide their expenditures on elections that do not specifically advocate for or against candidates.

11. In the 2000 election, the Brennan Center for Justice at the New York University School of Law found that despite the "independent" claims of issue advocates, 83 percent of their ads were clearly intended to endorse candidates. In the final sixty days of the campaign, 99.4 percent of such ads were targeted toward the election outcome (M. Green 2002b, 98).

12. Of the 248 congressional members who sat on committees that held hearings on the Enron scandal, 212 of them had received money from either Enron or from its auditing company, Arthur Andersen (Will 2002). In the 2000 election, Enron contributed $1.7 million, 70 percent of it in the form of soft money. Of Enron's political payoffs, 73 percent went to Republicans and 27 percent to Democrats (Jamieson and Waldman 2003, 7). The huge energy conglomerate has been the largest donor to George W. Bush's political campaigns, which helps to understand that president's sense of urgency in wanting to pass oil drilling rights legislation in the Alaskan wilderness. It may also explain his party's positions in rejecting the Kyoto Accord on global energy policy; the legislative efforts to remove CO_2 emission caps in U.S. power plants and other forms of energy deregulation; and the administration's support for increased oil drilling, refining, and transportation, and discouragement of exploration of renewable and alternative energy sources (Weinberg 2001).

13. Under the new rules, soft money cannot be used for political advertising (i.e., mentioning or depicting a candidate) purposes thirty days before a state primary or sixty days before the general federal election.

14. On the media side of the revolving door, the National Association of Broadcasters (NAB) has twenty registered lobbyists, seven of whom served on congressional staffs, the Federal Communications Commission (FCC), and the Federal Trade Commission. From 1996 to 1998, the NAB, together with ABC, CBS, A. H. Belo, Meredith Corporation, and Cox Enterprises, spent $11 million to defeat a range of bills mandating free airtime for political candidates (Lewis 2000b). Dennis Patrick, who is a former chair of the FCC, is now president of AOL Wireless. William Kennard worked for a high-powered legal firm in Washington, D.C., Verner Liipfert, which had a major presence in the communications industry, before he became chair of the FCC (Barsamian 2001, 7).

15. Among the principals of the Carlyle Group are former president George Bush Sr. (senior advisor); former secretary of defense and deputy director of the CIA, Frank Carlucci (Carlyle chair and CEO); former secretary of state and treasury, James Baker (senor counselor); White House budget advisor in the Bush Sr. and Clinton administrations, Richard Darman (managing director); retired general and former president of the Philippines, Fidel Ramos (Asia advisory board); and former prime minister of England, John Major (Carlyle Europe chair). Among its investors, at least until October 2001, were members of the Osama bin Laden family (Schneider 2003).

16. McCain went to bat for General Electric's NBC television interests by writing to the FCC to approve a broadcast license request by a company, Paxson Communications, in which it is seeking controlling interest—"a day after the senator flew on the company's corporate jet" (Lewis 2000b).

17. Better hidden from scrutiny than soft money given to parties are the advocacy ads that are put on the air directly by interest groups that voters often cannot identify. Among those that have taken to the airwaves to push their causes include one organization advertising under the name "Americans for Job Security," which actually represents a business coalition that wants to lower immigration barriers for foreign skilled labor; "Citizens for Better Medicare" is a front for the pharmaceutical industry; "The Alliance for Quality Nursing Home Care" is an organization of nursing home operators. Advocacy organizations spent more than $342 million between January 1, 1999 and August 31, 2000 (Kaplan 2000).

18. Philip Morris and the tobacco industry are well represented in the George W. Bush administration. Both Bush and Attorney General John Ashcroft are regarded as close to tobacco interests. Deputy Attorney General Larry Thompson worked for the law firm that represented Canadian Tobacco Manufacturers Council in a Canadian government racketeering lawsuit against RJR. Bush's senior political advisor, Karl Rove (see chapter 3), worked for five years as a political consultant to Philip Morris (Marsden 2001, 1ff).

19. During the 2002 congressional election campaign, the pharmaceutical industry, with more than 600 lobbyists in the capital, spent over $30 million, overwhelmingly for Republicans, and almost $500 million in lobbying over the previous six

years. The biggest benefactor of the industry in 2002, accepting direct contributions of $200,000, was Republican Nancy Johnson, chair of the House Ways and Means subcommittee on health. The industry's top CEOs met shortly after the election, at a conference of the Pharmaceutical Research and Manufacturers of America, to plan how to stall government efforts to reduce the cost of prescription drugs and encourage generic substitutes (Moyers 2004b; Pear and Oppel 2002, A1).

7

Professionalization, Election Financing, and Democracy

As a result of the war, corporations have become enthroned, and an era of corruption in high places will follow. The money power of the country will endeavor to prolong its rule by preying upon the prejudices of the people until all wealth is concentrated in a few hands and the Republic is destroyed.

—Abraham Lincoln (cited in Center for Responsive Politics 2001)

$\mathbf{W}$ars are extensions of politics and as such create the means and rationale for redistributing wealth in favor of the most privileged strata. A massive financial transfer in the form of tax reductions and state contracts and subsidies accompanied the U.S. invasion of Iraq under the George W. Bush administration. As any history textbook will reveal, the United States has been almost perpetually at war since its industrial ascendancy—and this violent pattern of dealing with other nations and people did not abate in the late twentieth century. This type of globalization does not meet the needs of most people in the world or even the United States and can hardly be considered a formula for fostering democratic political values at home or abroad.

During the Cold War and in the face of a perceived Soviet adversary, political intervention and destabilization were often substituted for direct invasion as a method of securing U.S. political, economic, and military objectives. In war as in politics, corporate profiteers rake in material largesse and live to fight another military or political campaign, while working-class soldiers and ordinary citizens overwhelmingly are the casualties. An increasing concentration of wealth in the U.S. political economy and its military- and political-industrial complex has made the United States a poorer civil society. The reproduction of American-style elections in other countries threatens to turn

215

many of them, often fragmented and fragile democracies, into unstable and corrupt regimes and subcenters for predatory global capitalism.

What lessons can be learned from American elections? Private financing means that only those candidates willing to be supplicants to large corporations and other monied interests or who can draw from their own very deep pockets can reasonably consider running for national office. Few involved in the political campaign industry will not concede that the primary color of American politics is green. Even gubernatorial and mayoral candidates in large states and municipalities in most cases are considered viable only with the imprimatur of the corporate suites. For federal officeholders, whether first time or incumbent, to be successful means that most will have or need to cultivate solid connections to corporate executives. And given the large number of officeholders who go on to work for corporations, with or without portfolio, one wonders how many politicians see government service merely as a stepping-stone to upward economic mobility.

Image and name recognition, even if unrelated to public office, work well in American politics. Celebrity status also goes a long way, to the benefit of people like Ronald Reagan, Arnold Schwarzenegger, Jesse Ventura, and Bill Bradley. The unfortunate result of politics by public relations is that many potentially strong public servants will either never seek to become or not be welcomed by the main parties as the people's standard-bearers. If he were running today, Abraham Lincoln probably would have had about as much chance of getting his party's nomination for president as Dennis Kucinich.

Elections have become media spectacles, and that's not surprising. For one thing, political campaigns hire many of the same people who work in product advertising and public relations and draw their funding from large, often global, business interests. Away from election season, political consultants frequently work as image advisors for corporations. Many politicians themselves move unself-consciously in their lifetimes through the revolving door of business and government. The separation of public and private occupation has broken down in the era of the deregulated, neoliberal economy. That big business seeks to control political outcomes is not new, but the degree of representation of corporate executives in the executive branch and the overt ways in which politics has turned into a commercial branding device (with ex-politicians using their status to become corporate lobbyists or even to sell potato chips and sex supplements) is unprecedented.

The breakdown of social, spatial, and political boundaries, intrinsic to the aggressive logic of neoliberalism, melds public and private spheres within transnational capitalism's insatiable quest for occupation and profit. In neoliberalism's fullest dystopian articulation, "all that is solid melts into air, all that is holy is profaned," as expressed by Marx and Engels in the *Manifesto of the Communist Party*. Everything is up for sale, including politicians and politics. Industrialism, with its technology- and process-centeredness, is extended to spaces once excluded from its reach by corporeal, policy, legal, or moral boundaries. Hyperindustrialism expands the reach of capital and its system of management into zones formerly reserved as public or personal. Household space and the information that can be harvested from it and its occupants are now integrated into the circuit of production, marketing, advertising, and consumption. Citizens as voters are objects of surveillance and sources of data on all manner of their habits that electioneering specialists, with their store of information-gathering and processing tools, can uncover, process, and reproduce for the multiple uses of the political campaign and its associated interests and operatives.

Globally, neoliberalism is a discourse in the service of economic transnationalism, to which many formerly nationalist- and socialist-oriented governments have conceded a major share of territory and state power. The Blair government in Britain is an enthusiastic supporter of neoliberal globalization, evident in its incorporation of American-style politics at home and foreign policy (its collaboration with the United States in the invasion of Iraq, for example). For neoliberalism and the regime of economic globalization to succeed, governments throughout the world that welcome foreign corporate investment and trade with the least resistance and the fewest of barriers (financial, economic, environmental, labor, cultural, political) would need to be championed. The capture of national elections with standardized commercial political strategies backed by private financing ensures such results. For international neoliberalism to succeed requires that local partners of global power interests invite private campaign professionals to help deliver them the elections they need to sell off state assets and commoditize the public sphere.

Earlier U.S. attempts to influence or control state power in different parts of the world through clandestine activities have largely been substituted by more open collaboration with local political parties and social movements, often engaging the services of American and/or other international political consultants. In countries where cooptation or collaboration does not succeed or where active political resistance is present (such as Venezuela, Haiti, Georgia, Serbia, and the Philippines), the CIA or the more indirect actions of the National Endowment for Democracy and "fellow traveler" organizations are usually deployed. Syndicated conservative columnist and Republican Party insider George Will acknowledges that the United States is an empire, should act like one, and make no apologies for it. Being an "empire is always about domination"—from which "Americans must not flinch." Specific acts of U.S.

aggression, such as the violations of international law committed against Iraqi prisoners, he says, is simply part of the "pornography [that] is, almost inevitably, part of what empire looks like" (Will 2004, 79).

Such explicit assertions of imperial power, rooted in the domination of world markets, represent the "bad cop" version of international political economy. The "good cop" centrists (mainstream Democrats) have no less a sense of America's "manifest destiny," though they tend to be less unilateralist in their worldly ambitions for the nation, preferring the company of European imperial allies. With this internationalist alignment, it will be difficult to change the direction of a globalized U.S. political-industrial complex; the Democrats have become less of a true opposition party to the Republicans. Writing in the mid-1990s, Lance Bennett described the two dominant parties as having so closely aligned on free trade issues "that the Democrats must make increasingly large concessions, selling out the interests of their traditional labor and social constituents just to compete for money they once attracted with relatively little effort" (Bennett 1996, 147). The political process appears designed to manipulate symbolic values and the public pulse, make the interests of the average voter—such as affordable health care and education; job and income security; physical safety; and a clean home, outdoor, and working environment—largely irrelevant, and transfer real power to corporate boardrooms.

If anything, American politics has become even more socially Darwinist than it already was in the Reagan era. Although the Reagan administration seems almost moderate compared to that of George W. Bush, his administration set in motion a collapse of the public-private divide and put a much greater emphasis on the professional makeover of politicians and other elites. The industrialization and professionalization of elections has not increased democratic participation and other measures of public engagement in civil society. Instead, the increased costs of running elections in this manner has opened the door to greater corporate dominion over the political process. Speaking to the transformation of elections globally, one leading student of politics notes that the intervention of foreign consultants and professional campaign techniques and technologies has brought about a situation in newly democratizing societies in which "[p]arty leaders have little interest in democratizing their parties' internal structures, and the whole institutional culture is different. Many parties are [now] in the pocket of a handful of wealthy sponsors who, similarly, have little interest in broadening the party's base" (Carothers 1999, 154). If this is true for newly democratizing countries, it is even truer in the United States, where money and corporate interests overwhelmingly dominate the electoral process and the system of government administration.

TECHNIQUES OF CONTROL

Those authors who see the evolution of campaigning in terms of modernization and professionalization miss the historical and political economic context that has shaped the changes in campaign methods, techniques, technologies, and citizen and party engagement. Philip Gould, a British political consultant for the (New) Labour Party and for social democratic parties in other countries, insists that the techniques employed in political campaigns are neutral and unrelated to the corporate agenda in Britain or elsewhere. He argues that "sophisticated communication techniques, and in particular advertising, can be used by a radical organisation without compromising either the message, or the policies underlying [it]" (quoted in McNair 1999, 118). Many Britons disagree with this benign portrayal of professional campaign management. A writer for the *Guardian*, who, noting, for example, how the import of oppositional research/rapid-response technology from the United States was influencing the style of British elections, sees such developments as "reinventing the Labour [Party] machine—and with it the creeping Americanisation of British politics" (Harriman 2001).

Political consultants generally do not view themselves as advocates for popular empowerment but rather as power brokers for getting politicians into office. They bring a range of techniques designed instrumentally to secure votes for their candidate and discourage turnout for the opposition. The biggest stakeholders in American or British elections are corporate managers, financiers, and stockholders for whom a negative outcome, such as a socialist victory, would be seen as disastrous. Anything other than corporate control of political outcomes is inconceivable in a transnational capitalist political economy. Indeed, any relatively independent political formation, left or right, is a threat to a corporatist regime of power.

Elites from think tanks, corporate headquarters, powerful interest groups, mass media, the ranks of the leading electioneering professionals, and politicians and public officials are linked by mutual and symbiotic relationships that sustain their privileged positions in society. Their combined wealth purchases the use of information and communication technologies and mass media as means of surveilling the electorate and political rivals. This is to ensure results that create legitimacy for the system and circulate power only among a narrow stratum of competing elites. In a society as densely mediated as the United States (and other industrial states), the public is heavily reliant upon hierarchical and mass media political accounts and descriptions. Television news, particularly the highly partisan analyses given by *Fox News* and MSNBC commentators, often act as the shock troops for right-wing political persuasion. In the United States, there is no major left-wing TV news outlet.

Except for the small minority of individuals who actively seek alternative, critical sources of information and interpretation, most Americans form their opinions from media that do little to rock their boats.

The contemporary political-industrial complex makes the political party, the organization through which citizens should be directly influencing political issue agendas, relatively powerless. Powerful political and economic interests, political candidates, and political professionals operate largely outside the national party apparatus. According to a close observer over many years, "party chairmen have become little more than cheerleaders on the sidelines, while the candidates and their free-agent political professionals play the game. And the single big party event, the national convention, is an essentially meaningless sham, orchestrated for television" (Witcover 1999, 277).

Are political campaigns mere weapons of mass deception? Murray Edelman (1988) describes elections and other political events as "spectacles" that distract and disable citizens from political engagement—that is, from the actual exercise of power. The appropriation of the electoral process by corporate money and professionalization to a great degree forecloses citizen participation in the political process. As a result, American citizens have become mere spectators of government and the electoral process, which defies the notion that they live in a democracy, even a representative democracy.

The instrumental forces that political professionals bring to the campaign are impressive in their capacities to profile voters and anticipate their voting behavior—and the scientific management of voting and political participation is still in an early phase. Attending Bush campaign rallies in 2004 required those who wanted tickets to agree to vote and volunteer for the candidate as well as fill out forms giving their e-mail and home addresses, phone numbers, and Social Security numbers. Those who simply wanted to hear the president speak without first assuring their political loyalty were turned away (Halbfinger 2004, A19). In the future, one can expect that both commercial and political surveillance and advertising will be specified to the level of household cable viewing in consonance with the electronic dossiers kept on individuals, with more sophisticated monitoring devices than those already employed in targeted print media. There are other possible designs for managing the electorate. With respect to the increasing industrialization of civil society, the dimension most fastidiously hidden from popular discourses about politics is the elite control of the electoral process. However, one of the more interesting political developments in recent years is the fact that some of the same instruments used by professional electioneers have been appropriated to create and deliver a different picture of politics for those segments of the voting public willing to tune in.

ELECTIONS FOR SALE

Do elections matter? No democratic society can dispense with them, but the existence of elections does not define meaningful democracy. Even the most authoritarian states conduct electoral exercises, in large part to confer a stamp of legitimacy upon their regimes. What should be obvious from the poor turnouts in U.S. federal elections is that these ritualized events have not established adequate public support for an elitist two-party system wedded to corporate power. But neither political elites nor the corporate media would ever make such an admission. Indeed, they've done about everything they can to maintain the status quo.

Do corporate-financed, professionally run elections nonetheless result in policies that serve the interest of the majority? Elitists believe they do (e.g., Dye and Ziegler 1993). Others see U.S. elections as symbolic events in a showcase democracy, one not based on rule by the people. Political scientist Tom Ferguson (1995) conceives of elections as forms of corporate investment to ensure their prevailing voice in the administration of society. In a recent poll, 84 percent of Americans expressed the belief that members of Congress "listen to those who give money to their political party in response to their solicitation for large donations" (cited in Lewis 2004, 83). Other public opinion polls have indicated that the public increasingly believes that government is largely run for the benefit of big business. The numbers in support of that supposition have risen over time: 25 percent in 1960, 50 percent in 1970, 70 percent in 1980, 77 percent in 1990, and 83 percent in 1994 (Bennett 1996, 227). These public responses suggest that Americans are not at all naive about the legislative patronage structure; they may feel at a loss and lack national leadership to do anything about it.

The political-industrial complex is a complicated set of interrelationships between corporations (including the mass media) and politicians who engage in the trade of administrative and legal acts in return for protection money paid by wealthy individuals, corporate lobbyists, and well-heeled political action committees. A highly porous network of corporate and government leaders and staffs fluidly move back and forth between the public to the private sector. The prize positions are in the executive branches of government and corporations. Money derived from the control of the Earth's resources continually greases the engine of political economic power and blocks serious efforts to bring about the radical changes that are needed in public policy and public consciousness to end war, promote justice, and preserve the ecosystem.

Some proposed solutions to the election financing issue include putting caps on election spending, providing federal matching funds but only for small private contributions, creating a genuinely nonpartisan Federal Election

Commission, and requiring broadcast networks and stations to give free airtime to political candidates. These are only modest reform proposals. In the absence of *effective* legal controls on private funding (and provisions for full public funding), political parties and candidates have little choice but to override the effects of the McCain-Feingold legislation. Bankers, developers, and other corporate interests in McCain's home state of Arizona have challenged that state's public financing law, because private spending in elections is exactly what preserves such groups' control over politics.

There is little hope, actually, that spending constraints can actually be implemented. Bypassing the McCain-Feingold objectives, liberal groups such as MoveOn.org and the Media Fund and conservative organizations such as the Club for Growth and the Republican Mainstream Committee played an active part in funding political advertising on behalf of their favored candidates in 2004. These and other "527" advocacy groups (named for the tax code section under which they fall) have helped compensate for restrictions on soft-money contributions to political parties and enabled the Democrats to balance out the initial enormous advantage in hard-money fund-raising by Bush and the Republicans in the 2004 election. Ironically, the Republicans—who opposed soft-money restrictions during the McCain-Feingold debates in Congress—now rail against the use of the 527s.

Short of a major upheaval, it is highly improbable that corporations would ever relinquish their grip on controlling the American political system. If U.S. elections are dominated by campaign financing, the marketing of candidates, and the technologies and techniques of media management, as one political scientist notes (Bennett 1996, 20–22), where do the citizen and the public interest fit in? Reforms such as McCain-Feingold cannot stop, only redirect the flow of money, just as sandbags will only force a river to find other channels. The ultimate source of the money-in-politics problem is the legal status of personhood that the courts have conferred upon U.S. corporations since the nineteenth century. The most important way of getting corporate money out of politics, therefore, is to stop treating them as individuals under the law and, instead, regulate their financial intervention in elections as a restraint on democracy.

What is clear is that the current form of elections is not about canvassing and responding to citizen demands. Republican consultant Douglas Bailey argues that campaigns are not intended to enlighten the public or set forth political principles but rather "for linking [politicians] up with the public mood" (cited in Greider 1992, 271). This suggests that consultants and politicians collaborate to stylize and market candidacies, not to articulate governing ideas. The main governing ideas are preset within the inner circles of power; the campaign is intended largely to enjoin public consent within a narrow range of options. Governments do legislate on matters of substance to particular groups (such as Medicare and other welfare benefits), but no bills will challenge the corporate structure of power or the legitimacy of elite governance as a whole. Corporations cannot leave electoral outcomes to chance, and this compels their financial investment in the campaign process, resulting in "low-intensity democracy."

WITHER ELECTORAL DEMOCRACY?

Conducting elections is therefore a necessary but inadequate basis for calling societies democratic. Progressive political change requires more than an election mechanism. A democracy worthy of the name requires a high level of citizen participation, dense civic structures, including media in the service of public education, and people able to collectively understand societal issues at least as far they pertain to themselves and to conceive and articulate a set of policy alternatives. Public interest and citizen organizations are the key to putting governing ideas on the table and coming up with proposals in which each member of the commonwealth feels a sense of engagement and ownership. A governing process is only as good as the input that goes into its formulation: "garbage in, garbage out," as the saying goes. What democratic theorists such as Macpherson (1977) argue is for nothing more radical than highly participatory and deliberative decision-making structures.

Elites, even when well intentioned as many are, cannot be entrusted with the responsibility of constructing the core questions of public debate, because they are for the most part out of touch with what concerns ordinary people. Polling is an ineffective and unreliable means of deciphering those concerns. Political parties, except perhaps in the few American caucus states where discussions precede selection of the party nominee, are less participatory institutions than ever. Politicians depend heavily on the support of corporations to establish their electability, and just as corporations have little interest in workplace democracy, they also have little concern for political democracy. What global corporations need are electoral outcomes that secure for them domestic and foreign investment opportunities and satisfactory profit margins.

What is the way out of this layered system of domination? Making elections more responsive to the public is a lofty goal that can perhaps be partially achieved in steps. Several public interest groups, such as Common Cause, the Center for Responsive Politics, and the Center for Public Integrity, have tried to reduce money and corporate wealth as a strategic advantage in politics. As difficult as that may be in a global corporate capitalist society such as the United States, it is an approach that points in the right direction—the restoration of public interest principles and restraints on the privileged stratum. If Tocqueville could be so impressed by the ethos of American democracy in the nineteenth century, why couldn't the United States again impress the world with a pledge to achieve more democratic ideals in the twenty-first century? A short list of objectives would include guaranteeing easily affordable educational opportunities, eliminating child-hood poverty and the ravages of infectious and sexually transmitted diseases, ensuring quality medical care for all, adopting strict standards for clean air and water, nontoxic food production, and environmentally safe and healthy workplaces, restoring biological diversity, and working toward other social and political public objectives.

Such commitments do not appear to be on the immediate horizon, and it will take a very broad-based coalition of forces to reorient American politics and political culture. A start was made with the insular ultraconservatism of the younger Bush government, which incited a strong domestic rejection of its one-sided business-oriented federal policies. Its unilateralist foreign policy style provoked a worldwide "blowback" against the United States. The gov-ernment's radical rightist turn requires a reexamination of core political val-ues and new directions. Outside of Ralph Nader, however, no political leader of national prominence is asking for reconsideration of the structure and qual-ity of American democracy, certainly not John Kerry. The Democratic Party is no less sworn to global neoliberalism and the transnational corporate agenda than the Republicans. Indeed, it was Clinton and Gore who led the move toward the World Trade Organization and the creation of the North American Free Trade Association.

No serious shift in the direction of democratic governance and no major al-teration of the America's increasingly polarized class structure and ethnic and gender divide can occur without confronting the hegemonic power of the cor-porate elite, and nothing less than a radical change in the political culture will set such a course in motion. Removing the financial privileges that corporate elites wield in politics would encourage a broader range of people and gov-erning ideas to enter politics. Publicly oriented organizations and their con-stituents would put up candidates. The two central parties would be far less dominant, and to the extent that their leaders wish to retain influence, they would have to make concessions to nonparty groups with alternative program proposals.

The grip on politics by two business-oriented parties could be loosened by the use of an instant runoff system in which voters get to rank their choices for office seekers and thereby vote their conscience rather than selecting the lesser of two evils. A system of proportional representation in choosing rep-resentatives, as in parliamentary systems, would promote more equitable power sharing and encourage coalition politics that give voice to multiple parties and views, including those committed to environmental preservation, world disarmament and peace, socially oriented development, and social justice in public policy. It would also protect traditional identity groups, such as religious institutions and property interests. In parliamentary systems, the head of government, the prime minister, is chosen by the party, and is not vested with the degree of power of the U.S. president, nor does he/she draw nearly as much upon the largesse of corporate interests. It is the party, not the prime minister, that is the key to winning executive control of government.

The U.S. two-party and winner-take-all system of government has driven politically creative and diverse ideas to the margins and led to a tight monopoly of plutocratic power. With a broader range of organizations and political ideas vying for representation, the public would not have to relate to politics as a professionally managed horse race managed by elite interests but as a form of civic engagement (and entertainment) performed by people much like themselves. Such a form of politics would raise people's interest and hopes for the future. The current political system, catering to narrow market opportunism, has in so many ways proven violative of citizens' trust. The low level of citizen participation provides a compelling argument for radically revising U.S. politics in ways that concentrate more direct control in the hands of ordinary working people, public interest associations, and nonprofit organizations that represent them in civil society—not only in the formal political process but at the site of employment and in other public and private institutions.

The central question is, who would lead such a change? Organized labor has tried to compete with corporate interest groups in the electoral process, suggesting a false parallel between the two, although unions have helped some Democrats gain the needed margin of victory. It is questionable, however, how long organized labor can sustain itself in this way, as transnational corporations continue to move union jobs overseas. In fact, union membership has precipitously declined over the years. Public interest groups, such as MoveOn.org, have attempted to level the playing field with broadcast and print ads critiquing the Bush administration, but they cannot compete financially with the war chest of the Republican Party. Michael Moore's populist documentaries, including his phenomenally successful *Fahrenheit 9/11*, may prove to be historically groundbreaking as a force in politics. A well-organized coalition of organized labor, environmental, women's, antiracist, and peace groups would pose a formidable challenge to the way big business, and such groups as the pharmaceutical industry, insurance companies, investment banking firms, and energy corporations, buy their way into political campaigns and congressional offices.

The breakdown of what was once conceived as the "American way of life," built upon a stable and secure middle class, threatens great disorder to the system of politics under which it has been governed. In Western societies, increasingly coordinated within a vast system of political and commercial surveillance and administrative and police power, various political groups and their cyber alter egos, led by people who are politically sophisticated and technologically savvy, have become a threat to the elite political order. Antiwar and other political action groups have learned to employ digital political guerilla-warfare tactics to undermine regimes by spreading news and information that is unfiltered by the dominant media and other established gatekeepers. People now have many informational media sources upon which they can educate and organize themselves if they so choose. When the corporate and commercial media no longer seem to speak to public interests, traditional institutions will begin to lose their legitimacy. Resistance to the world trade and investment system has been witnessed in places such as Seattle, Quebec City, Genoa, and Cancun, forcing leaders of the neoliberal order to retreat to more hidden and secure meeting places and weakening cohesion among their ranks.

It is impossible to predict whether the neoliberal agenda and the globalization of corporatist politics will continue to develop or what might replace it. Neoliberal policies have revealed themselves to be as averse to political as biological diversity. The existence of progressive pollsters and webmasters suggests that technologically mediated methods of conducting elections do not necessarily negate preservation of cultural, economic, and political sovereignty, although large-scale use of media and surveillance technologies in corporate capitalist countries, which require extremely heavy financing, tend to favor those with the ability to pay for them. The "professionalization" of political campaigns and its symbiotic relationships with corporate financing and the uses of information and communication technologies and mass media have contributed to an inactive and cynical electorate, who are more spectators than agents of politics—rendering a "democracy without citizens."

There was once a complacent assumption among many "digirati" that the Internet would transform politics by putting politicians and administrators more closely in touch with citizens. But that has largely failed to materialize. Electronic communication is a useful informational device, but it lacks the dimensionality of human communication. In most cases, politicians and administrators use their staffs to respond to e-mail inquiries and complaints in much the same perfunctory way as the communication previously handled through the postal system. This is as true in Britain as it is in the United States (Castells 2001, 155). Direct political participation and action remains the key to advancing democratic societies.

The threats to democracy that the electioneering system in the United States presents, especially the influence of big money—not to mention the baldly antidemocratic capture of power in the 2000 presidential election and the increased fears of political corruption arising from computerized voting— may send a cautious message to voters in other parts of the world who welcome U.S.-style elections. The world tensions that arose after 9/11 and the Bush government's conduct of the "war on terrorism" may make it more difficult in the future for American political consultants to bring their election toolboxes to other countries. From the days of Shea's rebellion, to the 1936–1937 GM workers' strike in Flint, Michigan, to Martin Luther King's march in Birmingham, and the twenty-first century antiwar protests in Washington, D.C., London, Berlin, Paris, Madrid, and Tokyo, the ongoing struggle for democracy has occurred most meaningfully at the sites and in the hands of ordinary people. In the era of neoliberalism, global corporatism, and campaign professionalization, there is no reason to think that this has changed.

References

Abrams, Jim. 1993. Endowment fund promotes democracy, spawns controversy. *Associated Press*, October 29. Available through LexisNexis.

Abramson, Jill. 1997. '96 campaign costs set record at $2.2 billion. *New York Times*, November 24, A18.

Aday, Sean. 2003. Presidential candidate discourse on network news. An Alliance for Better Campaigns report. At www.bettercampaigns.org/reports/display.php?ReportID=6.

Agee, Philip. 1992. Tracking covert actions into the future. *Covert Action Information Bulletin* 42 (Fall). At www.mediafilter.org/caq/CovOps.html.

Aguayo Quezada, Sergio. 1999. U.S. invasion. Trans. Tania Connaughton Espino. *Reforma (Mexico City)*, September 1. At www.globalexchange.org/countries/mexico/dem/reforma090199.html.

Ahrens, Frank. 2004. Tauzin expected to leave house for trade group. *Washington Post*, January 24. Online edition.

Alliance for Better Campaigns. 2000. Presidential candidate; discourse on network news. At www.bettercampaigns.org/reports/display.php?PageID=47.

———. 2001. Gouging democracy: How the 2000 television industry profiteered on campaign 2000. Executive summary. At www.bettercampaigns.org.

Alter, Jonathan. 2002. Between the lines online: Tuning out the TV lobby. *Newsweek*, March 1. Online edition.

Alvarez, Lizette. 2002a. In political din, South Dakotans long for "mute." *New York Times*, October 18. Online edition.

———. 2002b. Latinos are focus of new brand of ads. *New York Times*, October 28, A20.

American Correctional Association. 2001. At www.aca.org

American Prospect. 2002. Hard road for soft money. February 25. Online edition.

Andersen, Edwin. 2002. Argentina crying over "hired guns." *Insight*, May 20. Online edition.

Anderson, Perry. 1992. *English questions*. London: Verso.

Andrews, Edmund L. 2003. Senate panel backs bill to give tax windfall to U.S. companies. *New York Times*, October 2, A1, C4.

Ansolabehere, Stephen, and Shanto Iyengar. 1995. *Going negative: How political advertisements shrink and polarize the electorate*. New York: Free Press.

Aslam, Abid. 1999. The IMF just wants to be your friend. *Asia Times Online*, January 8. At www.atimes.com/media/AA08Ce01.html.

Associated Press. 2003. MLB's PAC contributes more than $250,000 to candidates, parties. May 13. At www.sportsline.com/mlb/story/6369132.

Bailey, Doug. 1998. What if . . . the president's consultant couldn't speak English? *National Journal.com*, May 20. At www.nationaljournal.qpass.com.

Baker, Kevin. 2003. We're in the army now. *Harper's* (October): 35–46.

Baldauf, Scott. 1999. The man behind the curtain of Bush campaign. *Christian Science Monitor*, March 26, 1.

Baldwin, Tom. 2002. Tory Party conference to be made in America. *Times (London)*, September 20. Online edition.

Barbash, Fred. 1997. British parties to campaign American-style. *Washington Post*, March 17. Online edition.

Barnes, James A. 1995. Privatizing politics. *National Journal* (June 3): 1330–34.

Barnett, Michael, and Kenneth Goldstein. 2002. Consultants abroad: American and political consultants and the transformation of democracy. Paper presented at the American Political Science Association, Boston, August 29–September 1.

Barnett, Steven, and Ivor Gaber. 2001. Media: Politics under pressure. *Guardian (London)*, April 23. Online edition.

Barnouw, Erik. 1968. *The golden web: A history of broadcasting in the United States*. Vol. 2, 1933 to 1953. New York: Oxford University Press.

Barsamian, David. 2001. *The decline and fall of public broadcasting*. Cambridge, Mass.: South End Press.

Bartle, John, and Dylan Griffiths. 2001. Introduction. In *Political communications transformed: From Morrison to Mandelson*, edited by J. Bartle and D. Griffiths. New York: Palgrave Publishers.

Bates, Eric, et al. 2001. Campaign inflation. *Mother Jones* (March/April): 46–55.

Batt, Tony. 1998. Consultant joins sides with gaming. *Las Vegas Review-Journal* (September 19). At www.lvrj.com.

Battersby, John. 1996. Parties take a rear seat in Israel vote. *Christian Science Monitor*, May 17, 7.

Beattie, Alan. 2003. Bush nominee defends US policy on AIDS spending. *Financial Times (U.S. edition)*, October 1, 2.

Bennett, W. Lance. 1996. *The governing crisis: Media, money, and marketing in American elections*. 2nd ed. New York: St. Martins Press.

Beresford, Quentin. 1998. Selling democracy short: Elections in the age of the market. *Current Affairs Bulletin* (February/March): 24–31.

Bernays, Edward L. 1947. Engineering of consent. *Annals of the American Academy of Political and Social Science* 250 (March): 113–20.

Bernstein, Carl. 1977. The CIA and the media: How America's most powerful news media worked hand in glove with the Central Intelligence Agency and why the Church Committee covered it up. *Rolling Stone* (October 20): 55–67.

Blizzard, Christina. 2001. Looking south for spin doctors. Comment. *Toronto Sun*, May 16. Online edition.

Blum, William. 1995. *Killing hope: U.S. military and CIA interventions since World War II*. Monroe, Maine: Common Courage Press.

———. 1997. Will humans ever fly? *Peace Review* 9 (1, March). Available on Academic Search Premier database.

———. 2000. *Rogue state: A guide to the world's only superpower*. Monroe, Maine: Common Courage Press.

———. 2002. The CIA and the Venezuela coup: Hugo Chavez—A servant not knowing his place. *Counter Punch*, April 12. At www.CounterPunch.org.

Blumenthal, Sidney. 1982. *The permanent campaign*. Rev. ed. New York: Simon & Schuster.

Blumler, Jay G., and Michael Gurevitch. 2001. "Americanization" reconsidered: U.K.-U.S. campaign communications comparisons across time. In *Mediated politics: Communication in the future of democracy*, edited by W. Lance Bennett and Robert M. Entman, 380–403. New York: Cambridge University Press.

Blumler, Jay G., Dennis Kavanagh, and T. J. Nossiter. 1996. Modern communications versus traditional politics in Britain: Unstable marriage of convenience. In *Politics, media, and modern democracy*, edited by David Swanson and Paolo Mancini, 49–72. Westport, Conn.: Praeger.

Bonner, Raymond. 1987. *Waltzing with a dictator: The Marcoses and the making of American policy*. New York: Times Books.

Bowler, Shaun, and David M. Farrell. 2000. The internationalization of campaign consultancy. In *Campaign warriors: Political consultants in elections*, edited by James Thurber and Candice Nelson, 153–74. Washington, D.C.: Brookings Institution Press.

Bowman, Karlyn. 2000. Polling to campaign and to govern. In *The permanent campaign and its future*, edited by Norman J. Ornstein and Thomas E. Mann, 54–74. Washington, D.C.: American Enterprise Institute and the Brookings Institution.

Brennan Center for Justice. 2001. Political television advertising. At www.brennancenter.org

———. 2002a. The purposes and beneficiaries of party "soft money." At www.brennancenter.org.

———. 2002b. Voter mobilization. At www.brennancenter.org

Brier, Stephen, et al. 1992. *Who built America?: Working people and the nation's economy, politics, culture and society*. Vol. 2. New York: Pantheon

Brown, Erika. 1999. Hired heads. *Forbes* (March 3): 234ff.

Bumiller, Elisabeth, and Eric Lichtblau. 2003. Attorney general is closely linked to inquiry figures. *New York Times*, October 2, A1, A22.

Business and Finance. 2002. Washington letter. A publication of the *Financial Times (London)*, May 13. Online edition.

Business Industry Political Action Committee (BIPAC). 2004. At www.bipac.org.

BusinessWeek. 2004. How to fix a rigged system (June 14): 74–75.

Butler, David, and Austin Ranney. 1992. Conclusion. In *Electioneering: A comparative study of continuity and change*, edited by David Butler and Austin Ranney, 278–86. Oxford: Clarendon Press.

Buzzflash. 2003. Will the 2004 election be stolen with election machines? An interview with Bev Harris, who has done the groundbreaking work on this issue, September 29. At www.buzzflash.com/interviews/03/09/29_harris.html.

Campaigns & Elections. 2004. Movers and shakers: Felipe Noguera (February): 17.

Campbell, Matthew. 1999. Ragin' Cajun brings out the Jewish vote. *Sunday Times (London)*, May 23.

Carlisle, Johan. 1993. Public relationships: Hill & Knowlton, Robert Gray, and the CIA. *Covert Action Quarterly* 44 (Spring). At www.mediafilter.org/caq/Hill&Knowlton .html.

Carney, James, and Michael Duffy. 1999. Who's that guy next to Karl Rove? *Time*, August 23. Online edition.

Carothers, Thomas. 1996. The resurgence of United States political development assistance to Latin America in the 1980s. In *The international dimensions of democratization: Europe and the Americas*, edited by Laurence Whitehead, 125–45. New York: Oxford University Press.

———. 1999. *Aiding democracy abroad: The learning curve*. Washington, D.C.: Carnegie Endowment for International Peace.

———. 2002. The end of the transition paradigm. *Journal of Democracy* 13, no. 1: 5-21.

Castells, Manuel. 2001. *The Internet galaxy: Reflections on the Internet, business, and society*. New York: Oxford University Press.

CBS. 1999. The lobbyist. *60 Minutes* transcript, August 22. At www.pattonboggs.com/aboutus/articles/60%5Fminutes.html.

Center for Responsive Politics. 1997. 1995–96 soft money update. June 4. At www.opensecrets.org.

———. 2001. A brief history of money in politics. At www.opensecrets.or/pubs/history/history2.html.

———. 2002. The Bush administration: Corporate connections. At www.opensecrets .org/bush/cabinet.asp.

Chaddock, Gail R. 2003. Republicans take over K Street. *Christian Science Monitor*, August 29. Online edition.

Chambat, Pierre. 2000. Computer-aided democracy: The effects of information and communication technologies on democracy. In *The information society in Europe: Work and life in an age of globalization*, edited by Ken Ducatel, Juliet Webster, and Werner Herrmann, 259–78. Lanham, Md.: Rowman & Littlefield.

Chomsky, Noam. 1989. *Necessary illusions: Thought control in democratic societies*. Boston: South End Press.

———. 1997. Market democracy in a neoliberal order. A talk reprinted in *Z* magazine (September). Online edition.

Clark, Charles. 1996. Political consultants. *CQ Researcher* (October 4): 867–87.

Cleaver, Harry. 1992. The inversion of class perspective in Marxian theory: From valorisation to self-valorisation. In *Essays in open Marxism*, edited by Werner Bonefeld, Richard Gunn, and Kosmas Psychopedis, 106–44. London: Pluto Press.

Cohen, Jeff. 2001, June 8. The return of Otto Reich: Will government propagandist join Bush administration? *Extra!* June 8. Online edition at www.fair.org/articles/otto-reich.html.

Cohen, Nick. 1999. Hold on a minute. Genetically modified politics. *Observer (London)*, February 7, 27.

Common Cause. 1997. Channeling influence: The broadcast lobby and the $70-billion free ride. At www.commoncause.org/publications/040297_rp16.html.

———. 1999. Overall campaign finance statistics. November 15. At www.common cause.org/publications/cycle_party_pres_facts.html.

———. 2000a. Follow the dollar reports. March. At www.commoncause.org/soft_ money/study99/chart1.html.

———. 2000b. Reporter's guide to money in politics campaign 2000. At www .commoncause.org/pressroom/profiles.html.

———. 2000c. You get what you pay for. September 7. At www.commoncause.org/ publications/sept00/softmoney/.

———. 2002. National parties raise record $300 million in soft money during first 18 months of 2001–2002 election cycle. At www.commoncause.org/moneyinpolitics/.

Congressional Research Service (CRS) Report for Congress. 2001. Campaign finance in the 2000 federal elections: Overview and estimates of the flow of money. March 16. At www.law.umaryland.edu/marshall/ElectronicResource/crsreports/crsdocuments/ RL30884_03162001.pdf.

Connell, Mike. 1997. New ways to reach voters and influence public opinion on the Internet. *Campaigns & Elections* (September): 64ff.

Conrad, Roger S. 1994. Winning votes on the information superhighway. *Campaigns & Elections* (July): 22ff.

Conry, Barbara. 1993, November 8. Loose cannon: The National Endowment for Democracy. Foreign policy briefing paper no. 27 for the Cato Institute. At www.cato.org/pubs/fpbriefs/fpb-027.html.

Constantino, Renato, and Letizio R. Constantino. 1978. *The Philippines: The continuing past*. Quezon City, Philippines: Foundation for Nationalist Studies.

Cooper, Michael. 2001. At $92.60 a vote, Bloomberg shatters an election record. *New York Times*, December 4, A1, A20.

Corn, David. 1996. G.O.P.'s new mouthwash. Editorial. *Nation* (September 30). Online edition.

———. 2002. Our gang in Venezuela? *Nation* (August 5, 12): 24–28.

Corporate Watch. 2002. Burson-Marsteller: A corporate profile. July. At www .corporatewatch.org/uk/profiles/burson/burson1.htm.

Corrado, Anthony. 2000a. Running backward: The congressional money chase. In *The permanent campaign and its future*, edited by Norman J. Ornstein and Thomas E. Mann, 75–107. Washington, D.C.: American Enterprise Institute and the Brookings Institution.

———. 2000b. Task force on financing presidential nominations of the Campaign Finance Institute. At www.CFInst.org.

———. 2002. Financing the 2000 presidential general election. In *Financing the 2000 election*, edited by David B. Magleby, 79–105. Washington, D.C.: Brookings Institution Press.

Corwin, Julie. 2002. The business of elections. *Radio Free Europe/RadioLiberty*. September 11. Available online through LexisNexis.

Croteau, David, and William Hoynes. 2001. *The business of media: Corporate media and the public interest*. Thousand Oaks, Calif.: Pine Forge Press.

Cunningham, William G. 1976. Citizen participation: Antagonists or allies? *Theory into practice* 15, no. 4: 274–83.

Damrosch, Lori F. 1989. Politics across borders: Nonintervention and nonforcible influence over domestic affairs. *American Journal of International Law* 83, no. 1: 1–50.

De Moraes, Lisa. 2000. Fox tries to defuse flap on Ellis. *Washington Post*, November 17. Online edition.

DeMont, John. 1997. Hitting the right target. *Maclean's* (May 5): 27.

Denton, Robert E., and Gary C. Woodward. 1990. *Political communication in America*. 2nd ed. New York: Praeger.

Denver, David, and Gordon Hands. 2001. The fall and rise of constituency campaigning. In *Political communications transformed: From Morrison to Mandelson*, edited by John Bartle and Dylan Griffiths, 71–86. New York: Palgrave Publishers.

Desert Sun (Palm Springs, Calif.). 2003. Power broker playing dual role as lobbyist, consultant sparks debate. June 29. Online edition.

Desmone, Rosanne. 1999. Calling the shots: How technology is making telephone campaigning more effective than ever. *Campaigns & Finance* (October/November): 40ff.

Deutsche Presse-Agentur. 1996a. U.S. political consultants take bow for Yeltsin victory. July 9. Online edition.

———. 1996b. U.S. Republicans reportedly helped Yeltsin engineer election win. July 7. Online edition.

Diamond, Edwin, and Stephen Bates. 1992. *The spot: The rise of political advertising on television*. 3rd ed. Cambridge, Mass.: MIT Press.

Dillon, Sam. 2000. The "sell me" politician the Mexicans bought. *New York Times*, July 3, A6.

Dobbs, Michael. 2000. U.S. advice guided Milosevic opposition. *Washington Post*, December 11. Online edition.

Donnelly, David, and Janice Fine. 2001. Preface. In *Are elections for sale?* edited by Joshua Cohen and Joel Rogers, xiii–xvii. Boston: Beacon Press.

Donnelly, David, Janice Fine, and Ellen S. Miller. 2001. Going public. In *Are elections for sale?* edited by Joshua Cohen and Joel Rogers, 3–30. Boston: Beacon Press.

Dreyfuss, Robert. 1999. George W. Bush: Calling for Philip Morris. *Nation* (November 8). Online edition.

Drohan, Michael. 2002. Another U.S. war—on the poor in Haiti. *New People* (July/August). Online edition at www.thomasmertoncenter.org/The_New_People/July-August2002/.

Dubose, Louis. 2001. Bush's hit man. *Nation* (February 8). Online edition.

Dye, Thomas R., and Harmon Ziegler. 1993. *The irony of democracy: An uncommon introduction to American politics*. 9th ed. Belmont, Calif.: Wadsworth.

Economist. 1997. Politicians for rent (March 5): 23ff.

———. 2002. Karl Rove's fading ambition (June 22). Online edition.

———. 2004. Spinning (April 3): 56.

Edelman, Murray. 1988. *Constructing the political spectacle.* Chicago: University of Chicago Press.

Eismeier, Theodore J., and Philip H. Pollock. 1988. *Business, money, and the rise of corporate PACs in American elections.* New York: Quorum Books.

Eliot, Stuart. 1997. P. & G. names one agency to handle billion-dollar TV operations. *New York Times*, November 19, C1, C8.

Engel, Matthew. 2002. US throws out "odious" party funding system. *Guardian*, March 22, 15.

Engelberg, Stephen. 1990. U.S. grant to 2 Czech parties is called unfair interference. *New York Times*, June 10, A8.

Enzensberger, Hans Magnus. 1974. *The consciousness industry: On literature, politics & the media.* New York: Seabury.

Epps, Garrett. 2004. Why should we settle for right-wing hot air? *Oregonian*, February 1, B1– B2.

Erickson, Allan. 2000. Fighting the other drug war. *Newsweek* (April 3). Online edition.

Ewen, Stuart. 1976. *Captains of consciousness: Advertising and the social roots of the consumer culture.* New York: McGrawHill.

———. 1996. *PR! A social history of spin.* New York: Basic Books.

Farnsworth, Stephen J., and S. Robert Lichter. 2003. *The nightly news nightmare: Network television's coverage of U.S. presidential elections, 1988–2000.* New York: Rowman & Littlefield.

Farrell, David M. 1996. Campaign strategies and tactics. In *Comparing democracies: Elections and voting in global perspective*, edited by Lawrence LeDuc, Richard G. Niemi, and Pippa Norris, 160–83. Thousand Oaks, Calif.: Sage.

———. 1998. Political consultancy overseas: The internationalization of campaign consultancy. *PS: Political Science and Politics* (June): 171–76.

Farrell, David M, Robin Kolodny, and Stephen Medvic. 2001. Parties and campaign professionals in a digital age: Political consultants in the United States and their counterparts overseas. *Harvard International Journal of Press/Politics* 6, no. 4: 11-30.

Faucheux, Ron. 1996. Campaign trends '96. *Campaigns & Elections* (July): 5.

FBIS (Foreign Broadcast Information Service). 2002. Translation of Alexis Papakhelas, newly released CIA records shed light on events leading up to Greece's 1967 coup. *Athens to Vima* (Greece). August 17: A6–A7. Document FBIS-WEU-2002-0818.

Federal Election Commission. 1997. PAC activity increases in 1995–96 election cycle. April 22. At www.fec.gov/press/pacye96.html.

Ferguson, Thomas. 1995. *Golden rule: The investment theory of party competition and the logic of money-driven political systems.* Chicago: University of Chicago Press.

Fitzgerald, Frances. 1972. *Fire in the lake: The Vietnamese and the Americans in Vietnam.* New York: Vintage Books.

Fones-Wolf, Elizabeth A. 1994. *Selling free enterprise: The business assault on labor and liberalism, 1945–60.* Urbana: University of Illinois Press.

Forsberg, Kenneth. 2001. A reform that lobbyists could love. *American Prospect* (October 22): 5.

Foster, Jody, and Christopher Muste. 1992. The United States. In *Electioneering: A comparative study of continuity and change*, edited by David Butler and Austin Ranney, 11–42. Oxford: Clarendon Press.

Fram, Alan. 2003. Millionaires are the rule in ranks of U.S. Senate. *Oregonian*, June 14, A4.

Frank, Thomas. 2000. *One market under God: Extreme capitalism, market populism, and the end of economic democracy*. New York: Anchor Books.

Franklin, Mark N. 1996. Electoral participation. In *Comparing democracies: Elections and voting in global perspective*, edited by Lawrence LeDuc, Richard G. Niemi, and Pippa Norris, 215–35. Thousand Oaks, Calif.: Sage.

Friedenberg, Robert V. 1997. *Communication consultants in political campaigns: Ballot box warriors*. Westport, Conn.: Praeger.

Gagliardi, Jason. 1999. A numbers man to count on. *South China Morning Post*, July 21, 17.

Galizio, Michael. 2002. Interview with author, April 11.

Gallavan, Erin, Shannon Rebholz, and Helen Sanderson. 2000. *Off the record: What media corporations don't tell you about their legislative agendas*. Washington, D.C.: Center for Public Integrity.

Gapper, John. 1997. Pollsters to give business advice. *Financial Times*, September 10, 7.

Garnham, Nicholas. 1990. *Capitalism and communication: Global culture and the economics of information*. London: Sage.

Gerard, Jasper. 2001. Labour pollster Gould finds a percentage in official contracts. *Sunday Times (London)*, April 22. Online edition.

Gerth, Jeff. 1984. C.I.A. has long sought to sway foreign voters. *New York Times*, May 13, A12.

Getter, Lisa. 2004. Kerry cuts into Bush's fund-raising advantage. *Oregonian*, May 21, A9.

Ginsberg, Benjamin. 1986. *The captive public: How mass opinion promotes state power*. New York: Basic Books.

Ginsberg, Benjamin, and Martin Shefter. 1999. *Politics by other means: Politicians, prosecutors, and the press from Watergate to Whitewater*. Rev. ed. New York: Norton.

Glasser, Susan B. 2000. Hired guns fuel fundraising race. *Washington Post*, April 30. Online edition.

Gould, Philip. 1998. *The unfinished revolution: How the modernisers saved the Labour Party*. London: Abacus.

Gozan, Julie. 1993. The torturer's lobby. *Multinational Monitor*, April. At www.multinationalmonitor.org/hyper/issues/1993/04/mm0493_05.html.

Graff, Steve. 1992. High-tech tools for campaigners. *State Legislatures* (May): 24–26.

Grech, Daniel A. 2003. Transcript shows Kissinger approved Argentina's dirty war. *Oregonian*, December 5, A18.

Green, Joshua. 2002. The other war room. *Washington Monthly* (April). Online edition.

Green, Mark. 2002a. The evil of access. *Nation* (December 30): 16–19.

———. 2002b. *Selling out: How big corporate money buys elections, rams through legislation, and betrays our democracy.* New York: Regan Books.

Greenberg Research. 2001a. Philip Gould. October 17. At www.greenbergresearch .com/ggcnop/ggc-page/gould.html.

———. 2001b. Stanley Greenberg Biography. At www.greenbergresearch.com/gri/ who/stanbio.html.

Greider, William. 1992. *Who will tell the people: The betrayal of American democracy.* New York: Simon & Schuster.

Grose, Thomas K. 1997. Lessons from the Yanks. *U.S. News & World Report* (May 5). Online edition.

Grove, Lisa. 2003. Political consultant. Interview with author, June 19.

Halbfinger, David M. 2004. Supporters get incentive plans at Bush rallies. *New York Times,* September 28, A1, A19.

Halimi, Serge. 1999. Big guns for hire. *Le Monde Diplomatique* (August). At www.en .monde-diplomatique.fr/1999/08/02spin.

Hamilton, Don. 2000. Costly campaigns on the Westside signal change. *Oregonian,* October 7, A1, A12.

Harbrecht, Douglas. 1990. Mary Matalin: The GOP's secret weapon. *Business Week* (May 21): 83.

Harriman, Ed. 2001. Putting the dirt back into politics. *Guardian (London),* May 31. Online edition.

Harris, Bev. 2003. Inside a U.S. election vote counting program. July 8. At www .scoop.co.nz/mason/stories/HL0307/S00065.htm.

Harrop, Martin. 2001. The rise of campaign professionalism. In *Political communications transformed: From Morrison to Mandelson,* edited by John Bartle and Dylan Griffiths, 53–70. New York: Palgrave Publishers.

Harry Walker Agency, Inc. 1998. Dr. Frank Luntz. At www. harrywalker.com.

Hartmann, Thom. 2002. *Unequal protection: The rise of corporate dominance and the theft of human rights.* Emmaus, Pa.: Rodale.

Harvey, David. 2000. *Spaces of hope.* Berkeley: University of California Press.

Harwood, John. 1999. A lot like home: Campaign strategists give foreign elections that American cachet. *Wall Street Journal,* March 24, A1, A18.

Heclo, Hugh. 2000. Campaigning and governing: A conspectus. In *The permanent campaign and its future,* edited by Norman J. Ornstein and Thomas E. Mann, 1–37. Washington, D.C.: American Enterprise Institute and the Brookings Institution.

Hellinger, Daniel. 1996. Democracy builders or information terrorists? *St. Louis Journalism Review* (September): 10–11.

Herman, Edward S., and Noam Chomsky. 2002. *Manufacturing consent: The political economy of the mass media.* New York: Pantheon.

Herrnson, Paul S. 1992. Campaign professionalism and fundraising in congressional elections. *Journal of Politics* 54, no. 3: 859–70.

Herszenhorn, David M., and Riva D. Atlas. 2002. WorldCom investor hires Giuliani consulting firm. *New York Times,* November 19, C2.

Hess, Stephen. 2000. The press and the permanent campaign. In *The permanent campaign and its future*, edited by Norman J. Ornstein and Thomas E. Mann, 38–53. Washington, D.C.: American Enterprise Institute and the Brookings Institution.

Hightower, Jim. 1998. *There's nothing in the middle of the road but yellow stripes and dead armadillos*. New York: HarperCollins.

———. 2003. Invasion of the privacy snatchers. June 3. At www.alternet.org/story .html?StoryID=16064.

Hill, Steven. 2002. *Fixing elections: The failure of America's winner take all politics*. New York: Routledge.

Himes, David. 1995. Strategies and tactics for campaign fund-raising. In *Campaigns and elections American style*, edited by James A. Thurber and Candice Nelson, 62–67. Boulder, Colo.: Westview Press.

Hockstader, Lee. 1999. A campaign spin in Tel Aviv. *Washington Post*, April 7. On-line edition.

Hollingsworth, Mark. 1991. *MPs for hire: The secret world of political lobbying*. London: Bloomsbury.

Holman, Craig B., and Luke P. McLoughlin. 2002. *Buying time 2000: Television advertising in the 2000 federal elections*. New York: Brannan Center for Justice at the New York University School of Law.

Hoogvelt, Ankie. 1997. *Globalization and the postcolonial world: The new political economy of development*. Baltimore: Johns Hopkins University Press.

Information Technology Association of American. 2001. At www.itaa.org/.

International Foundation for Election Systems. 2003. At ww.ifes.org.

Jackson, Paul. 2002. Right-guard. *Calgary Sun*, March 12. Online edition.

Jacobs, Lawrence R., and Robert Y. Shapiro. 2000. *Politicians don't pander: Political manipulation and the loss of democratic responsiveness*. Chicago: University of Chicago Press.

Jamieson, Kathleen H. 1992. *Dirty politics: Deception, distraction, and democracy*. New York: Oxford University Press.

———. 1996. *Packaging the presidency: A history and criticism of presidential campaign advertising*. 3rd ed. New York: Oxford University Press.

Jamieson, Kathleen H., and Paul Waldman. 2003. *The press effect: Politicians, journalists, and the stories that shape the political world*. New York: Oxford University Press.

Joan Shorenstein Center on the Press, Politics and Public Policy, The Vanishing Voter Project. 2000a. Looking back, Americans believe their role in the nominating process was secondary. June 14. At www.vanishingvoter.org.

———. 2000b. Tired and locked out of nominating process, Americans seek change. April 6. At www.vanishingvoter.org

Johnson, Dennis W. 2000. The business of political consulting. In *Campaign warriors: Political consultants in elections*, edited by James Thurber and Candice Nelson, 37–52. Washington, D.C.: Brookings Institution Press.

———. 2001. *No place for amateurs: How political consultants are reshaping American democracy*. New York: Routledge.

Justice, Glen. 2003. In new landscape of campaign finance, big donations flow to groups, not parties. *New York Times*, December 11, A25.

———. 2004. Bush drew record $259 million during primaries. *New York Times*, September 21. Online edition.

Kaplan, Sheila. 2000. When the grass has no roots. *U.S. News & World Report* (October 9). Online edition at www.usnews.com.

Kavanagh, Dennis. 1992. The United Kingdom. In *Electioneering: A comparative study of continuity and change*, edited by David Butler and Austin Ranney, 70–87. Oxford: Clarendon Press.

Kelley, Stanley. 1956. *Professional public relations and political power*. Baltimore: Johns Hopkins Press.

King, Anthony D. 1990. *Global cities: Post-imperialism and the internationalization of London*. London: Routledge.

Kirchheimer, Otto. 1966. The transformation of the Western European party systems. In *Political parties and political development*, edited by Joseph LaPalombara and Myron Weiner, 177–200. Princeton, N.J.: Princeton University Press.

Kissinger, Henry. 1979. *White House years*. Boston: Little, Brown.

Kitfield, James. 2001. Nice work, if you can get it. *National Journal* (September 1): 2658–65.

Kolbert, Elizabeth. 1992. Test-marketing a president. *New York Times Magazine*, August 30, 18–21ff.

Kostmayer, Peter H. 2001. Money turned this pol into a telemarketer. *Democracy Matters*. At www.democracymatters.org/ResearchCenter/Articles/MoneyTurned .htm.

Kramer, Michael. 1996. Rescuing Boris. *Time* (July 15). Online edition.

Lakoff, George. 1996. *Moral politics: What conservatives know that liberals don't*. Chicago: University of Chicago Press.

Lampman, Jane. 2003. Easing into Islamic democracy. *Christian Science Monitor*, May 29. Online edition.

Lardner, George, Jr. . 2001. Rove's first step toward shedding stock took 5 months. *Washington Post*, July 26. Online edition.

Leahy, Pat. 2004. King of spin. *Sunday Business Post*, March 7. Online edition.

Lee, Martin A., and Norman Solomon. 1990. *Unreliable sources: A guide to detecting bias in news media*. New York: Lyle Stuart.

Lemann, Nicholas. 2000. The word lab: The mad science behind what the candidates say. *New Yorker* (October 16): 100ff. Online edition.

Lenhart, Harry. 1997. The race to the bottom. *Oregon Business* (May): 30–37, 42.

Lewis, Charles. 2000a. How George W. Bush scored big with the Texas Rangers. *Public i*. At www. angelfire.com/ok5/pearly/htmls/bush-sec.5.html.

———. 2000b. Media money. *Columbia Journalism Review* (September/October). Online edition.

———. 2004. *The buying of the president, 2004*. New York: HarperCollins.

Lewis, Justin. 2001. *Constructing public opinion: How political elites do what they like and why we seem to go along with it*. New York: Columbia University Press.

———. 2002. Public opinion. In *Television studies*, edited by Toby Miller, 78–80. London: British Film Institute.

Lewis, Tom. 1991. *Empire of the air: The men who made radio*. New York: HarperCollins.

Lieberman, Trudy. 2001. *Slanting the story: The forces that shape the news.* New York: New Press. Excerpted in TomPaine.common sense online journal at www.tompaine .com/news/2001/04/25/.

Live Online. 2002. A moderated online discussion with Mark Green, author of *Selling out: How big corporate money buys elections. Washington Post,* October 30. At www.discuss.washingtonpost.com.

Living on Earth. 1997. Transcript, radio series, April 11. At www.loe.org/archives/ 970411.htm.

Loomis, Burdett A. 2000. The never ending story: Campaigns without elections. In *The permanent campaign and its future,* edited by Norman J. Ornstein and Thomas E. Mann, 162–84. Washington, D.C.: American Enterprise Institute and the Brookings Institution.

Lorimer, Doug. 2004. Venezuela: U.S. finances coup conspiracy. *Green Left Weekly,* February 25. At www.greenleft.org.au/back/2004/572/572p24.htm.

Los Angeles Times. 2001. Continental Airlines posts 3rd-quarter profit. November 1. Online edition.

Lynch, Michael W. 2002. The hard truths about attempts to ban "soft money." *Oregonian,* February 17, E1, E2.

Macpherson, C. B. 1977. *The life and times of liberal democracy.* Oxford: Oxford University Press.

Maggs, John. 2000. Not-so-innocents abroad. *National Journal* 32, no. 25 (June 17). Available online through Ebsco Host.

Mancini, Paolo. 1999. New frontiers in political professionalism. *Political Communication* 16:231–45.

Mancini, Paolo, and David L. Swanson. 1996. Politics, media, and modern democracy: Introduction. In *Politics, media, and modern democracy,* edited by David Swanson and Paolo Mancini, 1–26. Westport, Conn.: Praeger.

Margolis, Eric S. 2003. Shevy's big mistake: Crossing Uncle Sam. *Toronto Sun,* November 30. Online edition.

Mark, David. 2001. Politics down under. *Campaigns & Elections* (October): 8–9.

Marketing News. 2000. Wirthlin Worldwide. June 5. At www.wirthlin.com/news/ news.phtml.

Marquis, Christopher. 2002a. U.S. bankrolling is under scrutiny for ties to Chávez ouster. *New York Times,* April 25, A8.

———. 2002b. U.S. probes agency that funneled funds to Chávez foes. *New York Times,* April 26. Online edition.

Marsden, William. 2001. The mob and big tobacco: Corporate executives linked to organized crime. *Gazette (Montreal),* March 3, 1ff.

Mattelart, Armand, and Seth Siegelaub, eds. 1979. *Communication and class struggle.* Vol. 2. New York: International General.

Maxfield, Andrew, and Robert Schlesinger. 1997. As the world spins. *Mother Jones* (March/April): 15.

Mayhew, Leon H. 1997. *The new public: Professional communication and the means of social influence.* Cambridge: Cambridge University Press.

McChesney, Robert W. 1999. *Rich media, poor democracy: Communication politics in dubious times.* Urbana: University of Illinois Press.

McClintock, Pamela. 2002. Local stations give elections short shrift. *Variety* (October 16). Online edition.

McCormick, Thomas J. 1989. *America's half-century: United States foreign policy in the Cold War*. Baltimore: Johns Hopkins University Press.

Mcelvoy, Anne. 2000. Fanatic of the focus group. Profile: Philip Gould. *Independent (London)*, July 22, 5. Online edition.

McGrory, Mary. 2002. Democracy takes a hit. *Washington Post*, April 19. At www.washingtonpost.com.

McIntyre, Dave. 1999. Burglaries show influence of U.S. politics abroad. Deutsche Presse-Agentur (German Press Agency release), January 21. Online edition.

McManus, Terry. 1999. Political campaigns pivot on web. *Advertising Age* (December 13): 76.

McNair, Brian. 1999. *An introduction to political communication*. 2nd ed. New York: Routledge.

McWilliams, Wilson C. 2001. The meaning of the election. In *The election of 2000: Reports and interpretations*, edited by Gerald M. Pomper et al., 177–201. New York: Seven Bridges Press.

Medvic, Stephen K. 2000. Professionalization in congressional campaigns. In *Campaign warriors: The role of political consultants in elections*, edited by James A. Thurber and Candice J. Nelson, 91–109. Washington, D.C.: Brookings Institution Press.

Meetings & Conventions. 2000. If bosses motivate, workers stay (December): 26.

Mellman Group. 2003. At www.mellmangroup.com.

Mendelson, Sarah E. 2001. Democracy assistance and political transition in Russia. *International Security* 25, no. 4. Available online through Ebsco Host.

Mickiewicz, Ellen. 1998. Transition and democratization: The role of journalists in Eastern Europe and the former Soviet Union. In *The politics of news: The news of politics*, edited by Doris Graber, Denis McQuail, and Pippa Norris, 33–50. Washington, D.C.: CQ Press.

Miliband, Ralph. 1969. *The state in capitalist society*. New York: Basic Books.

Mills, C. Wright. 1956. *The power elite*. New York: Oxford University Press.

Milne, Kirsty. 1996. The memo-mad ad-man turned political strategist for Blair (and the Sandinistas). *New Statesman* (October 25): 24ff. Online edition.

Mitchell, Alison. 1998. The influence industry. *New York Times*, September 30. Online edition.

Monbiot, George. 2000. *Captive state: The corporate takeover of Britain*. London: Macmillan

———. 2001. What is . . . the Corporate Takeover? *The Oldie* (UK), November. Online edition.

Morgan, Dan. 2000. A made-for-TV windfall: Candidates' air time scramble fills stations' tills. *Washington Post*, May 2. Online edition.

Moyers, Bill. 2004a. *Now*. Transcript, February 6. At www.pbs.org/now.

———. 2004b. *Now*. Transcript, April 30. At www.pbs.org/now.

Mughan, Anthony. 2000. *Media and the presidentialization of parliamentary elections*. New York: Palgrave.

Multimedia News. 1998. Information Technology Association of America. June 24. At www.fiam.org/en/pages/mmnews.html.

Mulvihill, Maggie, Jack Myers, and Jonathan Wells. 2001. USA: Bush advisers cashed in on Saudi gravy train. *Boston Herald*, December 11. Online edition.

Myers, Dee Dee. 1993. New technology and the 1992 Clinton presidential campaign. *American Behavioral Scientist* (December): 181–84.

Myers, Steven L. 1999. Toppling dictators: Guns don't scare them? Try campaign spending. *New York Times*, November 7. Online edition.

———. 2003. A new role on Lithuania's horizon: A new scandal too. *New York Times*, December 28. Online edition.

Nagourney, Adam. 1999. Sound bites over Jerusalem. *New York Times Magazine*, April 25, 42ff.

Nagourney, Adam, and Michael Janofsky. 2003. Dean's surge in fund-raising forces rivals to reassess him. *New York Times*, July 3, A1, A16.

Napolitan, Joseph. 1999. Present at the creation (of modern political consulting). In *The Manship School guide to political communication*, edited by David D. Perlmutter, 19–26. Baton Rouge: Louisiana State University Press.

National Center for Policy Analysis. 1998. Putting prison inmates to work. May 5. At www.ncpa.org/press/mor505ad.html.

Negrine, Ralph, and Stylianos Papathanassopoulos. 1996. The "Americanization" of political communication: A critique. *Harvard International Journal of Press/Politics* 1, no. 2: 45–62.

Nelson, Candice J. 2002. Spending in the 2000 elections. In *Financing the 2000 election*, edited by David B. Magleby, 22–48. Washington, D.C.: Brookings Institution Press.

Nelson, Joyce. 1989. *Sultans of sleeze: Public relations and the media.* Monroe, Maine: Common Courage.

New Internationalist. 1985. Democracy incorporated. April. Online edition.

Newsweek. 2004. A wasted moment. (February 16): 4.

Nimmo, Dan. 1970. *The political persuaders: The techniques of modern election campaigns.* Englewood Cliffs, N. J.: Prentice-Hall.

Noguera, Felipe. 2000. Latin American trends. *Campaigns & Elections* (April): 26.

Nordlinger, Gary. 2000. Count the ways. *Campaigns & Elections* (April): 26.

Norris, Pippa. 2000. *A virtuous circle: Political communications in postindustrial societies.* Cambridge: Cambridge University Press.

———. 2001. Political communications and democratic politics. In *Political communications transformed: From Morrison to Mandelson*, edited by John Bartle and Dylan Griffiths, 163–68. New York: Palgrave Publishers.

Novotny, Patrick. 2000. From Polis to Agora: The marketing of political consultants. *Harvard International Journal of Press/Politics* 5, no. 3: 12–26.

Opensecrets. 2001. At www.opensecrets.org/2000elect/cgi-win/format.exe.

Oppel, Richard A. 2002. Records falling in waning days of soft money. *New York Times*, September 30, A1, A19.

———. 2003. Campaign documents show depth of Bush fund-raising. *New York Times*, May 5, A17.

Ottaway, Marina, and Theresa Chung. 1999. Toward a new paradigm. *Journal of Democracy* 10, no. 4: 99–113.

Overbeck, Ashley. 1999. A report on CIA infiltration and manipulation of the mass media. Unpublished paper. At www.geocities.com.

Parenti, Michael. 1995. *Democracy for the few*. 6th ed. New York: St. Martins Press.

Patterson, Thomas E. 2002. *The vanishing voter*. New York: Vintage.

Pear, Robert, and Richard A. Oppel, Jr. 2002. Election gives drug industry new influence. *New York Times*, November 21, A1, A28.

Perry, Roland. 1984. *The programming of the president: The hidden power of the computer in world politics today*. New York: Beaufort.

Petersen, Scot. 2000. Ragin' in the technical arena. *EWeek* (May 5): 43.

Peterson, Bill. 1985. U.S. campaign consultants branching out overseas. *Washington Post*, December 30. Online edition.

Petracca, Mark P. 1989. Political consultants and democratic governance. *PS: Political Science & Politics* 22, no. 1: 11–14.

Pew Research Center for the People and the Press. 1998. Don't blame us: The views of political consultants. June 17. At www.people-press.org.

Phelps, Douglas. 2001. Setting limits. In *Are elections for sale?* edited by Joshua Cohen and Joel Rogers, 49–59. Boston: Beacon Press.

Phillips, Andrew. 1999. The spin doctors look north. *Maclean's* (August 16): 38.

Phillips, Kevin. 2002a. The cycles of financial scandal. *New York Times*, July 17. Online edition.

———. 2002b. *Wealth and democracy: A political history of the American rich*. New York: Broadway Books.

Pinto-Duschinsky, Michael. 2001. Overview (project precis). In *Handbook on funding of parties and election campaigns*, edited by the International IDEA (Institute for Democracy and Electoral Assistance). Stockholm: International IDEA (forthcoming).

Plasser, Fritz. 2000. American campaign techniques worldwide. *Harvard International Journal of Press/Politics* 5, no. 4: 33–54.

———. 2001. Parties' diminishing relevance for campaign professionals. *Harvard International Journal of Press/Politics* 6, no. 4: 44–59.

Plasser, Fritz, and Gunda Plasser. 2002. *Global political campaigning: A worldwide analysis of campaign professionals and their practices*. Westport, Conn.: Praeger.

Plasser, Fritz, Christian Scheucher, and Christian Senft. 1999. Is there a European style of political marketing? A survey of political managers and consultants. In *Handbook of political marketing*, edited by Bruce I. Newman. Thousand Oaks, Calif.: Sage.

Platell, Amanda. 2002. "It's time for . . ." change in Tory camp. *PR Week* (October 4). Online edition.

PN&A (Phil Noble & Associates). 2001. At www.pnoble.com.

PoliticsOnline. 2001. At www.politicsonline.com.

Poor, Tim. 1992. Perot keeps an ear to his phone bank. *St. Louis Post-Dispatch*, July 12, 1B.

Post, Tom. 1991. The CIA on the stump. *Newsweek* (October 21). Online edition.

Postman, Neil, and Steve Powers. 1992. *How to watch TV news*. New York: Penguin.

Powell, Larry, and Joseph Cowart. 2003. *Political campaign communication: Inside and out*. Boston: Allyn & Bacon.

PR Watch. 1997. They're rich, they're powerful and they're running scared. Vol. 4, no. 1. At www.prwatch.org.

Prewitt, Kenneth, and Alan Stone. 1973. *The ruling elites: Elite theory, power, and American democracy*. New York: Harper & Row.

Prusher, Ilene R. 1999. Big U.S. export: Campaign gurus. *Christian Science Monitor*, May 19, 1.

Public Citizen. 2003. Enron's tangled web. June. At www.citizen.org.

Public Citizen. 2004. *Public Citizen* calls for ethics investigation of Tauzin. January 28. At www.citizen.org

Putnam, Robert D. 1995. Bowling alone: America's declining social capital. *Journal of Democracy* (January): 65–78.

Raney, Rebecca F. 1998. Company seeks to streamline political campaign donations. *New York Times*, September 30. Online edition.

Rath, Dan. 2000. Global marketplace. *Campaigns & Elections* (April): 27–28.

Reed, Stanley F. 2000. An afterword from the founder of *Campaigns & Elections*. *Campaigns & Elections* (April): 28.

Richardson, Valerie. 2004. U.S. woman targets Romania. *Washington Times*, March 8, A4.

Robbins, Tom. 2001. The best campaign money can buy. *Village Voice* (October 31–November 6). Online edition.

Robins, Kevin, and Frank Webster. 1999. *Times of the technoculture: From the information society to the virtual life*. New York: Routledge.

Robinson, William I. 1992. *A Faustian bargain: U.S. Intervention in the Nicaraguan elections and American foreign policy in the post–Cold War era*. Boulder, Colo.: Westview Press.

———. 1994. Low-intensity democracy: The new face of global domination. *Covert Action Quarterly* (Fall): 40–47.

———. 1996. *Promoting polyarchy: Globalization, US intervention, and hegemony*. Cambridge: Cambridge University Press.

Rodrick, Stephen. 1996. The secret life of Arthur J. Finkelstein. *Boston Magazine* (August). At www.bostonmagazine.com/archive/finkelstein.html.

Rosen, Jeffrey. 2003. Magic words. *New Republic* (September 29). Available online through Ebsco Host.

Rosenbaum, Martin. 1997. *From soapbox to soundbite: Party political campaigning in Britain since 1945*. New York: St. Martins.

Ross, John. 2000. Scent of fraud as long ruling PRI panics at prospect of losing presidential election. May 12. At www.globalexchange.org/countries/mexico/news/051200.html.

Rustow, Dankwart. 1970. Transitions to democracy: Toward a comparative model. *Comparative Politics*. Vol. 2, 337–63.

Rutherford, Paul. 2000. *Endless propaganda: The advertising of public goods*. Toronto: University of Toronto Press.

Sabato, Larry J. 1981. *The rise of political consultants.* New York: Basic Books.

Sabato, Larry J., and Glenn R. Simpson. 1996. *Dirty little secrets: The persistence of corruption in American politics.* New York: Times Books.

Sachs, Jeffrey. 2004. Don't fall for Washington's spin on Haiti. Op-ed piece. *Financial Times (U.S. edition),* March 1, 13.

Salmore, Barbara G., and Stephen A. Salmore. 1989. *Candidates, parties, and campaigns: Electoral politics in America.* 2nd edition. Washington, D.C.: Congressional Quarterly Books.

Samuels, David. 1995. At play in the fields of oppression. *Harper's* (May). Online edition.

Scammell, Margaret. 1998. The wisdom of the war room: US campaigning and Americanization. *Media, Culture & Society* 20: 251–75.

———. 1999. Political marketing: Lessons for political science. *Political Studies* 47:718–39.

Schedler, Andreas. 2002. The menu of manipulation: Elections without democracy. *Journal of Democracy* 13, no. 2: 36–50.

Schiller, Dan. 1999. *Digital capitalism: Networking the global market system.* Cambridge, Mass.: MIT Press.

Schiller, Herbert I. 1973. *The mind managers.* Boston: Beacon Press.

Schlesinger, Robert. ca. 1997. Money and politics: A primer (a Public Broadcasting System report on the Frontline series *The Fixers*). At www.pbs.org/wgbh.pa... online/shows/fixers/reports/primer.html.

Schmidt, Susan, and John Mintz. 2001. Shrub time: Bush aides disclose finances. *Washington Post.* June 2. At www.loper.org/~george/archives/2001/Jun/23.html.

Schmitter, Philippe C. 1996. The influence of the international context upon the choice of national institutions and policies in non-democracies. In *The international dimensions of democratization: Europe and the Americas,* edited by Laurence Whitehead, 26–54. New York: Oxford University Press.

Schneider, Greg. 2003. Connections and then some. *Washington Post,* March 16. Online edition.

Schneider, Stephen J. 2003. National Endowment for Democracy consultant. Interview with author, November 13.

Schrader, Esther. 1999. Mexico imports American-style campaigning. *Los Angeles Times,* August 27, A1, A16, A17.

Schwartzman, Paul. 1998. GOP's very own pit bull: A career of dogging liberals. *New York Daily News,* October 17, 15.

Securities Industry Association Press Release. 2001. Retail executives to discuss challenges of the new millennium. At www.sia.com/press/html/pr-retailexecs.html.

Selnow, Gary W. 1994. *High-tech campaigns: Computer technology in political communication.* Westport, Conn.: Praeger.

Sevastopulo, Demetri, and James Harding. 2004. Tauzin decision to take lobbying job provokes outrage among Democrats. *Financial Times (U.S. edition),* February 5, 1.

Shea, Daniel M., and Michael J. Burton. 2001. *Campaign craft: The strategies, tactics, and art of political campaign management.* Westport, Conn.: Praeger.

Shelley, Becky. 2000. Political globalisation and the politics of international non-governmental organisations: The case of village democracy in China. *Australian Journal of Political Science* 35, no. 2. Online edition.

Shiley, Dawn. 1999. SOCMA's INFORMEX: Manufacturer's choice for growing their businesses: 1999 exposition breaks records with over 500 booths sold. At www.socma.com/bond/archive/January2.html.

Sklair, Leslie. 2001. *The transnational capitalist class*. Oxford: Blackwell.

Smith, Joseph B. 1976. *Portrait of a cold warrior: Second thoughts of a top CIA agent*. New York: Ballantine Books.

Smith, Robert F. 1960. *The United States and Cuba: Business and diplomacy, 1917–1960*. New York: Bookman Associates.

Smyth, Julie C. 2003. Voting machine controversy. *Cleveland Plain Dealer*, August 28. Online edition.

Snow, Nancy. 1998. *Propaganda, Inc.: Selling America's culture to the world*. New York: Seven Stories Press.

Solomon, Norman. 1999. *The habits of highly deceptive media: Decoding spin and lies in mainstream news*. Monroe, Maine: Common Courage Press.

Spielmann, Peter J. 1988. American advisers export Yankee campaign know-how. *Associated Press*, October 12. Available through LexisNexis Academic Universe.

Stark, Steven. 1985. Serving TV winners. *Atlantic Monthly* (March): 24–29.

Stauber, John C., and Sheldon Rampton. 1995. *Toxic sludge is good for you! Lies, damn lies and the public relations industry*. Monroe, Maine: Common Courage Press.

Steel, Ronald. 1997. The hard questions. *New Republic* (September 8–15): 27.

Steinhauer, Jennifer. 2002. With Bush at fund-raiser, political capital for mayor. *New York Times*, January 24, A27.

Stevenson, Mark. 2000a. No red carpet for American campaign consultants in Mexico. *Associated Press*, January 24.

———. 2000b. America's newest export industry: Political advisers. *Associated Press*, January 29.

Stoffer, Harry. 1998. Poll: Chrysler will benefit in Daimler deal. *Automotive News*, June 22, 28.

Stone, Peter. 1997. Business pushes for fast-track. *National Journal*, September 27. Online edition

Strother, Dane. 1999. Television ads. In *The Manship School guide to political communication*, edited by David A. Perlmutter, 186–95. Baton Rouge: Louisiana State University Press.

Strother, Ray. 1999/2000. A successful secret. *Campaigns & Elections* (December/January): 17.

Sussman, Gerald. 1997. *Communication, technology, and politics in the information age*. Thousand Oaks, Calif.: Sage.

Swanson, David L., and Paolo Mancini. 1996. Patterns of modern electoral campaigning and their consequences. In *Politics, media, and modern democracy*, edited by David Swanson and Paolo Mancini, 247–76. Westport, Conn.: Praeger.

Swint, Kerwin C. 1998. *Political consultants and negative campaigning: The secrets of the pros*. Lanham, Md.: University Press of America.

Tait, Nikki. 1999. Welfare to work drive "still faces barriers." *Financial Times (U.S. edition)*, August 5, 3.

Taylor, Frederick W. 1911. *The Principles of Scientific Management*. At www.melbecon.unimelb.edu.au/het/taylor/sciman.htm

Taylor, Paul. 2002. The case for free air time. A paper of the Alliance for Better Campaigns at www.freeairtime.org.

Theimer, Sharon. 2003. NRA looks to buy news outlet to skirt election restriction. *Oregonian*, December 7, A4.

Thompson, Elaine. 1998. Political culture. In *Americanization and Australia*, edited by Philip Bell and Roger Bell, 107–22. Sydney: University of New South Wales.

Thurber, James A. 1995. The transformation of American campaigns. In *Campaigns and elections American style*, edited by James A. Thurber and Candice Nelson, 1–13. Boulder, Colo.: Westview Press.

———. 1998. The study of campaign consultants: A subfield in search of theory. *PS: Political Science & Politics* (June): 145–49.

Thurber, James A., and David A. Dulio. 1999. Industry portrait: Political consultants. *Campaigns & Elections* (July): 26ff.

Tischler, Eric. 1999. 1999 winter conference Nashville. *Corrections Today* 61, no. 2: 32–35.

Tompkins County (New York) Green Party. 2003. Corporate money was the winner in 2002 elections. February 7. At www.tcgreens.org.

Traynore, Ian. 2003. Analysis: How Shevardnadze went from Glasnost hero to hated lame duck—and who will succeed him. *Guardian*, November 24. Online edition.

Tu Thanh Ha. 1993. Prominent U.S. campaign consultant signs on with PCs. *Gazette (Montreal)*, September 25. Online edition.

Tucker, Neely, and Juliet Eilperin. 2003. Campaign law fails to pass court test. *Oregonian*, May 3, A1, A9.

United States Senate. (1980). Committee on Governmental Affairs, 96th Congress, 2nd Session. *Structure of corporate concentration: Institutional shareholders and interlocking directorates among major U.S. corporations*. Washington, D.C.: U.S. Government Printing Office.

US Newswire. 2000. Richard B. Wirthlin honored for lifetime contributions to campaign consulting. May 23. Online edition.

Van der Schriek, Daan. 2003. Georgia: "How good the revolution has been!" *World Press Review*, December 7. Online edition.

Vidal, Gore. 2001. Foreword. In *Are elections for sale?* edited by Joshua Cohen and Joel Rogers, vii–xii. Boston: Beacon Press.

Virtual Truth Commission. 1998. Telling the truth for a better America: National Endowment for Democracy. At www.geocities.com/~virtualtruth/ned.htm.

Wall Street Journal. 2003. Worldwatch. April 16. Online edition.

Warner, Tom. 2004a. Saakashvili may win 80% of vote in Georgia. *Financial Times*, January 4, 4.

———. 2004b. Poll landslide for Saakashvili. *Financial Times*, January 5, 3.

Wattenberg, Martin P. 1994. *The decline of American political parties, 1952–1992*. Cambridge, Mass.: Harvard University Press.

Wayne, Leslie. 2000. Political consultants thrive in the cash-rich new politics. *New York Times*, October 24, A1, A21.

——. 2001. Trading on their names. *New York Times*, May 23. Online edition.

Wayne, Stephen J. 2003. *Is this any way to run a democratic election? Debating American electoral politics.* 2nd ed. Boston: Houghton Mifflin.

Wedel, Janine R. 2001. *Collision and collusion: The strange case of Western aid to Eastern Europe.* New York: Palgrave.

Weinberg, Adam. 2001. Globalization of campaign funding: The problem of private money in politics. At www.democracymatters.org.

Weiner, Mark. 2003. Political consultant. Interview with author, May 1.

Weiner, Tim. 2003. Enter consultant Giuliani, his fee preceding him. *New York Times*, January 16, A4.

Weir, Fred. 1996. Betting on Boris: The West antes up for the Russian election. *Covert Action Quarterly* (Summer): 38–41.

Weissman, Robert. 2000. The money trail: Corporate investments in U.S. elections since 1990. *Multinational Monitor* (October): 25–29.

Welfare to Work. 2001. At www.welfaretowork.org/.

West, Darrell M. 2000. How issue ads have reshaped American politics. In *Crowded airwaves: Campaign advertising in elections*, edited by James A. Thurber, Candice J. Nelson, and David A. Dulio, 149–69. Washington, D.C.: Brookings Institution Press.

West, Darrell M., and Burdett A. Loomis. 1999. *The sound of money: How political interests get what they want.* New York: Norton.

White House news release. 2004. April 13. At www.whitehouse.gov.news/releases/20040413-5.html.

White, Michael. 2000. Full text: Philip Gould's leaked memo. *Guardian (London)*, July 19. Online edition.

Wilkinson, Tracey. 1999. Israeli voters can't escape candidates' slick TV ads. *Oregonian*, May 2, A16.

Will, George F. 2002. Soft money, odd thinking. *Newsweek* (February 11). Online edition.

——. 2004. US must not flinch from action over Iraqi abuses. *Australian Financial Review*, May 13, 79.

Wilson Quarterly. 2000. Campaign warriors: The role of political consultants in elections. (Summer): 119.

Winston, Brian. 1986. *Misunderstanding media.* Cambridge, Mass.: Harvard University Press.

Wirthlin Worldwide. 2001. Dr. Richard B. Wirthlin. At www.wirthlin.com/aboutww/people/rwgrbw.htm.

Witcover, Jules. 1999. *No way to pick a president.* New York: Farrar, Straus and Giroux.

WNYC. 2003. The father of public relations (part of the New York-based radio series *On the Media*). Transcript, January 17.

Zolotov Jr., Andrei. 2002. Hollywood spins Yeltsin spin doctors. *Moscow Times*, June 3. Online edition.

Index

About the Author

Gerald Sussman is joint professor of urban studies and communications at the School of Urban Studies & Planning and the Department of Communication, Portland State University. Formally trained in political science (international political economy and comparative politics), he is the author of *Communication, Technology, and Politics in the Information Age* (Sage, 1997) and co-editor of *Global Productions: Labor in the Making of the "Information Society"* (Hampton, 1998) and *Transnational Communications: Wiring the Third World* (Sage, 1991). He also has written or edited three monographs on the political economy of international communications and broadcasting and numerous journal articles and book chapters on politics and media. Professor Sussman can be reached at sussmang@pdx.edu.